Jeb Bush
vs. Hillary Clinton
On The Issues

6th edition, April 12th, 2015

Edited by Jesse Gordon,
OnTheIssues.org

Dedication

To the young boy Kessel; we once shared so much love;
and to the young man Julien for whom I hope the same.

Hillary vs. Jeb On the Issues

Hillary Clinton and Jeb Bush agree on some issues and disagree on many others. This book outlines their stances on the issues, in a side-by-side manner for each issue, on many of controversial topics that they will address in the campaign and will face as President.

We gather the two candidates' issue stances from their political biographies and memoirs; from debates in previous elections; from public speeches; from campaign websites; and from political analysis websites. All of the excerpts appear, with many additional issue stances, on our website, www.OnTheIssues.org.

As of her announcement in early 2015, Hillary is the frontrunner for the Democratic nomination, but will likely face at least one primary opponent. This book details the issues which Hillary will debate in the primaries, likely against a progressive opponent.

Jeb, while always listed among the frontrunners, likely will face a large number of primary opponents. This book details the issues which Jeb will debate in the primaries, against a Tea Party opponent, a libertarian opponent, a religious-right opponent, or (most likely) all three.

This book also addresses the issues that Hillary and Jeb would debate against each other, if both were to win their respective primaries. Hillary has a well-established record on both domestic and foreign affairs, and we outline Hillary's stances on the issues that will arise in 2016. Jeb has a well-established domestic record, but less so on foreign affairs; based on heavy research, this book presents a comprehensive outline of Jeb's foreign policy stances as of early 2015.

In early 2015, the mainstream media speculated endlessly on whether Jeb and Hillary are running at all. We stated categorically in 2014 that yes, they are both running. They prepared appropriately in 2014; both published books outlining their core campaign issues (*Hard Choices,* by Hillary Clinton, reviewed on pp. 202-3; and *Immigration Wars,* by Jeb Bush, pp. 204-7). We detailed in those two book reviews the evidence that the candidates are running. Hillary's public announcement came on April 12, 2015; and Jeb's will soon follow. But those announcements are just for publicity: the campaigns already began long before that!

This was the first book in our series of books about the 2016 election, and we debated internally when to publish. We decided to publish as soon as possible after the 2014 elections, since that is the unofficial start of the 2016 presidential season.

But won't Jeb's and Hillary's issues stances change over the course of 2015? No, not likely. Candidates don't often change issue stances because then they are accused of "flip-flopping" and have to explain why they "evolved" (for example, see how Hillary evolved on gay marriage, p. 118). Of course, Jeb will develop and enunciate more specific opinions on foreign affairs over time, but we think we have captured his core values here. We have updated our content several times, but those updates are merely nuances, not about changes to core issue stances.

We considered publishing earlier but we had to wait until Jeb had at least *some* foreign policy stances. Governors like Jeb do not have voting records, and Jeb's governorship ended in 2007. Many of Jeb's opponents will be Senators who *do* have voting records; we will publish additional books in this series as the contenders become better known.

Jeb's and Hillary's issues stances are presented in a side-by-side format, so that you can directly compare the two, as if they debated on each topic. Sometimes we present their original words, in context, and sometimes we present some political analysis explaining the political context. Our "Notes" explain any background information required to understand the policy analysis, since politicians often speak in jargon. We also sometimes present more than one excerpt on one topic: those are intended for you to compare how the politicians have changed over time (or remained consistent over time), or to compare what the politicians *SAY* to what they *DO*. Keep it on your coffee-table for those inevitable arguments during the political season, to see what they *REALLY* mean!

The purpose of this book, and the mission of our website, is to inform voters about candidates' issue stances — what they believe about the issues, and what they have done to implement those beliefs. The mainstream media report on candidates' politics: who's ahead this week; who "won" the last debate; who has endorsed whom. We reject the "horse race politics" that dominates the mainstream media, and instead focus on what matters: Hillary on the issues versus Jeb on the issues.

— Jesse Gordon, Editor-in-Chief, jesse@OnTheIssues.org
First edition: December 10, 2014
Sixth edition: April 12, 2015

Table of Contents

Hillary vs. Jeb on Entitlement Issues............72

Hillary vs. Jeb on Social Issues 106

Hillary vs. Jeb on National Security Issues 136

Hillary vs. Jeb
on Domestic Issues

Domestic issues focus on joint state-federal jurisdiction or joint state-federal enforcement. On the Democratic side, the progressive wing of the Democratic Party focuses on domestic issues (and social issues) while Hillary does not. On the Republican side, the Tea Party does not focus on these issues, while the libertarian wing of the Republican Party does. Libertarians agree more with Hillary than they do with Jeb, on issues such as criminal prosecution, marijuana legalization, and Internet policy. Hence Jeb might draw a libertarian primary challenger focusing on those issues (such as Sen, Rand Paul, R-KY). This chapter includes the following sections:

- *Gun Control (pp. 12-15):* Bush and Clinton follow their respective party lines on these issues: Jeb Bush supports gun rights alongside enforcement against criminal use of guns; Hillary Clinton supports leaving the issue to the states but restricting gun sales at the federal level. Jeb has been more activist on these issues, pushing Florida's "stand your ground" law; Hillary generally offers platitudes rather than specifics; this is not her core issue. If elected president, she will likely be opportunistic: silent on this issue unless there is a new school shooting, which will prompt some reactive restriction.

- *Crime (pp. 16-19):* Jeb is "tough on crime": he supports stricter sentencing and faster executions. Hillary opposes mandatory sentencing but supports the death penalty (i.e., she is a moderate on crime). Jeb's tough stance invites a Fourth-Amendment-oriented libertarian challenge in the Republican primaries; Hillary's moderate stance invites an anti-death-penalty progressive challenge in the Democratic primaries.

- **Drugs (pp. 20-23):** Hillary focuses on alternatives to prison for drug offenders; Jeb supports prison for drug users and treats drugs as just another crime issue. Jeb opposes medical marijuana legalization, which Hillary supports. This issue is currently being addressed at the state level rather than the federal level: but the president still decides whether federal enforcement applies in states with legal pot. Jeb as president would likely undo Obama's non-enforcement policy.

- **Infrastructure / Environment (pp. 24-31):** Hillary considers infra-structure construction to be a useful form of federal investment (including investment in environmentally-oriented infrastructure). Jeb opposes government investment in infrastructure; i.e., he considers infrastructure as another stimulus program to be avoided. See economic aspects of environmental issues on pp. 56-61, and international aspects on pp. 172-175.

- **Technology / Internet (pp. 32-37):** Jeb and Hillary view the Internet from very different perspectives. Jeb focuses on pro-business and moral aspects. Hillary focuses on freedom of speech and open access, but criticizes WikiLeaks and Edward Snowden heavily. Jeb agrees with Hillary in criticizing WikiLeaks.

- **Citizen Rights / Voting (pp. 38-41):** Hillary supports more accessible voter registration; Jeb disagrees, as demonstrated in his actions in 2000. Voting rights was a big issue in the 2014 election, with Democrats claiming that Republicans limit voting for minorities and youth, who vote heavily Democratic. How the courts rule on Voter ID requirements in 2015 will determine how this issue is addressed in the 2016 election. Also see campaign finance issues on pp. 64-5.

Hillary Clinton on Domestic Issues

Jeb Bush on Domestic Issues

Hillary Clinton on Gun Rights

Rein in idea that anybody can have a gun anywhere, anytime

As Hillary Clinton mulls running for president in 2016, she has been careful to shy away from broad, sweeping policy declarations. But not when she delivered harsh criticism of gun culture in America and denounced the idea that "anybody can have a gun, anywhere, at any time." Clinton didn't dispute Americans' right to own guns. But she said access to guns in the U.S. had grown "way out of balance."

"We've got to rein in what has become an almost article of faith that anybody can have a gun anywhere, anytime," she said. "And I don't believe that is in the best interest of the vast majority of people."

Citing a number of shootings that arose from minor arguments over loud music or texting, she drew a comparison: "That's what happens in the countries I've visited where there is no rule of law and no self-control." She added: "That is something that we cannot just let go without paying attention."

Source: Wall Street Journal, "Anywhere, Anytime Gun Culture," May 6, 2014

NOTES: *Federal discussions on gun control often focus on the "D.C. handgun ban" because Congress has direct control over the gun laws of the District of Columbia. One such law was at issue in the case called "District of Columbia v. Heller," decided by the Supreme Court in 2008. The ruling determined that the 2nd Amendment does define an individual right to gun ownership, as opposed to a "collective right" for a state-run and state-armed National Guard. Much discretion was left to the states and to Congress, but Heller opens up the issue to further Supreme Court cases. Hence, gun control issues are still primarily the subject of Congressional legislation.*

Jeb Bush on Gun Rights

Stand-your-ground bill: Deadly force OK when threatened

In 2005, the governor signed into law another piece of NRA legislation on the topic of gun control. The bill was written by the NRA and expanded the rights of Floridians to use deadly force when threatened in public places. This proposal, known as the "stand your ground bill," expanded the rights of people to use guns or other deadly force to defend themselves without first trying to escape even in places outside their homes. The law stipulated that a person "has no duty to retreat and has the right to stand his or her ground and meet force with force, including deadly force."

The bill was opposed by police chiefs in high crime areas like Miami and Broward County who claimed it would lead "drivers with road rage or drunken sports fans who get into fights leaving ball games to assume that they had total immunity." The Brady Campaign to Prevent Gun Violence argued that it could be used to defend people who shoot in the emotional rage associated with domestic violence and other high-stress events.

Source: Aggressive Conservatism in Florida, by Robert Crew, p. 80,
Dec. 11, 2009

NOTE: *Many states have "Stand Your Ground" laws, justifying the use of deadly force when threatened, in contrast with the legal principle of an "obligation to retreat" first. The Florida version of the "stand your ground" law gained national attention in February 2012 in the case of Trayvon Martin shooting case. Martin, an unarmed black teenager, was shot and killed by a "neighborhood watch" coordinator, George Zimmerman. Citing the "stand your ground" law, Zimmerman was not initially charged, but was later arrested. He was acquitted of both murder and manslaughter in July 2013. Since then, the mainstream media report regularly on Zimmerman's new arrests & police encounters, including a "road rage" incident in Sept. 2014.*

Hillary Clinton on Gun Crimes

Against illegal guns; crack down on illegal gun dealers

I am against illegal guns, and illegal guns are the cause of so much death and injury in our country. I also am a political realist and I understand that the political winds are very powerful against doing enough to try to get guns off the street, get them out of the hands of young people. I don't want the federal government preempting states and cities like New York that have very specific problems.

We need to have a registry that really works with good information about people who are felons, people who have been committed to mental institutions. We need to make sure that that information is in a timely manner, both collected and presented. We do need to crack down on illegal gun dealers. This is something that I would like to see more of. We need to enforce the laws that we have on the books. I would also work to reinstate the assault weapons ban. We now have, once again, police deaths going up around the country, and in large measure because bad guys now have assault weapons again.

Source: Philadelphia primary debate, April 16, 2008

Backed off a national licensing registration plan on guns

Gun rights groups have long considered Clinton their foe. Her 2000 Senate campaign centered on a push to keep guns off the streets, and she was a forceful advocate of creating a national gun registry. But eight years later, she positioned herself as more conservative than him on gun control. She backed off the proposal for a national registry

Source: Wall Street Journal, "Anywhere, Anytime Gun Culture," May 6, 2014

NOTE: *The Newtown, Connecticut shootings in December 2012 reignited the debate on gun regulation. On December 14, 2012, Adam Lanza, 20, fatally shot twenty children and six adult staff members in a mass murder at Sandy Hook Elementary School. Several bills were proposed in the 2013-14 Congressional session: banning the sale of semi-automatic firearms, and restricting large-capacity magazines.*

Jeb Bush on Gun Crimes

Use a Gun and You're Done

During the commission of a crime:

- Pull a Gun—Mandatory 10 Years
- Pull the Trigger—Mandatory 20 Years
- Shoot Someone—25 Years to Life (whether they live or die)

New Mandatory Minimum Prison Sentences for:

- Three Time Convicted Violent Felons
- Drug Traffickers
- Aggravated Assaults/Batteries on Law Enforcement Officers or an Elderly Person
- Repeat Sexual Batterers

Source: Governor's web site, www.MyFlorida.com, "Initiatives,"
Nov. 7, 2001

Violent gun crime rate is down by more than 25%

Public safety has been protected, and convicted criminals will continue to serve at least 85 percent of their sentences. Over the last two years, the violent gun crime rate is down by more than 25 percent, translating into 18 fewer gun assaults each day in this state in 2000 compared to 1998.

Source: State of the State address to 2002 Florida Legislature,
Jan. 22, 2002

Hillary Clinton on Criminal Sentencing

Grapple with hard truths about race and justice

Hillary Clinton called for grappling with "hard truths" about racial discrimination in the justice system, and said "weapons of war" have no place on the streets of American communities. Clinton said she wanted to address "the pain and frustrations that many Americans are feeling" following grand jury decisions not to indict the police officers who killed Michael Brown in Ferguson, Missouri and Eric Garner in Staten Island, New York City. Clinton spoke for more than five minutes on the subject, saying she's "very pleased" that the U.S. Department of Justice is investigating those cases, while calling for dramatic reform overall.

"Each of us has to grapple with some hard truths about race and justice in America. Because despite all the progress we've made together, African-Americans, and most particularly, African-American men, are still more likely to be stopped and searched by police, charge with crimes, and sentenced to longer prison terms," she said.

Source: MSNBC, 'Race and justice,' by Alex Seitz-Wald Dec. 4, 2014

Address the unacceptable increase in incarceration

Q: Some people say your husband's crime bill is one of the primary factors behind the rising incarceration rate for blacks and Latinos. It earmarked $8 billion dollars for prisons and continued a trend to harsher sentencing. Do you regret how this has affected the black community?

A: I think that the results—not only at the federal level but at the state level—have been an unacceptable increase in incarceration across the board & now we have to address that. At the time, there were reasons why the Congress wanted to push through a certain set of penalties and increase prison construction and there was a lot of support for that across a lot of communities. It's hard to remember now but the crime rate in the early 1990s was very high. But we've got to take stock now of the consequences, so that's why I want to have a thorough review of all of the penalties, of all the kinds of sentencing, and more importantly start having more diversion and having more second chance programs.

Source: Iowa Brown & Black Presidential Forum, Dec. 1, 2007

Jeb Bush on Criminal Sentencing

1990s: punishment over therapy; 2010s: that hardens people

Bush once called for building prisons and emphasizing "punishment over therapy" for juvenile offenders. Today, he supports reforming the criminal justice system, arguing that incarceration can harden low-level lawbreakers into career criminals.

Bush "does not flip-flop," a Bush adviser said. "He learns. When he learns, he changes." Bush was particularly influenced by the experience of governing: he suddenly had access to measurements of what worked, and what did not, on issues like juvenile justice

Source: New York Times interview, "Evolving Views", Jan. 11, 2015

Ran as "tough on crime" candidate for governor

Bush's first campaign against Lawton Chiles was dominated by his efforts to appeal to the "tough on crime" constituency and to portray his opponent as "soft."

Governor Bush continued to focus support for "get tough on crime" laws. These include a variety of mandatory sentencing laws such as the 10-20-Life Act, the Three Strikes Violent Felony Offender Act, and the Habitual Offender Accountability Act, all passed in the glow of Bush's 1st-term victory. Despite evidence that the 10-20-Life law had no effect on the state's crime rate (Stoddard, 2006) Bush continued into his last year in office to cite these laws as some of the primary accomplishments of his administration.

Source: Aggressive Conservatism in Florida, by Robert Crew, p. 72-3, Dec. 11, 2009

Hillary Clinton on Death Penalty

Longtime advocate of death penalty, with restrictions

Clinton has been a longtime advocate of the death penalty. Clinton cosponsored the Innocence Protection Act of 2003 which became law in 2004 as part of the Justice for All Act. The bill provides funding for post-conviction DNA testing and establishes a DNA testing process for individuals sentenced to the death penalty under federal law. As first lady, she lobbied for President Clinton's crime bill, which expanded the list of crimes subject to the federal death penalty.

Source: Pew Forum on Religion and Politics 2008, Jan. 1, 2008

Require DNA testing for all federal executions

Clinton co-sponsored the Innocence Protection Act: To reduce the risk that innocent persons may be executed.

- Authorizes a person convicted of a Federal crime to apply for DNA testing to support a claim that the person did not commit the Federal crime of which the person was convicted; or any other offense that a sentencing authority may have relied upon when it sentenced the person with respect to such crime.

- Prohibits a State from denying an application for DNA testing made by a prisoner in State custody who is under sentence of death if specified conditions apply.

- Provides grants to prosecutors for DNA testing programs.

- Establishes the National Commission on Capital Representation.

- Withholds funds from States not complying with standards for capital representation.

- Provides for capital defense incentive grants and resource grants.

Source: House Resolution Sponsorship 01-HR912 on Mar 7, 2001

Jeb Bush on Death Penalty

Fewer death-row appeals; faster executions

One of Bush's central themes during the 1994 campaign was his desire to streamline the execution process for death row inmates. He proposed limiting death row inmates to only one appeal with the state, a measure he hoped would speed up the state's execution process. Bush named his plan "one trial, one appeal," and released it in spring 1994.

Enacting the "one trial, one appeal" plan would have required Florida voters to approve an amendment to the state's constitution, but this hurdle didn't dissuade Bush. In November, he reiterated his goal, saying, "I want to accelerate, not slow down, the enforcement of the death penalty in Florida."

Source: New York Times interview, "Evolving Views", Jan. 11, 2015

Called special legislative session for death penalty law

When he miscalculated on how many votes were necessary to rewrite rules for the court system in the death penalty special session, he turned to the Republican Party's rich donors to send private [police] out to retrieve missing GOP legislators. One was dragged away from a pregnant wife on the brink of childbirth, another from his sister's funeral.

The reaction to this style of leadership varied, and was not always predictable. To many, even in the much-reviled press, Jeb was a breath of fresh air. He said what he was going to do, and then he did it, without the mealy-mouthed games that are so common among elected officials.

Source: America's Next Bush, by S.V. Dáte, p.131, Feb. 15, 2007

NOTE: *The death penalty is currently implemented in 32 states (down from 34 in 2012). It was re-legalized by a Supreme Court decision in 1977. Since then, 1,392 people have been executed. About 3,000 inmates remain on 'Death Row.' Texas is by far the national leader in executions— it has executed 518 people as of November 2014, or 37% of the national total. (Oklahoma is a very distant second with 111). Florida is fourth, with 89 executions, but has 404 people on death row as of Nov. 2014 (only California has more, with 745).*

Hillary Clinton on War on Drugs

Divert non-violent drug offenders away from prison

We need diversion, like drug courts. Non-violent offenders should not be serving hard time in our prisons. They need to be diverted from our prison system. We need to make sure that we do deal with the distinction between crack and powder cocaine. And ultimately we need an attorney general and a system of justice that truly does treat people equally, and that has not happened under this administration.

Source: Democratic Primary Debate at Howard University, June 28, 2007

Address drug problem with treatment and special drug courts

Q: What is your approach to the "Drug War"?

CLINTON: I have spoken out on my belief that we should have drug courts that would serve as alternatives to the traditional criminal justice system for low-level offenders. If the person comes before the court, agrees to stay clean, is subjected to drug tests once a week, they are diverted from the criminal justice system. We need more treatment. It is unfair to urge people to get rid of their addiction and not have the treatment facilities when people finally makes up their minds to get treatment.

LAZIO: The truth is that under the Clinton administration, there has been a dramatic and troubling increase in drug abuse by our children. And that has not been addressed. I crossed party lines in 1994 and built a coalition of Republicans that passed the crime bill. If it were not for that, we would not have drug courts right now. We would not have community policing. We need to have somebody in Washington who has the ability to get the job done.

Source: Senate debate in Manhattan, Oct. 8, 2000

Jeb Bush on War on Drugs

Illegal drugs moving over US-Mexico border has intensified

The movement of illegal drugs and weapons across the US-Mexican border has intensified. On the Mexican side of the border, full-scale war among paramilitary drug cartels has left 50,000 people dead over the past 6 years.

Given Mexico's inability to control the drug cartels and the massive drug market in the US, spillover effects are inevitable. The most vivid example is the horribly failed Operation Fast and Furious, in which weapons obtained from US authorities were linked to at least a dozen violent crimes in the US. Given that the cartels control an estimated 90% of the illegal drugs entering the US, their effects extend to American gangs, crime syndicates, and drug addicts.

The president should be authorized to deploy military or National Guard forces if necessary to counter the cartels' threat and secure the US border. Preferable to US military deployment would be efforts to increase the effectiveness of Mexican authorities in dealing with the cartels on their side of the border.

Source: Immigration Wars, by Jeb Bush, p. 50-53, March 5, 2013

Reduce drug use by 50% by prevention & enforcement

One of the most serious challenges our state faces is the scourge of drugs. [My drug control strategy] reflects our will and determination to reverse the years of lost human, social, and economic potential wrought by the illegal drug trade and to bring down appreciably the numbers of our citizens caught in the grip of drug abuse My administration is determined to reduce drug use in Florida by 50%. This ambitious goal can only be achieved with the commitment of our efforts and resources on many fronts-in awareness, prevention, treatment, and law enforcement.

Drug Control Strategy 1999; Introductory Letter, July 2, 1999

Hillary Clinton on Marijuana Legalization

Medical marijuana now; wait-and-see on recreational pot

[This week], New York lawmakers approved legislation that would make it the 23rd state in the country to permit medical marijuana use, according to the Marijuana Policy Project. Voters in Alaska and possibly Oregon will decide in November whether to join Colorado and Washington in allowing the sale of marijuana for recreational use.

As the momentum behind marijuana legalization grows, the issue is becoming inescapable for potential presidential contenders in 2016. The latest to weigh in was Hillary Clinton, who was asked about marijuana last week during her book tour. She seemed slightly more open to medical marijuana than she was during the 2008 campaign, saying it was appropriate in limited cases, but that more research was necessary.

"On recreational, you know, states are the laboratories of democracy," Mrs. Clinton told CNN interviewer Christiane Amanpour. "We have at least two states that are experimenting with that right now. I want to wait and see what the evidence is."

Source: Beth Reinhard in Wall Street Journal, "Third Way," June 14, 2014

NOTE: *Marijuana is legal or partially legal in 27 states as of Nov. 2014 (up from 23 states in 2013): Alaska, Arizona, California, Colorado, Connecticut, Delaware, Hawaii, Illinois, Maine, Maryland, Massachusetts, Michigan, Minnesota, Mississippi, Montana, Nebraska, Nevada, New Hampshire, New Jersey, New Mexico, New York, North Carolina, Ohio, Oregon, Rhode Island, Vermont, Virginia, and Washington. Medical marijuana is also legal in numerous foreign countries. Medical marijuana alleviates symptoms associated with glaucoma, cancer, HIV/AIDS, and numerous mental diseases.*

Jeb Bush on Marijuana Legalization

No medical marijuana; it's just a guise toward legalization

Jeb Bush is siding with opponents of an initiative on Florida's November election ballot to make medical marijuana legal, despite strong public support for its use as a treatment for debilitating illnesses. Bush issued a statement saying the legalization of medical marijuana would hurt the state's family-friendly reputation: "Florida leaders and citizens have worked for years to make the Sunshine State a world-class location to start or run a business, a family-friendly destination for tourism and a desirable place to raise a family or retire," Bush said. "Allowing large-scale, marijuana operations to take root across Florida, under the guise of using it for medicinal purposes, runs counter to all of these efforts," he added. "I strongly urge Floridians to vote against Amendment 2 this November," he said.

Florida Governor Rick Scott signed a law in June allowing the limited use of a special non-euphoric strain of marijuana, known as Charlotte's Web. The amendment, if approved by voters, would allow marijuana to be more broadly prescribed by doctors.

Source: David Adams on Reuters: "Jeb Bush joins opposition," Aug. 14, 2014

Mandatory prison sentences for drug offenses

- Create mandatory prison sentences for persons convicted of drug trafficking.

- Mandatory minimum prison sentences of 3, 7, 15, 25 years, life or death will be imposed depending on the type and amount of the controlled substance.

- A minimum of three years will be mandated for any person convicted of possession, sale, importation, etc., of at least 25 pounds of cannabis, 4 grams of morphine, opium or heroin, or 28 grams of cocaine.

- Penalties increase as the type and amount of the drugs increase or if use of the drug results in someone's death.

Source: Governor's web site, www.MyFlorida.com, Nov. 7, 2001

Hillary Clinton on Transportation Infrastructure

Infrastructure investment creates jobs
AND improves security

Q: You've co-sponsored legislation to establish a national commission on infrastructure. Is our government actually doing anything better at making us collectively safer?

A: We have to make investments in infrastructure. This will create jobs, not only if we once again focus on our bridges, our tunnels, our ports, our airports, our mass transit—it will put millions of people to work—but it is also part of homeland security. We need to have a better infrastructure in order to protect us. And it's not only the physical infrastructure, it is the virtual infrastructure, like a national broadband system that our police and firefighters can actually access and use to be safe. So I think that we've got to look at this, with the disaster that we see, from the levees of New Orleans to the bridge in Minneapolis to what happened to us in New York City on 9/11, as the highest priority, and it will be at the top of my list when I'm president.

Source: AFL-CIO Democratic primary forum, Aug. 8, 2007

NOTE: *In 2008, Barack Obama backed proposed legislation for a National Infrastructure Reinvestment Bank. Obama suggested that the Bank would borrow $60 billion to invest in infrastructure over 10 years, while leveraging "up to $500 billion" of private investment. It would invest in high-speed trains to provide an alternative to air travel, energy efficiency, and clean energy, among other kinds of public infrastructure. The Bank would complement existing federal programs to fund infrastructure, such as the Highway Trust Fund or State Revolving Funds. It would invest primarily in surface transport infrastructure, which is likely to include highways, mass transit, and high-speed rail. Obama repeated the call in Sept. 2010, but no legislation resulted. Sen. Clinton voted NO on restoring $550 million in funding for Amtrak (S.Amdt.3015 to S.Con.Res.83; vote number 52 on Mar 15, 2006).*

Jeb Bush on Transportation Infrastructure

Enraged by citizen initiative mandating high speed rail

[Some] citizen initiatives absolutely enraged him: one in 2000 that mandated a high-speed rail system among the major Florida population centers. Jeb did not have a moral aversion to trains, fast or slow. [What enraged Jeb was than the] voters had passed a constitutional amendment over Jeb's objections.

The high-speed rail amendment had a champion, a longtime proponent of fast trains who happened to be a millionaire and was not afraid to take on Jeb. The proponents went to the voters to force Jeb to reconsider a decision he had made in 1999: undoing the long-standing state policy to bring high-speed rail to Florida. True, after more than a decade, the project seemed mired in endless delays.

But set aside for a moment the relative merits of keeping or canceling the bullet train. Jeb failed to understand that there was a much more reasonable way to build a consensus that high-speed rail should be terminated, than the method he chose, which was to decree this by fiat.

Source: America's Next Bush, by S.V. Dáte, p.148-149, Feb. 15, 2007

NOTE: *High-speed rail is common throughout Europe and East Asia, but has only one line in the United States, the Amtrak Acela line from Boston to New York City and Washington DC. President Obama made high-speed rail a goal in January 2009, but no projects are underway as of 2013. High-speed rail projects are proposed in California, Pennsylvania, Texas, and elsewhere. Replacing the projects canceled by Jeb Bush in 2000, a Florida high-speed rail project was approved by the Florida legislature in 2009, but canceled by Governor Rick Scott in 2011; a replacement was proposed as of 2012.*

Hillary Clinton on Hurricane Recovery

Overcome almost criminal indifference to Katrina rebuilding

Q: Would you support a federal law guaranteeing the right to return to New Orleans and other Gulf regions devastated by Hurricane Katrina?

KUCINICH: Absolutely. The aftermath underscores everything that's wrong in this country about race.

GRAVEL: Yes.

CLINTON: I have proposed a 10-point Gulf Coast Recovery Agenda, because it's sort of as a chicken and an egg issue. First, we've got to get the hospitals back up, [then] the law enforcement and the fire departments. This administration has basically neglected with almost criminal indifference the rebuilding of the Gulf Coast, in particular New Orleans and the parishes. Even if we were to give people a right, there is nothing to return to. We have got to rebuild New Orleans, and it's not only the protection from the levees, it is all the infrastructure.

EDWARDS: This is an issue I care about personally and deeply.

OBAMA: Halliburton or Bechtel getting the contracts to rebuild is a further compounding of the outrage.

Source: Democratic Primary Debate at Howard University, June 28, 2007

Jeb Bush on Hurricane Recovery

2004: Universal praise for handling spate of hurricanes

Jeb drew almost universal praise for his handling of the spate of hurricanes that hit Florida in 2004. All the traits that make him such a scary leader in other areas actually work to good effect, when it comes to managing disasters. He did those things that should happen when a storm strikes. Implement an effective, thorough evacuation. And, afterward, come in quickly with massive quantities of help: search and rescue teams, water, ice, food, law enforcement—in more or less that order.

A skeptical view might see this as pure political survival: the Florida hurricanes struck a broad cross section of constituents, many if not most of them white, middle class, and Republican. This view, though, misses a key component of Jeb's personality, which is that he loves a tough challenge. He really would have responded just as vigorously if the storm had struck a predominantly black, Democratic town. Katrina serves as the perfect illustration of the difference between Jeb and Big Brother.

Source: America's Next Bush, by S.V. Dáte, p. 21-22, Feb. 15, 2007

During hurricanes, prosecutes gas stations for price gouging

In that unprecedented 2004 autumn, when 4 powerful storms slammed the state within 6 weeks, Jeb's government first immersed itself into the gasoline distribution market. One hand reached out, requesting that certain areas be given priority—even as the other closed into a fist, threatening gas station owners who price gouged with prosecution.

When asked how it could be defined as price gouging if the hurricane in question had not struck anywhere near the service station with the higher-priced gas: "I would consider it price gouging even if it's in Alaska. It's price gouging if you are raising your price, irrespective of cost, beyond a certain threshold. The same commodity, if you buy it at X and you sell if at Y for a profit, that's great. But when you take advantage of the situation and raise prices even more, I think that's price gouging." Just to make sure I was hearing this right, I asked what a reasonable profit would be on a gallon of gasoline. His answer: "2 or 3 cents."

Source: America's Next Bush, by S.V. Dáte, p.168-169, Feb. 15, 2007

Hillary Clinton on Environmental Protection

Protect Obama's environmental actions

Steps that President Barack Obama has taken to help the environment must be protected, former Secretary of State Hillary Rodham Clinton said, but she avoided the contentious issue of the Keystone XL pipeline in remarks to a group that vigorously opposes it. Clinton spoke at a dinner of the League of Conservation Voters, which has come out strongly in urging elected officials to reject the project. Her speech followed a private fundraising event for Mary Landrieu (D-LA), a senator who supports the Keystone XL pipeline.

Clinton told the audience that this is an exciting time for environmental action, and mentioned progress like the agreement the U.S. reached with China a few weeks ago over cutting emissions, which Clinton said must be safeguarded. The steps "that President Obama has taken must be protected at all costs," Clinton said.

Source: Huffington Post, "Obama's Environmental Actions," Dec. 2, 2014

Remove PCBs from Hudson River by dredging 200 miles

Clinton signed a letter to the EPA Administrator:

We would like to convey our strong support for EPA's proposal to remove sediment contaminated by polychlorinated biphenyls (PCBs) from the "hot spots" in the upper Hudson River. This clean-up plan is a crucial first step towards restoring the Hudson's tremendous social, ecological, and economic value for the people of NY and NJ.

PCBs pose a serious threat to public health; they are probable human carcinogens and are known to cause neurological, reproductive, and endocrine disorders. This contamination also adversely impacts longstanding commercial, recreational, and cultural activities on the Hudson River. EPA's remediation plan is a critical first step.

Source: Letter to EPA Administrator Christine Todd Whitman on April 6, 2001

Jeb Bush on Environmental Protection

1990s: Compensate landowners;
2010s: state-run conservation

In the past, Jeb used to emphasize the rights of big landowners who felt cheated by environmental programs. Now, he is a champion of state-sponsored conservation, celebrated for his $2 billion program to restore the Everglades. Bush insists that he will not contort himself to satisfy ideologues, but his views have already changed—in presentation, in tone, in language and, at times, in substance.

A useful case study: the environment. In 1994, Bush supported a state constitutional amendment, also backed by big corporations, to compensate landowners hurt by conservation efforts. He [supported] cutting funds to purchase environmentally fragile lands and declared that "excessive regulation does not mean we are going to improve the quality of water, air or land-use planning." But Bush met with conservation experts and toured important environmental sites across Florida. When he was elected four years later, "his heart changed," an adviser said.

Source: New York Times interview, "Evolving Views", Jan. 11, 2015

Everglades are "crown jewel" of
Florida environmental legacy

The "unwavering commitment of Governor Bush and the Florida legislature" to saving the Everglades was cited by Bush's first secretary of Environmental Protection as the "crown jewel" in Florida's environmental legacy. This legislation involved both the state of Florida and the federal government and was just the kind of big-government spending plan that Bush had deplored throughout his campaigns for office and subsequently as governor. Nevertheless, when President Clinton signed the Comprehensive Everglades Restoration Plan, Bush attended the ceremony in Washington and said, "the restoration of America's Everglades has been one of my administration's top priorities" and said later that it was *THE* highest environmental priority.

Source: Aggressive Conservatism in Florida, by Robert Crew, pp.157-158,
Dec. 11, 2009

Hillary Clinton on Nuclear Power

Voted against and consistently opposed to Yucca Mountain

I voted against Yucca Mountain in 2001. I have been consistently against Yucca Mountain, looking at all the reasons why Yucca Mountain is not workable. The science does not support it. We do have to figure out what to do with nuclear waste. I have consistently and persistently been against Yucca Mountain, and I will make sure it does not come into effect when I'm president.

Source: Democratic debate in Las Vegas, Jan. 15, 2008

NOTE: *Yucca Mountain is a federally-owned mountain in Nevada which the federal government has proposed as a long-term repository for nuclear waste. Yucca Mountain was selected because, in theory, it is geologically stable enough to survive intact for the thousands of years until the nuclear waste becomes harmless. The site was first proposed under Pres. Reagan in 1985-1987; Congress canceled the program under Pres. Obama in April 2011. Lawsuits are continuing into 2015.*

Expand nuclear power plant in Czech Republic

Secretary of State Hillary Rodham Clinton lobbied the Czech government to approve an American bid for a $10 billion expansion of a nuclear power plant, even as a rival Russian offer seems to be the favorite. Clinton made her pitch for the American energy giant Westinghouse Electric Company.

Speaking to reporters, she stressed the need for the Czech Republic to wean itself off of a dependency on Russia for fuel. "We are encouraging the Czech Republic to diversify its energy sources and suppliers," Clinton said. Revitalizing the Temelin nuclear power plant is a big part of the Czech agenda to radically boost its nuclear power production, defying global skepticism about the use of atomic energy in the aftermath of last year's meltdown at Japan's Fukushima plant.

Source: Politico.com, "U.S. bid for Czech nuclear project,"
by Deepti Hajela, Dec. 2, 2014

Jeb Bush on Nuclear Power

Use federal funds for nuclear cleanup, with state input

Bush signed the Southern Governors' Association resolution:

- Whereas, in order to protect the health, safety and welfare of our citizens by maintaining safe and clear strategies for the transportation, disposition and environmental clean-up of the nation's nuclear materials, including nuclear weapons materials, at DOE nuclear energy and weapons complexes; now, therefore, be it

- Resolved, that the Southern Governors' Association urges Congress and the President in any national energy policy:

- provide full funding for all of DOE's past and present commitments related to clean-up operations at DOE nuclear energy and weapons complexes and disposition plans for nuclear materials, including nuclear weapons materials;

- provide full funding for all state public health and environmental sampling and analysis activities at DOE nuclear energy and weapons complexes;

- and provide clear instruction to DOE that states' rights must be respected and that plans regarding DOE sites for processing of DOE research and weapons waste must be made in consultation with the various states concluding in mutually agreeable terms.

Source: Resolution of Southern Governor's Assn. on Energy Policy on Sep 9, 2001

NOTE: *The last new nuclear plant to come on-line in the US was in 1996, due to both political and economic issues. Pres. Obama promoted new nuclear plants during as part of a comprehensive energy plan; the NRC accordingly approved a new nuclear plant design in Dec. 2011, the first in decades. Since then, construction permits have been issued to dozens of new reactors, with construction underway at five of them (this compares to 100 existing reactors at 62 different nuclear plant sites). Proponents describe this as the beginning of a "nuclear renaissance."*

Hillary Clinton on Net Neutrality

Ensure net neutrality: no corporate-tiered Internet

Clinton co-sponsored against no corporate-tiered Internet: "A bill to amend the communications act of 1934 to ensure net neutrality":

- Broadband service providers shall not interfere with the ability of any person to use a broadband service to access or offer any lawful content via the Internet;

- only prioritize content or services based on the type of content or services and the level of service purchased by the user, without charge for such prioritization.

Sen. DORGAN. "Broadband operators announced their interest in acting in discriminatory ways, planning to create tiers on the Internet that could restrict content providers' access to the Internet unless they pay extra for faster speeds or better service. Under their plan, the Internet would become a new world where those content providers who can afford to pay special fees would have better access to consumers. This fundamentally changes the way the Internet has operated and threaten to derail the democratic nature of the Internet."

Source: Internet Freedom Preservation Act (S.215) on Jan 9, 2007

Regulate Internet as utility to avoid "Internet fast-lanes"

Clinton lent her support to net neutrality as federal regulators consider Obama-backed rule change that would ban Internet "fast lanes."

- Give federal regulators more power over the Internet

- Ban Internet "fast lanes" for some content producers while slowing down data arrival time for others

- Clinton said she believed that her former boss was "right" to get involved and she would vote in favor of net neutrality

Clinton said she would vote for net neutrality if she were in a position to "because as I understand it, it's Title II with a lot of changes within it, in order to avoid the worst of the utility regulation."

Source: London Daily Mail, "Open Internet rules," Feb. 24, 2015

Jeb Bush on Net Neutrality

Regulating the Internet is craziest ideas I've ever heard

Bush weighed in on the Federal Communications Commission's (FCC) recent move to impose utility-style rules for the Internet, which have been blasted by Republicans and major cable companies. "The idea of regulating access to the Internet with a 1934 law is one of the craziest ideas I've ever heard," he said.

The comments were the first remarks Bush had made about net neutrality, though they mirrored the opinions of other Republicans after the FCC last month reclassified broadband Internet as a "telecommunications service" similar to phone lines under the 1934 Communications Act.

Bush also echoed a common refrain that President Obama had "steamrolled" the FCC by openly endorsing the tough utility-style rules in a high profile video and through staffers' work at the White House. Republican have worried that the FCC — a legally independent agency — has lost its legitimacy due to the new Web rules. "I hope that Congress acts" to reverse the rules, Bush added.

Source: TheHill weblog, "Craziest Idea," by Julian Hattem, March 9, 2015

NOTE: *Net Neutrality is the principle behind an "open Internet": that Internet service providers may not discriminate between different kinds of online content. In the view of its proponents, Net Neutrality guarantees a level playing field for all websites and Internet technologies. Proponents of Net Neutrality include Internet content providers such as Yahoo.com, eBay.com, and Amazon.com. In the view of its opponents a free market should allow content providers to guarantee speedy delivery of their data by paying an extra fee. Opponents include hardware providers such as AT&T and Comcast, plus conservative and libertarian think tanks such as Americans for Tax Reform and the Cato Institute.*

Hillary Clinton on Internet Freedom

Balance Internet freedom of speech against defamation

In 1998, reporters questioned Clinton on how the White House viewed the Internet's decentralizing effects, in the context of White House sex scandal stories on the web:

Q: I wonder if you think this new Internet media is necessarily an entirely good thing?

A: Every time technology makes an advance, we are all going to have to rethink how we deal with this, because there are always competing values. As exciting as these new developments are, there are a number of serious issues without any kind of editing function or gate-keeping function. What does it mean to have the right to defend your reputation, or to respond to what someone says? I'm a big pro-balance person.

Q: Sounds like you favor regulation.

A: We've got to see whether our existing laws protect people's right of privacy. So I think we have to tread carefully.

Source: Vast Right-Wing Conspiracy, by Amanda Carpenter, p.110-112, Oct. 11, 2006

When ideas are blocked, the Internet is diminished for all

If SOPA/PIPA are passed, the U.S. government and copyright holders can sue any website associated with infringing intellectual property. For you and me, this means if someone posts a YouTube song,or a book quote, an image to our blog, *WE* could be sued or shut down.

Hillary Clinton captured the problem best in her response to SOPA/PIPA: "When ideas are blocked, information deleted, conversations stifled, and people constrained in their choices, the Internet is diminished for all of us," Clinton stated. "There isn't an economic Internet and a social Internet and a political Internet. There's just the Internet." This week, SOPA was shelved (though many believe it's not gone for good).

Source: alibrown.com blog, Jan. 18, 2012

Jeb Bush on Internet Freedom

Practice technology in context of virtue; not isolated pleasure

[With e-mail], not only do we lose the human contact with the persons we are communicating with, but also the time spent online or tuning out with your Walkman is time spent away from your spouse, your children, your neighbor. We are becoming socially disconnected from our fellowman.

We spend too much time downloading gobs of useless information and this is becoming a serious problem for our culture. The social canyons created by rushing rivers of technology and modernization must be bridged. But we must be careful not to undo the good things these rivers have brought us.

We must reengage ourselves in our social settings, in our neighborhoods and communities, but do so in a way that acknowledges the advances made by our society. We should practice our technology in the context of character and virtue. Use it for the benefit of mankind, not to stimulate isolated pleasure. We must continue our technological revolution but we cannot use it as a substitute for social interaction.

Source: Profiles in Character, by Jeb Bush & B.Yablonski, p. 71-73
Nov 1, 1995

NOTE *(opposite page): SOPA and PIPA refer to two bills before Congress in 2012 on Internet regulation. SOPA, the House's Stop Online Piracy Act, has 28 sponsors, and PIPA, the Senate's Protect IP Act, has 40 sponsors. Proponents claim the bills would better protect electronic copyright ("IP," or Intellectual Property); opponents argue that SOPA and PIPA would censor the Internet. Internet users and entrepreneurs oppose the two bills; google.com and wikipedia.com held a "blackout" on Jan. 18, 2012 in protest. Jeb Bush has offered no opinion on SOPA and PIPA.*

Hillary Clinton on Government Secrecy

Make sure surveillance doesn't go too far, like Snowden did

During the promotional tour for her book "Hard Choices," Clinton stood behind the US surveillance programs and criticized former government contractor Edward Snowden for leaking sensitive information. Most of what Snowden disclosed, she said, "concerned the surveillance that the US undertakes, totally legally, against other nations."

While she has backed reforms to "make sure that it doesn't go too far," Clinton told NPR that "collecting information about what's going around the world is essential to our security."

"There were other ways that Mr. Snowden could have expressed his concerns," such as reaching out to Congress, Clinton continued. "I think everyone would have applauded that because it would have added to the debate that was already started. Instead, he left the country, taking with him a huge amount of sensitive information," she said, adding that during her trips to Russia, she would leave all electronics on the State Department plane with the batteries out to prevent hacking.

Source: M. R. Wilson in TheHill.com, "Clinton vs. Warren," Aug. 24, 2014

WikiLeaks tears at fabric of government

Clinton blasted the release of confidential diplomatic cables by online whistle-blower WikiLeaks and vowed to ensure that such a breach never happens again. "Let's be clear. This disclosure is not just an attack on America—it's an attack on the international community," Clinton said. Such leaks, she said, "tear at the fabric" of responsible government.

"There is nothing laudable about endangering innocent people, and there is nothing brave about sabotaging the peaceful relations between nations," she added. Clinton emphasized that she wanted to "make it clear to the American people and to our friends and partners that we are taking aggressive steps" to hold those who leaked the documents to account.

Source: Scott Neuman on NPR, "Clinton on WikiLeaks," Nov. 29, 2010

Jeb Bush on Government Secrecy

WikiLeaks is abhorrent but showed seriousness of Iran threat

Bush commented on the heels of a disclosure of secret U.S. diplomatic communications made by WikiLeaks. Several documents indicated that Arab states, including Saudi Arabia, had pressed the U.S. to bomb Iran.

Bush called the latest WikiLeaks disclosure of tens of thousands of confidential diplomatic cables "abhorrent" and "absolutely disgusting." But the Florida Republican said the content of the cables do reveal the true source of the ongoing instability roiling the Middle East.

"It does show that Iran poses the greatest threat in the region, when countries that publicly say Israel is the greatest threat, privately say the obvious, which is that Iran is the greatest threat," Bush told Newsmax. "It should bring home the fact that this should be a higher priority in terms of our own foreign policy." Bush also said sanctions against Iran, whose nuclear-arms program he termed "a huge threat," should be further strengthened as well.

Source: David A. Patten and Kathleen Walter on Newsmax.com, Nov. 29, 2010

NOTES: *From 2006 to 2013, WikiLeaks posted more than 250,000 classified documents online. The documents offered an unprecedented look at the American diplomatic process—and most well-known, in April 2010 releasing a video documenting a war crime by U.S. forces in Baghdad (obtained from Pfc. Bradley Manning, who in 2013 was sentenced to 35 years in prison for disclosing the classified video). WikiLeaks' Julian Assange is a hero to progressives who believe in open government and oppose secrecy, but a traitor to many others.*

The progressive hero / traitor mantle passed to Edward Snowden in March 2013, with the release of over 100,000 documents from the National Security Agency (NSA), exposing a massive program of domestic surveillance of U.S. citizens. When the U.S. government filed charges, Snowden fled to Russia, where he is seeking asylum in Latin America. As with Julian Assange, opponents claim that Snowden breached national security; supporters claim Snowden exposed illegal federal activities.

Hillary Clinton on Open Government

Administration secrecy shreds the Constitution

Our Constitution is being shredded. We know about the secret wiretaps, the secret military tribunals, the secret White House e-mail accounts. We've seen US attorneys fired to silence them because they didn't bring bogus lawsuits against Democrats during election years. We've seen information taken off of government websites. It is a stunning record of secrecy and corruption, of cronyism run amok. It is everything our founders were afraid of, everything our Constitution was designed to prevent.

Source: Take Back America 2007 Conference, June 20, 2007

Transparent government includes federal agency blogs

I want to have a much more transparent government, and I think we now have the tools to make that happen. You know, I said the other night at an event in New Hampshire, I want to have as much information about the way our government operates on the Internet so the people who pay for it, the taxpayers of America, can see that. I want to be sure that, you know, we actually have like agency blogs. I want people in all the government agencies to be communicating with people, because for me, we're now in an era—which didn't exist before—where you can have instant access to information, and I want to see my government be more transparent. I want to make sure that we limit, if we can't eliminate all the no-bid contracts, the cronyism, I want to cut 500,000 government contractors.

Source: Meet the Press: 2008 "Meet the Candidates" series, Jan. 13, 2008

NOTES: *The voter registration issue has been brewing since 2000, and may result in legislation prior to the 2016 election. Republicans favor "Voter Identification" requirements, on the grounds of ensuring the integrity of the vote. Democrats respond that individual fraud is extremely rare and has not ever affected an election outcome. The partisan reason for these stances is that voter identification discourages voting by youth, minorities, and the elderly, all of whom disproportionately favor Democrats. In general, Hillary supports more open voter registration, while Jeb opposes it.*

Jeb Bush on Open Government

Longer time and more fees to see public records

Even lower in his esteem than the other two branches of government were the members of the press and the public who attempted to obtain information about his administration that he did not wish to be generally known. He built new barriers to the state's public records law, forcing requesters to wait weeks or months, and then pay hundreds and thousands of dollars, to obtain information that should have been theirs for the asking. He instituted a regime of message control—rewarding journalists who carried his official line, punishing those who did not, but also attempting to censor outside entities, like a chamber of commerce study group that found far less than advertised in his touted educational gains.

Source: America's Next Bush, by S.V. Dáte, p. 41-42, Feb. 15, 2007

OpEd: Foundation for Florida's Future hides campaign donors

The Foundation for Florida's Future did keep Bush in the public eye, but at some cost. It generated controversy for Bush on two issues. First, the foundation was attacked for failure to identify those who had made financial contributions, suggesting that they were simply disguised campaign contributions. Secondly, it was criticized for the proportion of its funds it devoted to programmatic concerns.

The FFF raised more than $1.7 million in 1995 & 1996, primarily in $5,000 amounts. While the foundation released the names of its donors, it did so only in general categories related to the size of their donation. Thus in 1995 FFF released the names of 131 donors of $5,000 or more, but would not connect name to specific amounts. [That left] reporters to ask, "Who gave $50,000, a sum 100 times greater than the $500 limit for the Bush re-election campaign?"

Source: Aggressive Conservatism in Florida, by Robert Crew, p. 10,
Dec. 11, 2009

Hillary Clinton on Voter Registration

Same-day voter registration; no oppressive ID requirements

Q: What would you do to ensure that all Americans are able to cast a free and unfettered vote and that that vote be counted?

A: I introduced a piece of legislation called the "Count Every Vote Act." We heard firsthand from people in Cleveland who had been disenfranchised, all the people who waited for 10 or 12 hours because the precincts they were in only had two voting machines, whereas down the road, in a more affluent and whiter precinct, people could vote in a couple of minutes. We need to end the disparities in resources. We need to have same day voter registration and earlier absentee voting. We need to make it clear that we'd like to try a holiday or a weekend for voting because more people will be able to get off work and actually do it. And we need to end the oppressive ID requirements that are turning people away from the polls and restore the voting rights of ex-felons.

Source: NAACP Presidential Primary Forum, July 12, 2007

Voter suppression revives old demons of discrimination

Hillary Clinton delivered a forceful and impassioned defense of the Voting Rights Act, condemning laws and other moves in some states that she said are reviving "old demons of discrimination."

Clinton said: "Anyone that says that racial discrimination is no longer a problem in American elections must not be paying attention. We do—let's admit it—have a long history of shutting people out: African Americans, women, gays & lesbians, people with disabilities. And throughout our history, we have found too many ways to divide and exclude people from their ownership of the law and protection from the law."

Clinton criticized the Supreme Court's recent decision to strike down Section 4 of the Voting Rights Act, urging Congress to reconsider the 1965 landmark law and calling on citizen activists to mobilize.

Source: Philip Rucker in Washington Post, "Demons of Discrimination," Aug. 12, 2013

Jeb Bush on Voter Registration

Scrubbed voter registration rolls to eliminate felons

Just as he had in 2000, Gov. Bush pushed ahead with an aggressive scrubbing of the voter registration rolls to eliminate felons, who under a dated, Jim Crow-era state law cannot regain their right to vote unless they first undergo a tedious clemency process. Needless to say, a disproportionate number of the felons are black, and blacks disproportionately vote for Democrats.

Jeb not only defended the creation of the list, but also the clearly unconstitutional law that prevented the list from being released as a public record. It took a lawsuit by CNN to get the matter before a judge—who needed about 5 seconds to declare the law unconstitutional and order Jeb to turn over the master voter roll to anybody who wanted it. And it took about 5 days for reporters to notice that there was something unusual about the felon list: it included virtually no Hispanics. Of course, Florida Hispanics tend to vote disproportionately for Republicans, but Jeb and his people said that that had nothing to do with the glitch.

Source: America's Next Bush, by S.V. Dáte, p.123-124, Feb. 15, 2007

No conspiracy of hackers manipulating electronic voting

After the 2000 election, Jeb Bush promised to replace much of the state's hated voting technology, including Palm Beach County's butterfly ballots along with their notorious hanging chads.

The new system the counties chose was touch-screen voting machines. But that didn't work out too well. The costs were high. The glitches were constant. And worst of all, no one seemed to trust the electronic counts. Without paper records, how did voters know their choices were being accurately recorded? How could anyone be sure some evil hacker wasn't manipulating the results? Jeb dismissed those fears as "conspiracy theories." But in the run-up to the 2004 presidential election, the Republican Party of Florida sent out fliers urging their voters to use absentee ballots because of the disturbing absence of a paper trail from the Election Day machines.

Source: The Party's Over, by Gov. Charlie Crist, p. 92, Feb. 4, 2014

Hillary vs. Jeb on Economic Issues

Economic issues focus on the recession recovery and all fiscal matters. Jeb and Hillary mostly follow their respective party opinions on these issues, but are both moderates who are willing to compromise on economic issues. That means that both might draw primary opponents who are more extreme on economic issues. This chapter includes the following sections:

- *Corporations (pp. 46-49):* Both Jeb and Hillary say they oppose corporate welfare, but both their critics say they encourage corporate welfare. Hillary portrays herself as a consumer advocate; Jeb portrays himself as a deregulator; but neither makes corporate issues a major focus of their policies. Hillary will feel pressure in the primaries from the progressives on this issue, because they believe Hillary is too beholden to corporate interests. The progressives dream would be nominating Sen. Elizabeth Warren (D-MA, who ran a consumer protection agency), but the actual anti-corporate progressive primary candidate will likely be Sen. Bernie Sanders (D-VT, who has spent a long career on anti-corporatism), and then Dr. Jill Stein (Green-MA) in the general.

- *Budget & Economy (pp. 50-55):* Jeb and Hillary differ strongly on how to handle the Great Recession, following their party lines: Hillary supported the bank bailout and the stimulus package, but wanted more help for people struggling with their mortgages; Jeb supported the bank bailout but opposed the stimulus package and the automaker bailout. The issue for 2016 is how to extend (or terminate) the Great Recession programs for the post-Recession period.

- *Economic aspects of energy & environment (pp. 56-61):* Hillary's balance of environment vs. economy is to invest in green energy while restricting oil drilling, like most Democrats. Jeb does respect environmental protection (see Jeb's Everglades defense, p. 29), but Jeb and just about all Republicans greatly disrespect "green energy." Jeb claims that green energy is a form of "crony capitalism," i.e. that it is just another federal program that provides an excuse to enrich Democratically-favored industries, but is more moderate than many in the GOP. Jeb treats offshore drilling as an environmental protection issue, and hence mostly opposes it, unlike most Republicans, who support it. See international aspects of environmental issues on pp. 172-175, and infrastructure aspects on pp. 24-31.

- **Government Reform (pp. 62-65):** On the policy side, this section focuses on the size of the federal government, which Jeb thinks should be more privatized, while Hillary prefers less privatization. On the political side, Hillary would restrict campaign finance (despite that her PAC is one of the largest) while Jeb would loosen campaign finance. The 2016 campaign will be the first run under the new *Citizens United* unlimited PAC money rules; Hillary opposes that while Jeb has been silent on the issue so far. Also see voting issues on pp. 38-41.

- **Tax Reform (pp. 66-71):** including income taxes, tax rates, and bracket redistribution. Hillary would raise capital gains taxes and freeze inheritance taxes. Directly opposite, Jeb would reduce capital gains and inheritance taxes, which is the mainstream Republican view. But Bush differs from many Republicans by declining the "No New Taxes" pledge that many candidates sign. Jeb's father, the senior George Bush, famously broke his no-new-taxes pledge, and Jeb's compromising attitude on taxes means he may draw a primary opponent from among economic conservatives.

Hillary Clinton on Economic Issues

Jeb Bush on Economic Issues

Hillary Clinton on Corporate Regulation

We need bankruptcy reform, but we need the right kind

In the Senate, Clinton voted for an overhaul to the bankruptcy system that would have made debt forgiveness more difficult for borrowers to obtain. She said in 2008 that she regretted the vote.

The credit card lobby pushed hard for the legislation, which did not prevail when Clinton voted for it in 2001, but did become law after another attempt by Congress in 2005. (Clinton did not vote in that round; she missed the vote to be with Bill Clinton after his heart surgery.)

"The right kind of reform is necessary," Clinton said in a press release about the legislation in 2001. "We're on our way toward that goal, and I hope we can achieve final passage of a good bankruptcy reform bill this year" During her initial presidential campaign, she said she would have voted against the 2005 bill that eventually passed.

Source: M. R. Wilson in TheHill.com, "Clinton vs. Warren," Aug. 24, 2014

FactCheck: Yes, Bush shrunk CPSC; but it shrank before Bush

When discussing the safety concerns about toys imported from China, Clinton accused the Bush administration of crippling the Consumer Product Safety Commission, saying, "The reason we have such few recalls... is because this administration has basically de-fanged" the CPSC.

It's true that Bush has made some controversial appointments to the CPSC. And during the Bush administration, the commission has gone from 480 to 401 full-time employees (including only one full-time toy tester). But not all of this can be pinned on Bush. CPSC has been shrinking for decades. Between 1980 and 1982, during Ronald Reagan's administration, the agency went from 978 employees (its peak number) to only 649. Even during Bill Clinton's time in office, the agency went from 515 to 480 employees.

Source: FactCheck on Democratic radio debate on NPR, Dec. 4, 2007

Jeb Bush on Corporate Regulation

Champion enterprise zones and business deregulation

The past four years have not been kind to small businesses. Republicans should bring their message of low taxes and moderate regulatory policies to Hispanic communities whose economic future depends on such policies.

In particular, licensing regulations often disproportionately hamper Hispanic businesses that tend to operate informally. Republicans should champion enterprise zones, deregulation of entry into occupations and businesses that require few skills and little capital, and lower business taxes. More important, they should engage Hispanic business and community leaders in identifying & eradicating barriers to enterprise. As Democrats continue compounding the inherent risks of small businesses by piling on taxes & regulations at every level of government, Republicans should be seen as ardent defenders of small businesses.

Source: Immigration Wars, by Jeb Bush, p.216, March 5, 2013

NOTES: *The federal government "bailed out" the Big Three automakers early in the 2008 Great Recession. The bailout consisted of direct loans to General Motors and Chrysler, and a line of credit for Ford Motors. President Bush's loan to GM and Chrysler (originally $17 billion and ultimately $64 billion) was contingent upon the two automakers following federal government restructuring of their companies, and later improving fuel efficiency standards. The purpose of the bailout was to avoid bankruptcy and a large surge in unemployment of auto workers. It was criticized (mostly by Republicans) as "government intervention."*

The U.S. Treasury sold its last GM stock from the bailout loan in December 2013, repaying taxpayers $39 billion out of the total $50 billion invested (a 20% loss). When Chrysler stock was sold in 2011, taxpayers were repaid $11.1 billion out of a $12.4 billion (a 10% loss). Ford received a $5.9 billion loan in 2009, which is still being repaid. In theory, six million jobs were saved.

Hillary Clinton on Corporate Welfare

Enough with corporate welfare; enough with golden parachutes

Let's finally do something about the growing economic inequality that is tearing our country apart. The top 1% of our households hold 22% of our nation's wealth. That is the highest concentration of wealth in a very small number of people since 1929. So let's close that gap. Let's start holding corporate America responsible, make them pay their fair share again. Enough with the corporate welfare. Enough with the golden parachutes. And enough with the tax incentives for companies to shift jobs overseas.

Source: Take Back America 2007 Conference, June 20, 2007

Outraged at CEO compensation

[In Bill's cabinet, Labor Secretary] Robert Reich was gladdened by Hillary's passionate condemnation of corporate-executive compensation. "These are real issues, Bill," she said, pointing out that the average CEO of a big company "is now earning 200 times the average hourly wage. Twenty years ago the ratio was about forty times. People all over this country are really upset about this."

Source: For Love of Politics, by Sally Bedell Smith, p.220, Oct. 23, 2007

Corporate lawyer at Rose Law while Bill was Arkansas Attorney General

It was Hillary who decided that she wanted to be financially secure, and took the steps to accomplish that. Upon Bill's election as attorney general, Hillary was now willing to consider corporate law. Bill recommended the Rose Law Firm. Rose was the ultimate establishment law firm, representing the most powerful economic interests in the state. The firm's partners were all white men. Hillary, with her view of the law as an instrument for social reform, would be a radical departure

Source: A Woman in Charge, by Carl Bernstein, pp.127-9, June 5, 2007

Jeb Bush on Corporate Welfare

Fight corporate welfare: snouts out of public trough

Responsibility and self-government [also apply to] programs that are considered by many to be corporate welfare. Limited government does not mean limited for only one portion of society, one economic class. We cannot ask government to do less for the many while doing more for the few. Limited government is about the fair distribution of limited resources, meaning that as we criticize social spending for being no solution to our social problems, we should also criticize unnecessary corporate entitlements as no cure for our competitiveness problems. Creating barriers to competition and sanctuaries for profit is no answer. Many industries realize that they profit from a bigger, more involved government. Yet a return to limited self-government would not be complete without pushing these corporate snouts out of the public trough. Limiting the role of government must be a process that is rational, equitable, and principled.

Source: Profiles in Character, by Jeb Bush, p.172-173, Nov. 1, 1995

Stop rewarding portfolio Americans over paycheck Americans

In order to spur the economy, Bush said ObamaCare needs to be repealed. "Our current policy rewards portfolio Americans at the expense of paycheck America while enabling the greatest sustained deficits in American history," Bush said. "Conservatives need to advance economic freedom by working to repeal ObamaCare and replacing it with a system that is consumer-directed, less coercive and significantly less costly."

Source: Tal Kopan on Politico.com, "Crony Capitalism" , Oct. 29, 2013

Hillary Clinton on Recession Bailout

Government action to tackle recession, not tax cuts

Q: Why would you be better fit than the Republican nominee to turn this economy around as we seem to be headed for a downturn, if not a recession?

A: Well, it is the case that the economy is becoming a greater and greater concern because, obviously, it's not working for the vast majority of Americans. I've been out there since March talking about this mortgage crisis and urging much more aggressive action to stem the foreclosures that are beginning to cascade around the country. But at some point you've got to have government action to really tackle these problems. The stimulus package is a start, but it's not nearly enough. What we have to do is have an economic policy that once again creates jobs with rising incomes. Obviously, I disagree with the Republicans about the tax cuts for people making more than $250,000 a year. I think we should let those expire and use that money on universal health care and other needs that people have that are really directly related to the state of the economy.

Source: Fox News interview: "Choosing the President" series, Feb. 3, 2008

Help people; don't just bail out banks

Q: We've seen all this turmoil in the markets caused by the credit crunch and the crisis in the mortgage markets. The Federal Reserve lowered the discount rate for banks. Should they lower rates for everyone else, yes or no?

A: I'm glad they did what they did. But it can't be just left to a bail-out for the banks. We've got to figure out how we're going to [help] people facing foreclosures. And I have recommendations on that, that do not lend themselves to an easy yes or no.

Source: Democratic primary debate on "This Week," Aug. 19, 2007

Jeb Bush on Recession Bailout

Bank bailouts were needed to avoid financial unraveling

Q: Should McCain have opposed the bailout?

A: I don't know. Maybe if he had opposed the bailout based on some actual principles he could express, that would have shown leadership.

Q: You have defended the early bailouts, those implemented by your brother?

A: If there wasn't any support, given the intricate nature of all these credit-default swaps, you could have had an unraveling of the financial system. So I'm not sure there was another choice. There may have been a different means of doing it.

Source: Tucker Carlson interview of Jeb Bush in Esquire, Aug. 1, 2009

Auto bailout was government intervening; bank bailout was ok

Former Florida Gov. Jeb Bush was invited to speak to the House Budget Committee by the committee's chairman, Rep. Paul Ryan, R-Wisc., author of a federal budget despised by Democrats in part for its proposed changes to the Medicare program for seniors. Bush's remarks focused on removing barriers to free enterprise, but throughout the hearing, he was free with his opinions on all sorts of other policy matters.

Bush said that until the hearing, he hadn't been asked his opinion on the automotive bailout or the bank bailouts. He told the committee he didn't support the auto bailout—what he describes as "a form of capitalism where the government intervenes in a very muscular kind of way." The positions puts him in line with Romney. Bush did say, however, say that he thought some aspects of the bank bailout were necessary.

Source: Tampa Bay Times, "Jeb Bush cools VP chatter," June 1, 2012

Hillary Clinton on Mortgage Crisis

Foreclosure moratorium mitigates agony; doesn't prolong it

Q: Does your plan prolong the subprime agony?

A: No. I think it helps to mitigate the agony. What I hear as I go in and out of people's homes and talk to so many who have already lost their homes, they're in foreclosure, they see these interest rates that are about to go up and they know they can't pay them, is that we take action now. The mortgage crisis is not only destroying home ownership, it is having a ripple effect across the world. So my moratorium for 90 days is a work-out. It's not a bailout. I want people to be able to see whether they can stay in their homes paying a rate that is affordable for them. The interest rate freeze is merited. If you're a homeowner who has been at the bottom of this incredible scheme that was established, you're left holding the bag and you don't have the house anymore.

Source: Congressional Black Caucus Democratic debate, Jan. 21, 2008

Freeze mortgage interest rates for five years

Q: How do you pay for stimulus to the economy?

A: This stimulus shouldn't be paid for. The whole point of stimulus is going to require an injection of federal funding. I want to freeze interest rates for five years, and I want to have a $30 billion package that will go in and try to stabilize the housing market and stabilize communities that are going to be affected by that.

Q: Do people who opted for cheap mortgages bear responsibility?

A: The bankers, the mortgage lenders, the brokers, all bear a lot of the responsibility, because many of the practices that were followed were just downright predatory and fraudulent. There is no doubt about that. A lot of people got into subprime loans who frankly could've been in a conventional fixed-rate loan.

Source: Meet the Press: 2008 "Meet the Candidates" series, Jan. 13, 2008

Jeb Bush on Mortgage Crisis

Mortgage bankers got us into this mess; they should solve it

Former Florida Governor Jeb Bush spoke before attendees of the Mortgage Bankers Association conference in Chicago. He advised advocacy: "Advocate and persuade. There is real hostility toward business in Washington. There's not a lot of love. In those kinds of circumstances, most business organizations go into a fetal position. That doesn't work," he said. Bush spoke against turning a blind eye, and instead encouraged proactivity.

"The problem that got us into this mess was the real estate problem, but there is very little going on to solve the real estate problems," he said. "Who better to advocate a policy to get us out of this mess? Why not defend your positions in the marketplace of ideas? Business has gotten way too timid. The natural inclination is to cower. I would encourage you to stand up."

Source: Elizabeth Ecker in Reverse Mortgage Daily, Oct. 12, 2011

NOTE: *"TARP" refers to the Troubled Asset Relief Program, Pres. Bush's 2008 program to purchase assets from financial institutions to alleviate the subprime mortgage crisis. Congress initially approved $700 billion; the Dodd-Frank Act reduced that to $475 billion. The purpose of the bank bailout was to avoid "collapse of the financial system" because some banks were "too big to fail." It was criticized (mostly by Democrats) as "rewarding the bankers who caused the recession." TARP money went to mortgage banks and mortgage insurance companies, not to individual mortgage holders.*

The Treasury has been earning interest on most of the TARP money invested or loaned. As of December 2014, it has earned $271 billion. Including interest revenue, the government has profited $46 billion as of December 2014.

Hillary Clinton on Budget Deficit

Look back to 1990s to see how I'd be fiscally responsible

Q: Would it be a priority of your administration to balance the federal budget every year?

A: Well, fiscal responsibility is a very high priority for me. We don't have to go back very far in our history, in fact just to the 1990s, to see what happens when we do have a fiscally responsible budget that does use rules of discipline to make sure that we're not cutting taxes or spending more than we can afford. I will institute those very same approaches. You can't do it in a year. It'll take time. But the economy will grow again when we start acting fiscally responsible. And then we can save money in the government by cutting out private contractors, closing loopholes, getting the health care system to be more efficient. We'll do all of this at the same time, but the results will take awhile for us to actually see.

Source: Des Moines Register Democratic debate, Dec. 13, 2007

NOTE: Spending totals in FY2015's $3.8 trillion budget:
- ***Non-discretionary spending:***
- *$897 billion (23%) Social Security payments*
- *$860 billion (23%) Medicare/Medicaid/SCHIP payments*
- *$251 billion (7%) interest on the National Debt*
- *$659 billion (17%) other 'mandatory' payments*
-
- ***Discretionary spending:***
- *$606 billion (16%) national defense*
- *$543 billion (14%) other 'discretionary spending'*

When politicians discuss cutting "non-discretionary non-defense" spending, they are focusing on only 14% of the budget, and really mean "don't cut spending." The Sequester cuts the budget across-the-board and hence is described as cutting mostly entitlements and defense, which is true because entitlements and defense are most of the budget.

Jeb Bush on Budget Deficit

Bipartisan compromise to reduce the deficit significantly

Jeb Bush seems to be bucking the trend. He is seeking to return the party to its ideological moorings—toward the centrism of his grandfather. Even before the GOP's ignominious defeat in November, Jeb was offering tough love to his party, suggesting that Republicans stand up to Grover Norquist and craft a bipartisan compromise to reduce the deficit significantly. But will Republicans listen? There are many reasons to believe they won't.

Hence, in evaluating Jeb's prescriptions for fiscal responsibility, today's Republicans should recall the Bushes' past political palm reading. While Jeb's prescriptions are in the party's long-term interest, they will be difficult to execute, given the strength of the party's coalition members.

Can Jeb sway a resistant party base? It's quite possible: His family's odyssey has reflected the party's shifts for 50 years, and he's uniquely positioned to convince his peers.

Source: Jeff Smith, CNN Opinion, "Sway the GOP on taxes," Dec. 11, 2012

__NOTE:__ The annual budget deficits don't get paid off each year — they just accumulate year after year, into the National Debt, which is currently at $17.9 trillion as of the end of 2014. The 2015 budget includes a deficit of $565 billion (more spending than revenue). We pay interest in that debt — amounting to $251 billion in Fiscal Year 2015. Congress determines the "__debt ceiling__," which is the total amount that the federal government can be in debt. The actual debt must remain lower than the "debt ceiling" or the government may not borrow more money.

The "__fiscal cliff__" refers to the set of policy changes that took place on Jan. 1, 2013, including the expiration of the Bush tax cuts; the implementation of the "__sequester__" (across-the-board spending cuts); and the raising of the national debt borrowing limit. Alarmists claim that allowing the current policy set will send the US back into recession, hence the alarmist metaphor of "going over the cliff".

Hillary Clinton on Environment vs. Economy

$5B for green-collar jobs in economic stimulus package

Former Sen. JOHN EDWARDS [to Clinton]: One difference between what I have proposed & what my two colleagues have proposed is I have done something that not only stimulates the economy, but creates long-term benefits, investment in green infrastructure, which creates jobs

CLINTON: I do believe that the green-collar job piece of [the economic stimulus package] is important. That's why I have $5 billion to do it. There are programs already. In Oakland CA, Mayor Dellums is working to have a green-collar job program. We could put hundreds and hundreds of young people to work right now, putting solar panels in, insulating homes. That would give them jobs and it would move us more quickly to a green economy. And I think that if you look at this from a jobs and justice, a stimulation and long-term planning effort, we need to lay down the markers now. We've got to hold the line against President Bush with his ill-advised approach to stimulating the economy.

Source: Congressional Black Caucus Democratic debate, Jan. 21, 2008

Support green-collar job training

Q: What policies would you implement to make businesses invest in energy-efficient technologies?

A: I have supported a green building fund and green-collar job training with the AFL-CIO that will put a lot of people too work. And it's important that we do this, because we can create millions of new jobs.

Source: AFL-CIO Democratic primary forum, Aug. 8, 2007

Jeb Bush on Environment vs. Economy

Restrict Eminent Domain;
most severe of all government powers

The power of government to take property is perhaps the most severe of all governmental powers. State government must be frugal in the exercise of this power, and conscientious when it is expanded.

In this particular bill, eminent domain authority is expanded to benefit the North Broward Hospital District. This is undoubtedly a worthwhile and needed project, [and] the hospital has begun negotiations with local property owners to purchase their properties.

My objection to this well-intended bill, however, is that the hospital has begun this process [under the old rules, and] to change these rules [in the middle of the process] would not be in the spirit of fair play.

Additionally, this bill would set a dangerous precedent for one-time expansions of eminent domain authority. I believe this is a poor basis for creating new statutes. If the expansion of quick-take authority is an issue that needs addressing, the Legislature should do so as a policy debate for statewide application.

Source: Approval notification on Senate Bill 1230, June 7, 2000

Let industries "self-audit"; compensate for "takings"

Supports the following principles concerning the environment:

- Support "self-audit" legislation which creates incentives for industries to audit themselves and clean up pollution

- Require full compensation when environmental regulations limit uses on privately owned land

- Request added flexibility from the federal government in enforcing and funding federal environmental regulations

- Supports extending the Preservation 2000 program in Florida.

Source: Florida National Political Awareness Test, July 2, 1998

Hillary Clinton on Oil Drilling

Ban drilling in the Arctic National Wildlife Refuge

Vote to adopt an amendment that would strike a provision in the concurrent resolution that recognizes revenue from oil drilling in the Arctic National Wildlife Refuge (ANWR). The amendment says: "To ensure that legislation that would open ANWR, other federal lands, and the Outer Continental Shelf to oil drilling receives full consideration and debate in the Senate, rather than being fast-tracked under reconciliation procedures; to ensure that receipts from such drilling destined for the federal treasury are fairly shared with local jurisdictions; and does not occur unless prohibitions against the export of Alaskan oil are enacted."

Source: Arctic National Wildlife Refuge anti-drilling Amendment;
Bill S.Amdt.168 to S.Con.Res. 18 ; vote number 52 on Mar. 16, 2005

Get tough with energy speculators and with OPEC cartel

Q: You've said you want to get tough with OPEC?

A: I would go after the energy traders and speculators. I voted to quit filling up the Strategic Petroleum Reserve. I have advocated a gas tax holiday that is paid for, out of the record profits of the oil companies. And it's an enormous burden on people who drive any considerable distance.

Q: But what kind of leverage do you have on OPEC?

A: Nine countries that are members of OPEC are members of the WTO, where they have agreed to certain rules that I believe OPEC by definition violates. Also, we have never used antitrust laws in our country to really go at the heart of what is a monopoly cartel.

Source: CNN Late Edition with Wolf Blitzer, May 18, 2008

NOTE: *"ANWR" refers to the Arctic National Wildlife Refuge, a protected area in northern Alaska that contains substantial supplies of oil and gas. Conservatives favor drilling ANWR to extract the oil, while liberals favor maintaining its protected status.*

Jeb Bush on Oil Drilling

Drilling in Gulf of Mexico hurts Florida tourism industry

The Interior Department faces opposition from Jeb Bush to its proposal to auction off rights to a six-million-acre field in the Gulf of Mexico. "I am confident," Governor Bush wrote in a letter to the secretary of the interior, "that the new administration will recognize the need to protect sensitive natural resources located both offshore and along Florida's coastline for the benefit of the entire nation."

The area that Jeb Bush seeks to stop from being auctioned is not covered by the existing moratorium [on other off-shore drilling]. It actually lies off the coast of Alabama, but close enough to Florida to worry state environmentalists. "Florida's economy is based upon tourism and other activities that depend on a clean and healthy environment," Jeb Bush wrote in his letter to Washington. "As a result, we have the nation's best beaches, abundant fisheries, and pristine marine waters. Protection of those resources is of paramount importance to the state of Florida."

Source: David Sanger, NY Times, p. A17, Jan. 25, 2001

2005: 125-mile no-drill zone; then 75 miles ok for drilling

In 2001, Jeb trumpeted the deal he had won to back off federal plans to permit drilling in the Eastern Gulf: a new drilling moratorium that he proclaimed would protect Florida's beaches, a major source of the state's top industry, tourism: "As a result, there will be no new drilling in the Lease Sale 181 Area under my watch," Jeb announced.

In 2005, Jeb was ready to deal away half of that protected water. Instead of preventing drilling anywhere in a 200-mile-wide strip around Florida—the entire extent of the US's economic zone—Jeb was ready to give up the outer 75 miles of that in exchange for a permanent 125-mile zone that would be under state control.

Jeb argued that higher oil and gas prices made Florida's outright ban untenable—Jeb suggested acidly that he could take up such an idea with his fairy godmother—and that a permanent ban of any kind was better than a series of moratoria that could eventually end.

Source: America's Next Bush, by S.V. Dáte, p.365-366, Feb. 15, 2007

Hillary Clinton on Renewable Energy

Tax oil profits to fund renewable energy

At a Sept. 2005 global warming conference, Hillary offered her own solution: "I would advocate a much more concerted effort on our government's part to fund an extensive research project into alternative forms of energy." Hillary [soon afterwards] unveiled a clean-energy plan, "Energy Independence 2020."

After praising solar power and wind technology, Hillary turned her attention to her villains—the oil companies—and discussed the legislation that would force them to change their ways. Unless they diversified away from fossil fuels and into preferred, renewable technologies, her bill would require that they be assessed heavy windfall-profits taxes. This new revenue source, estimated at $50 billion, would finance a government energy fund that invested in innovative energy research.

Source: Her Way, by Jeff Gerth & Don Van Natta, p.276-283, June 8, 2007

Renewable energy is key to world's environmental progress

Clinton talked about the importance of sustainability and climate issues on the international policy agenda: "We have an interest in promoting new technologies and sources of energy—including renewables—to reduce pollution; to diversify the global energy supply; to create jobs; and to address the very real threat of climate change," said Clinton.

Clinton said the world is in a state of profound change when it comes to energy. She lauded improvements and expansions in renewable and traditional energy that have occurred under the Obama administration: "Our use of renewable wind and solar power has doubled in the last four years. Our oil and natural gas production is surging. That means we are less reliant on imported energy," she said.

Though using varied energy sources is important, Clinton said that renewable energy is key to the world's economic and environmental progress, as well as its security interests. "The transformation to cleaner energy is central to reducing the world's carbon emissions and it is the core of a strong 21st century global economy," she said.

Source: ThinkProgress.org on speech at Georgetown Univ., Oct. 19, 2012

Jeb Bush on Renewable Energy

Replace crony capitalism with free-market strategy

Bush laid out ways conservatives can advance the "American idea" that the dinner's namesake advocated. Bush advocated free market principles, especially in energy policy.<p>"We should let market forces, not crony capitalism, decide where to invest and how to incentivize citizens to conserve," Bush said, advocating approval of the Keystone XL pipeline, "rational" regulations on fracking, and opening federal lands to drilling. "A real energy strategy could add an additional 1% growth over the long haul."

Source: Tal Kopan on Politico.com, "Crony Capitalism" on Oct. 29, 2013

Set goal of 25% renewable energy by 2025

Bush endorsed a Congressional resolution that it is the goal of the United States that, not later than January 1, 2025, the agricultural, forestry, and working land of the US should provide from renewable resources not less than 25% of the total energy consumed and continue to produce safe, abundant, and affordable food, feed, and fiber. [Governors signed letters of endorsement at www.25x25.org, including Jeb Bush].

Rep. SALAZAR: "Our resolution establishes a national goal of producing 25% of America's energy from renewable sources—like solar, wind and biofuels—by 2025. The "25x'25" vision is widely endorsed, bold, and fully attainable. If implemented, it would dramatically improve our energy security, our economy, and our ability to protect the environment.

"I am pleased that the "25x'25" vision has been endorsed by 22 current and former governors. The Big Three automobile manufacturers—Ford, Chrysler, and General Motors—are all behind "25x'25" So are many agricultural organizations, environmental groups, scientists, and businesses. It is time for Congress to take a more active role in our clean energy future. Establishing a national goal—"25x'25" is the first step."

Source: 25x'25 Act (S.CON.RES.3 / H.CON.RES.25) on Jan. 17, 2007

Hillary Clinton on Government Privatization

Cut government contractors
and end privatization of government

I stood with AFSCME against the privatization of Social Security and now I want to stand with you against the privatization of our government. The Bush administration has been privatizing government services. In fact, now we have more government contractors and grantees by three times the number than the entire military and Civil Service personnel. We have to stop that. And I have proposed cutting government contractors by 500,000 as soon as I'm sworn in and saving $8 billion to $10 billion.

Source: AFSCME Democratic primary debate in Carson City Nevada, Feb. 21, 2007

New Democrat:
Government is not the solution to all problems

I'm a New Democrat. I don't believe government is the source of all of our problems or the solution to them. But I do believe that when people live up to their responsibilities, we ought to live up to ours to help them build better lives. That's the basic bargain we owe one another in America today.

Source: Announcement Speech, SUNY Purchase, Feb. 6, 2000

NOTE: *"Privatization" is a politicized word that means the same thing as term "out-sourcing" in the business world. The EPA, for example, is largely "privatized": most federal environmental work is implemented by private contractors selected through a competitive bidding process. The NIH, in another form of "privatization," provides grants for scientific research and development, also selected through a competitive application process. The EPA and NIH focus on enforcing regulations and overseeing contract and grant completion.*

Jeb Bush on Government Privatization

Privatize & outsource government; fee holidays for contractors

Senate Bill 1016 is a broad piece of legislation dealing with the regulation of professions. It also implements a number of the Administration's priorities reflecting a smaller, more efficient government. Among these priorities, Senate Bill 1016 provides a "fee holiday" for 14 professions, ranging from electrical contractors to veterinarians to surveyors. Over the course of the next two years, the fee holidays will provide over $18 million in savings to these professions.

Senate Bill 1016 also encourages the privatization and outsourcing of certain governmental activities. It calls for the privatization of elevator inspections and contains provisions known collectively as the Management Privatization Act. These provisions will allow for the outsourcing of licensing and investigative functions of regulated professions.

Source: Approval notification on Senate Bill 1016, June 23, 2000

Mature society can empty government buildings of workers

Like other governmental conservatives, Governor Bush disliked and distrusted government and promoted the idea that smaller government—combined with more privatizing of governmental services— was more efficient government. He argued that "the most efficient, effective and dynamic government is one composed primarily of policymakers, procurement experts and contract managers." He expressed his general philosophy about government in his 2003 Inaugural Address when he stated that "There would be no greater tribute to our maturity as a society than if we make these [governmental] buildings around us empty of workers, monuments to a time when government played a larger role than it deserve or could adequately fill."

Source: Aggressive Conservatism in Florida, by Robert Crew, p. 30, Dec. 11, 2009

Hillary Clinton on Campaign Finance Reform

Stand for public financing and getting money out of politics

Where I stand is for public financing. I'm going to do everything I can to get public financing, to get the money out of American politics. The point is that you've got to say no. You've got to say no. We will say no consistently in order to have a positive agenda that is actually going to make a difference. Do you have to stand up to the lobbyists? Yes. But the lobbyists represent the interests that are paying the lobbyists. So to go and focus on the lobbyists kind of misses the point.

Source: Congressional Black Caucus Democratic debate, Jan. 21, 2008

HILL-PAC is one of politics biggest money-raisers

Since she entered the senate in 2001, no senator has raised more money than Clinton has—$51.5 million, according to the Center for Responsive Politics. Her personal political action committee, HILL-PAC, is one of the biggest money-raisers and spenders in the business. For her 2008 presidential bid, she set a goal of $100 million raised through the primaries. To reach her target, she's decided to forgo public financing, just as Bush did in 2000 and 2004.

Source: The Contenders, by Laura Flanders, p. 21, Nov. 11, 2007

Consider Constitutional Amendment against Citizen's United

While eying a potential presidential run that would surely be boosted by deep-pocketed super PACs, Hillary Clinton said that she's open to supporting a constitutional amendment to overturn the Supreme Court's *Citizens United* decision, which opened the door to the outside groups and the flood of money that poured into the political process with them: "I would consider supporting an amendment among these lines that would prevent the abuse of our political system by excessive amounts of money if there is no other way to deal with the Citizen's United decision," she said in response to a question on the measure.

Source: Alex Seitz-Wald on MSNBC, "Citizens United," July 21, 2014

Jeb Bush on Campaign Finance Reform

Complete transparency for campaigns & PAC donations

Florida is so flush with special-interest cash that our state is drowning in it. Even former Gov. Jeb Bush—a staunch defender of money in politics—believes reform is needed.

I asked the former governor about the current state of money in Florida politics. His response: "I am for complete transparency within 24 hours for all groups, committees, organizations, campaigns, PACs, etc." Right now, donations can remain secret for months.

Personally, I'd go further than Jeb Bush and crack down on these unlimited donations and secretive, under-regulated committees in general. But at a minimum, Bush is right that complete—and rapid—transparency is needed.

Source: Orlando Sentinel, "Megadonors taint Florida politics",
by Scott Maxwell, Aug. 18, 2012

No campaign spending limits; no public financing

Q: Do you support requiring full and timely disclosure of campaign finance information?

A: Yes.

Q: Do you support imposing spending limits on state level political campaigns?

A: No.

Q: Do you support partial funding from state taxes for state level political campaigns?

A: No.

Source: Florida Gubernatorial NPAT Test, Nov. 1, 1998

NOTE: *"Citizens United" refers to a 2010 Supreme Court case which allowed unlimited spending by "'super-PACs" on behalf of any candidate, as long as the TV ads are not coordinated with the campaign itself. Super-PACs dominate the spending in the 2012 presidential primaries and 2014 midterm elections, and will continue to do so in the 2016 elections.*

Hillary Clinton on Capital Gains Tax

Perhaps raise capital gains tax, but at most to 20%

Q: You favor an increase in the capital gains tax, saying, "I certainly would not go above what existed under Bill Clinton, which was 28%." It's now 15%. That's almost a doubling if you went to 28%.

OBAMA: What I've said is that I would look at raising the capital gains tax for purposes of fairness.

Q: Sen. Clinton, would you say, "No, I'm not going to raise capital gains taxes"?

CLINTON: I wouldn't raise it above the 20% if I raised it at all. I would not raise it above what it was during the Clinton administration.

Source: Philadelphia primary debate, on eve of PA primary, April 16, 2008

End Bush tax cuts;
take things away from rich for common good

When Hillary spoke at a private San Francisco fundraiser in 2004, an A.P. reporter caught a particularly illuminating comment by Clinton about the 2001 tax cuts. "We're saying that for America to get back on track, we're probably going to cut that short not give it to you," she said. "We're going to take things away from you on behalf of the common good." In Clinton's eyes, government redistribution—not private entrepreneurship—is the key to economic growth.

Votes against the Bush tax cuts

- 11/17/2005: YES on raising capital gains taxes on wealthy individuals
- 2/13/2006: YES on allowing capital gains tax cuts to expire

Source: Vast Right-Wing Conspiracy, by Amanda Carpenter, p. 52-53, Oct. 11, 2006

Jeb Bush on Capital Gains Tax

Remove Intangibles Tax on stocks, bonds & dividends

Over the course of his administration the Bush legislation produced $19.1 billion in tax cuts. The centerpiece of Bush's tax-reform effort was the abolition of the state's Intangible Personal Property Tax.

When Governor Bush came into office, Florida was one of only a handful of states that utilized some form of an intangibles tax. This tax was levied on stocks, bonds, mutual funds, money market funds, and other such investments. "By design, the tax is aimed at the state's wealthier residents" and in the absence of an income tax was initiated to derive at least some revenue from the personal income of wealthy citizens and corporations. While it was the most progressive of the taxes employed by the state, it was described by the governor as "evil and insidious," "counterproductive and unfair." Governor Bush worked to reduce it in every legislative session between 1999 and 2006, when it was finally abolished. Its elimination accounted for nearly 30% of the tax cuts he initiated.

Source: Aggressive Conservatism in Florida, by Robert Crew, p.102-3, Dec. 11, 2009

Cutting "intangibles tax" helps "seniors and savers"

Saying that you're helping the rich doesn't play well, so Jeb and his people came up with a host of other reasons to eliminate the state's one tax on the rich: the tax's inefficiency; its alleged "unfairness."

Jeb knew it would be tough to create any public empathy for the actual "victims" of this tax, and so he and his people invented a new description for them: "seniors and savers." They produced statistics to show that a disproportionate number of people who paid this tax were elderly. And indeed, many of them probably were "savers."

Source: America's Next Bush, by S.V. Dáte, p.279-280, Feb. 15, 2007

Hillary Clinton on Inheritance Tax

Freeze estate tax at 2009 level of $7 million per couple

I'm in favor of doing something about the AMT. How we do it and how we put the package together everybody knows is extremely complicated. I want to get to a fair & progressive tax system. The AMT has to be part of what we try to change when I'm president There are a lot of moving pieces here. There are kinds of issues we're going to deal with as the tax cuts expire. I want to freeze the estate tax at the 2009 level of $7 million for a couple. I'm not going to get committed to a specific approach.

Source: Democratic debate at Drexel University, Oct. 30, 2007

NOTE: *The 'Estate Tax' or 'Inheritance Tax' is called the 'Death Tax' by its opponents, beginning in 2001 under President Bush. While polls indicate broad support for eliminating the estate tax, few Americans are directly affected by it. Opponents point out that some family businesses would have to sold to pay the estate tax. In 2001, 98% of descendants avoid taxes altogether because the first $675,000 of an estate was exempt from taxation. That exemption rose to $5 million in 2011-2012, with a one-year repeal in 2010, and is slated to return to $1 million in 2013. According to the Internal Revenue Service, about 3,000 estates are worth more than $5 million each and hence would be subject to the tax in 2011-2012.*

The most popular sales tax on the Republican side is the 'FairTax,' which would replace the current progressive marginal rates with a single 'flat' rate (plans vary from 10% to 17%), applied after a deductible base. Flat Tax plans can achieve lower rates by removing the mortgage interest and charitable deductions. Jeb has mixed views on sales taxes; endorses repealing the estate tax; and has been silent so far on the FairTax.

Jeb Bush on Inheritance Tax

Supports estate tax repeal, but not at states' expense

Even as they deal with declining revenue growth from a softening economy, states are scrambling to plan for the potential loss of $50 billion to $100 billion over 10 years from the repeal of the federal estate tax enacted last month. The loss in revenue would come because states for 75 years have tied their own estate and inheritance taxes to the federal estate tax.

Governors are also chafing under a Congressional timetable that calls for the states to lose their tax revenues by 2005 while stretching the repeal of the federal estate tax more gradually over 10 years. Jeb Bush warned about anticipated revenue shortfalls [in Florida], including the expected loss of $210 million from the estate tax in the 2002-03 fiscal year. "While I support the eventual repeal of the estate tax," Mr. Bush, the president's brother, wrote, "shifting the burden merely allows Washington to spend more, while requiring us to spend less."

Source: Kevin Sack, NY Times, June 21, 2001

1987: supported sales service tax; 1998: opposed it

As Gov. Bob Martinez's Secretary of Commerce in 1987-88, perhaps Jeb's most memorable episode was his public support for the issue that proved to be Martinez' undoing: an expansion of the sales tax onto services, rather than just goods. Martinez originally endorsed the plan and then—under pressure from advertisers—called a special session for its repeal. The governor was never able to recover from this phenomenal flip-flop, and was easily defeated in 1990. In early 1987, Jeb came out solidly behind his boss: "If this is a way to broaden taxation and at the same time lower the rate, a lot of people would really go for it."

Even as he was publicly supporting the services tax, he had privately sent Martinez a letter telling him it was a bad idea. And in 1998, Jeb was able to produce the letter when his Democratic opponent started talking about the services tax and how Jeb had once supported it.

Source: America's Next Bush, by S.V. Dáte, p. 79-80, Feb. 15, 2007

Hillary Clinton on Tax Reform

Wealthy should go back to paying pre-Bush tax rates

Q: If either one of you become president, and let the Bush tax cuts lapse, there will be effectively tax increases on millions of Americans.

OBAMA: On wealthy Americans.

CLINTON: That's right.

OBAMA: I'm not bashful about it.

CLINTON: Absolutely. It's just really important to underscore here that we will go back to the tax rates we had before George Bush became president. And my memory is, people did really well during that time period. And they will keep doing really well.

Source: Democratic debate in Los Angeles, Jan. 30, 2008

Absolutely no tax increase on people earning under $250K

Q: Can you make an absolute pledge that there will be no tax increases of any kind for anyone earning under $200,000 a year?

CLINTON: I will let the taxes on people making more than $250,000 a year go back to the rates that they were paying in the 1990s.

Q: Even if the economy is weak?

CLINTON: Yes. And here's why: #1, I do not believe that it will detrimentally affect the economy by doing that. We used that tool during the 1990s to very good effect and I think we can do so again I am absolutely committed to not raising a single tax on middle class Americans, people making less than $250,000 a year. In fact, I have a very specific plan of $100 billion in tax cuts.

Q: Absolutely no middle-class tax increases of any kind?

CLINTON: No, that's right. That is my commitment.

Source: Philadelphia primary debate, on eve of PA primary, April 16, 2008

Jeb Bush on Tax Reform

Compromise on taxes ok, as part of a spending cut package

Q: You have taken some heat for your suggestion that you might be willing to accept higher taxes as part of a grand bargain, if you also got serious spending cuts, and you also gotten some entitlement reform. Anti-tax advocate Grover Norquist said: "People are looking for someone who's tough and you are saying, 'I'll fold.'"

BUSH: What we ought to be focused on in Washington is to build consensus on the things where there's an agreement. Maybe that would be on creating sustained economic growth which creates more revenue than any tax increase. But I don't think that you should automatically say, "No. Heck, no." We have to find in a divided country ways to forge compromise. [Reagan] did exactly that, he forged consensus, he compromised, he didn't violate his principles. So, the idea that you have to have this doctrinaire view [like Grover Norquist's "No taxes" pledge], but you're not necessarily going to be able to solve these pressing problems that we have.

Source: Fox News Sunday interview, March 10, 2013

No pledge on taxes; trade-offs on taxes means leadership

Perhaps the greatest sin in the modern conservative movement is George H. W. Bush's 1990 budget deal where he traded tax increases for budget savings. Jeb Bush has cited his father's compromise as the epitome of presidential leadership.

In his positions on fiscal policy, Jeb Bush has given comfort to the suspicious. When asked about the hypothetical trade-off posited during a 2012 GOP debate, where no GOP candidate would accept a dollar of tax increases in exchange for 10 dollars in spending reductions, Jeb Bush took a different view. "If you could bring to me a majority of people to say that we're going to have $10 in spending cuts for $1 of revenue enhancement—put me in, coach," he said at the time.

Source: John Dickerson on Slate.com, "Hard on the GOP," March 31, 2014

Hillary vs. Jeb on Entitlement Issues

Entitlement issues focus on the recession recovery and all forms of entitlements. The term "entitlements" implies that these programs are guaranteed and immutable, but in reality, they are subject to Congressional changes just like any other law. The duration of unemployment benefits, for example, has been changed regularly since the Great Recession began. And ObamaCare, the newest (and potentially largest) entitlement, can and likely will be changed by new laws as the program comes into full force. Even Social Security, once considered the "third rail" of politics because even *discussing* changing the program entailed political suicide, has been open to modification since George W. Bush publicly discussed it as president. This chapter includes the following sections:

- *Health Care (pp. 76-83):* including federal healthcare and ObamaCare issues; plus Medicare/Medicaid and state issues. The two candidates disagree on the central issue of ObamaCare, but Jeb is not a hard-core repealist on the subject: he says we should let ObamaCare fail on its own. Hillary, similarly, is not a hard-core ObamaCare supporter: if elected, she would tweak the law, although Jeb would likely tweak it a lot more. The same applies to Medicare/Medicaid: Hillary supports the programs, but does not recommend "Medicare for all" as do many progressives. Jeb would convert Medicaid to a voucher system, and other changes: more changes than Hillary, but again keeping the core program in place. A key question for Jeb in 2015 is whether his anti-ObamaCare stance is strong enough, or if a Tea Party opponent will challenge him on this issue in the primary (since "repealing and replacing" ObamaCare is a core tenet of the Tea Party, with which Jeb does not agree).

- *Jobs (pp. 84-89):* including unemployment and union issues. Depending on the state of the Great Recession, federal job assistance might become an issue in 2016 (such as extending unemployment insurance, or jobs-creation programs). If the unemployment rate continues slowly falling as it has throughout 2014, there will not be any jobs-based issues in 2016 except the usual ongoing issues (unions and affirmative action). Jeb would restrict unions and cut taxes instead of extending unemployment compensation; Hillary supports the opposite on both issues. Hillary is a hard-core activist on affirmative action issues (such as equal pay for women); Jeb is moderately anti-affirmative action.

- **Education (pp. 90-99):** This is a core issue for both Jeb and Hillary, so we include a lot of excerpts on a lot of aspects. Hillary first got involved with education reform in the 1980s in Arkansas; many aspects of "Common Core" came from Arkansas to federal programs via Bill Clinton's presidency. Jeb agrees with the national standards of Common Core; this issue invites a Tea Party primary opponent, since opposing Common Core is a hot issue within the Tea Party and other GOP factions. Jeb, like his brother George, has pushed hard for school choice (which Hillary opposes); that is the goal of those who would abolish Common Core, so Jeb might blunt the GOP primary attack by supporting both issues.

- **Social Security (pp. 100-101):** including the current Trust Fund and changes for the future. Jeb supported privatization of many state programs while Governor of Florida, but has not applied that philosophy to Social Security. Hillary has unambiguously opposed privatization, but has not made this a core issue.

- **Welfare & Poverty (pp. 102-105):** including homelessness, welfare payments, and other poverty programs. Jeb and Hillary agree on most aspects of this issue: both support workfare (initiated by Pres. Bill Clinton in the 1990s), and both support collaborating with faith-based organizations (initiated by Pres. George W. Bush in the 2000s). More on religion in our Social Issues chapter (p. 107ff)

Hillary Clinton on Entitlement Issues

Jeb Bush on Entitlement Issues

Hillary Clinton on ObamaCare

Non-employer system better;
but don't turn back ObamaCare

Hillary Clinton showed more signs of flexibility on how Obamacare is implemented, but she insisted the law is too important to "turn the clock back." Clinton said, "I have said many times that if we were starting from scratch, we wouldn't have built an employer-based system," But since that's the system we have, she said, it's important to make it work.

Clinton suggested she's open to different ways of achieving the health law's goals. She praised Arkansas for carrying out a new approach to expanding Medicaid coverage, by using the federal money to buy private health insurance for more than 100,000 low-income residents.

But the main goal, Clinton said, should be to keep moving ahead with the law. And in a subtle swipe at the Obama administration, she suggested that the law's supporters haven't done the best job explaining what Americans stand to gain from it. "We have to do a better job than has been done, quite frankly, in explaining the benefits," Clinton said.

Source: David Nather on Politico.com, "Obamacare important," March 5, 2014

2007: recast 1990s disaster as experience to make it happen

[In 2007] Hillary had recast her awful history with health care reform, unveiling her long-awaited plan in mid-September and getting rave reviews for her substantive prowess, the detail and clarity of her presentation, and her self-deprecating allusions to her disastrous attempt to overhaul the system as First Lady.

She's watched as Obama's campaign was hammered for producing a proposal that was an obvious rip-off of hers. She'd begun to defuse her rival's message, where she said, "change is just a word without the strength and experience to make it happen."

Source: Game Change, by Heilemann & Halpern, p. 98-99, Jan. 11, 2010

Jeb Bush on ObamaCare

ObamaCare is flawed to its core

Jeb Bush said that President Barack Obama's health care law "is flawed to its core" and will be a "big problem" for Democrats heading into the 2014 elections. "I don't think it will work," Bush said of ObamaCare. Bush added, "If the objective is, don't worry about the budget, we'll just finance it the same way we're financing our deficits right now, build a bigger debt, you could see this thing surviving," he said. "But it will have failed what the promises were. It will have failed the American people. And I don't think it will bend the cost curve."

Bush has emerged over the years as a strong proponent of what he calls "consumer-directed health care." He noted that he underwent knee surgery a month ago and forced himself into the conversation on billing. "The whole experience is opaque," he said. "It's like smoke comes up, you don't know what's really happening, the third party pays."

Source: Bill Glauber of the Milwaukee Journal Sentinel on Nov. 4, 2013

Let ObamaCare fail due to its own dysfunction

Q: This government shutdown started with House Republicans saying that they wanted to gut ObamaCare and they were willing to not fund the government until that happened. Your thoughts?

BUSH: Tactically it was a mistake to focus on something that couldn't be achieved. I would argue that allowing ObamaCare to be implemented, two things would happen. One, it would be so dysfunctional if it was implemented faithfully. Or it couldn't be implemented because the government is not capable of doing it. It looks like that, the latter rather than the former, may be happening. I think the best way to repeal ObamaCare is to have an alternative. We could do this in a much lower cost with improved quality based on free market principles. And show how ObamaCare, flawed to its core, doesn't work. It might actually be a politically better approach to see the massive dysfunction.

Source: ABC This Week interview, Oct. 20, 2013

Hillary Clinton on Medicare/Medicaid

Recommended "managed competition"; not expanding Medicare nor single-payer system

[On the 1994 healthcare taskforce], some proposed a "single payer" approach, modeled on the European and Canadian health care systems. The federal government, through tax payments, would become the sole financier—or single payer—of most medical care. A few favored a gradual expansion of Medicare what would eventually cover all uninsured Americans, starting first with those aged 55 to 65.

Bill and other Democrats rejected the single-payer and Medicare models, preferring a quasi-private system called "managed competition" that relied on private market forces to drive down costs through competition. The government would have a smaller role, including setting standards for benefit packages and helping to organize purchasing cooperatives. The cooperatives were groups of individuals and businesses forget for the purpose of purchasing insurance. Together, they could bargain with insurance companies for better benefits and prices and use their leverage to assure high-quality care.

Source: Living History, by Hillary Rodham Clinton, p.150, Nov. 1, 2003

Voted NO on means-testing to determine Medicare Part D premium

CONGRESSIONAL SUMMARY: To require wealthy Medicare beneficiaries to pay a greater share of their Medicare Part D premiums.

SUPPORTER's ARGUMENT FOR VOTING YES: Sen. ENSIGN: This amendment is to means test Medicare Part D the same way we means test Medicare Part B. An individual senior making over $82,000 a year would be expected to pay a little over $10 a month extra.

LEGISLATIVE OUTCOME: Amendment rejected, 42-56

Source: Bill S.Amdt.4240 to S.Con.Res.70 ; vote on Mar 13, 2008

Jeb Bush on Medicare/Medicaid

Move Medicaid from "defined benefit" to defined contribution

Bush proposed an overhaul of Medicaid that reflected another major philosophical shift in the state's program, moving it from a "defined benefit" to a "defined contribution" basis. The proposal had two significant features. The first was acceptance of a lump sum of money from the federal government to fund the state's program in exchange for flexibility to determine eligibility and benefits levels. The state took on the responsibility for meeting the health-care needs of its residents regardless of whether the costs to do so exceeded the amount negotiated between Tallahassee and Washington. If costs exceeded negotiated levels, Florida would be able to use the flexibility granted by the federal government to impose benefit restrictions and cap program enrollment in order to contain costs. This provision was designed to permit the state to more accurately predict and control its costs.

The second major change was to provide each person with a risk-adjusted allotment of funds (a voucher which the state called a premium) with which to purchase health care. Using this voucher, enrollees were required to purchase a health-care plan from a participating managed-care organization. The benefit package offered had to be actuarially equivalent to the existing Medicaid benefit.

To entice companies to insure some of Florida's sickest and poorest citizens, the state proposed to cap Medicaid benefits, and set a ceiling on spending for each recipient. Managed-care companies and other health-care networks would design alternative health plans that Medicaid patients would use. Beyond that, different managed-care networks could attract patients by offering additional services. However, patients would have a choice only among managed-care plans and no longer have access to traditional fee-for-service health care.

Source: Aggressive Conservatism in Florida, by Robert Crew, p. 38, Dec. 11, 2009

Hillary Clinton on Mental Health

Sponsored bill for mental health service for older Americans

OFFICIAL CONGRESSIONAL SUMMARY: A bill to provide for mental health screening and treatment services, and to provide for integration of mental health services and mental health treatment outreach teams.

SPONSOR's INTRODUCTORY REMARKS: Sen. CLINTON: This bill is an effort to improve the accessibility and quality of mental health services for our rapidly growing population of older Americans. As we look forward to increased longevity, we must also acknowledge the challenges that we face related to the quality of life as we age. Chief among these are mental and behavioral health concerns.

It is estimated that nearly 20% of Americans age 55 or older experience a mental disorder. It is anticipated that the number of seniors with mental health problems will increase from 4 million in 1970 to 15 million in 2030. The Positive Aging Act would fund grants to states to provide screening and treatment for mental health disorders in seniors.

Source: Positive Aging Act (S.1116/H.R.2629) on May 25, 2005

Committed to mental-health treatment, including suicide

Clinton touted her commitment to mental-health treatment, and even answered a question about what, all these years later, she thinks she might have done to prevent her friend Vince Foster's suicide. "Obviously, I've thought a lot about that," she began. She didn't say a lot beyond that "the ones I've known personally" who've taken their own lives "were all men, and particularly in the case you're talking about there was a reluctance to seek help." But she did readily reply, and the crowd was spared the look that any reporter asking that question would have received.

Source: Washington Post, "Early Intervention," by Melinda Henneberger, May 6, 2014

Jeb Bush on Mental Health

Slashed every request for adult mental health

Bush's lowest spending priorities were for Florida's agencies dealing with its most vulnerable citizens.

One embarrassing consequence of his lack of attention to social services agencies emerged in the days just before Bush left office when his secretary of the Department of Children and Families was fined and threatened with jail time for failure to provide enough beds to treat county jail inmates with severe mental illness. Records from the department showed that it had called repeatedly for funds for adult health and that Bush had slashed every request—in 1 year by 93% (Hunt, 2006; Rushing, 2006). To avoid court sanctions, the governor was forced to ask the Legislative Budget Commissions, an organization that authorizes appropriations when the legislature itself is not in session, for an additional $16.6 million for hundreds of new beds for these individuals.

Source: Aggressive Conservatism in Florida, by Robert Crew, p.107,
Dec. 11, 2009

NOTE: *ObamaCare suggested some mental health coverage but the details are left to each state. Mental health is one of ObamaCare's "10 Essential Health Benefits." This is an example of healthcare issues that were not fully worked out under ObamaCare, and will be left ot the 2016 election to decide.*

Hillary Clinton on Medical Malpractice

Voted NO on limiting medical liability lawsuits to $250,000

This bill would "provide improved medical care by reducing the excessive burden the liability system places on the health care delivery system." It would limit medical lawsuit noneconomic damages to $250,000 from the health care provider, and no more than $500,000 from multiple health care institutions.

Proponents of the motion recommend voting YEA because:

- Many doctors have had to either stop practicing medicine due to increased insurance premiums.

- Patients are affected as well—due to rising malpractice rates, more and more patients are not able to find the medical specialists they need.

- The cost of medical malpractice insurance premiums are having wide-ranging effects. It is a national problem, and it is time for a national solution.

- These bills are a commonsense solution to a serious problem, and it is time for us to vote up or down on this legislation.

Opponents of the motion recommend voting NAY because:

We have virtually no evidence that caps on economic damages will actually lower insurance rates. And in my view, these caps are not fair to victims. If we want to reduce malpractice insurance premiums we must address these problems as well as looking closely at the business practices of the insurance companies. What we shouldn't do is limit the recovery of victims of horrible injury to an arbitrarily low sum.

This is a complicated issue. This is the kind of issue that needs to be explored in depth in our committees so that a consensus can emerge. So I will vote no on cloture, and I hope that these bills will go through committees before we begin floor consideration of this important topic.

Source: Medical Care Access Protection Act; Bill S. 22; May 8, 2006

Jeb Bush on Medical Malpractice

Compromised on limiting medical malpractice awards

Jeb stood in the Capitol rotunda, a pained smile on his face, explaining how he was glad that he and lawmakers were able to come to a reasonable compromise on his plan to limit pain and suffering jury awards to medical malpractice victims.

Jeb was saying this, but it was obvious that he wasn't enjoying it, probably because everyone knew it wasn't true. The "compromise" was hardly that—more like a near-total capitulation on Jeb's part. Behind him, state senators stood in the familiar semicircle of solidarity, but they were scarcely able to contain their glee.

Then, after hands were shaken and the senators had withdrawn to their private office, there were laughs and high fives all around. "This is probably the first time he's ever been spanked," crowed one. Said another: "I don't want to gloat. Well, yes I do."

Source: America's Next Bush, by S.V. Dáte, p.129, Feb. 15, 2007

NOTE: *"Tort Reform" refers to changing the rules about civil litigation, typically to cap damage awards. In a political context, it usually applies to medical malpractice lawsuits, but in a legal context, it also applies to personal injury and product liability lawsuits. The term "tort" means "at fault;" when a doctor is found at fault, a jury can currently award unlimited damages. Awards in the millions of dollars put upward pressure on malpractice insurance rates; hence many conservatives favor tort reform as a means to reduce healthcare costs. Proposed solutions include capping lawsuit compensation or restricting "frivolous lawsuits." Trial lawyers—the recipients of legal fees from tort awards—heavily favor Democratic candidates, so Republicans would like to limit their legal fees.*

Hillary Clinton on Union Policy

Stand up for unions; organize for fair wages

Let's make sure the people who work hard every day can actually support their families and save for the future. That means standing up for our unions again—understanding that there's a connection between unions and the middle class. When I'm president, we're going to stand up for unions. We're going to make sure they can organize for fair wages and good working conditions. And we're going to appoint people to the Department of Labor who are actually pro-labor for a change.

Source: Take Back America Conference, June 20, 2007

Voted YES on restricting employer interference in union organizing

To enable employees to form & join labor organizations, and to provide for mandatory injunctions for unfair labor practices during organizing efforts. Requires investigation that an employer:

- discharged or discriminated against an employee to discourage membership in a labor organization;

- threatened to discharge employees in the exercise of guaranteed collective bargaining rights; and

- adds to remedies for such violations: back pay plus liquidated damages; and additional civil penalties.

Proponents support voting YES because: The principle at stake here is the freedom that all workers should have to organize for better working conditions & fair wages. There are many employers around the country who honor this freedom. Unfortunately, there are also many employers who do not. These employers attempt to prevent workers from unionizing by using tactics that amount to harassment, if not outright firing. In fact, one in five people who try to organize unions are fired. These tactics are already illegal, but the penalties are so minor, they are not effective deterrents.

Source: Employee Free Choice Act; Bill H.R.800 ; vote on Jun 26, 2007

Jeb Bush on Union Policy

School choice is about unions versus kids

There are many people who say they support strong schools but draw the line at school choice. "Sorry, kid. Giving you equal opportunity would be too risky. And it will upset powerful political forces that we need to win elections."

I have a simple message for these masters of delay and deferral: Choose. You can either help the politically powerful unions. Or you can help the kids. Now, I know it's hard to take on the unions. They fund campaigns. But you and I know who deserves a choice.

Source: Republican National Convention speech, Aug. 29, 2012

Employ American Workers Act led to lost ideas & lost jobs

Buried inside [the 2009 stimulus] was a union-backed provision called the Employ American Workers Act, which restricted H-1B visas for any company that received federal recovery assistance. "Within days of the president signing it into law," recounts a professor at the Tuck School of Business at Dartmouth College, "a number of US banks reneged on job offers extended months earlier to foreign-born MBA students." The net result, says Slaughter: "Lost ideas. Lost jobs. Lost taxes."

Source: Immigration Wars, by Jeb Bush, p. 93, March 5, 2013

NOTE: *Gov. Scott Walker (R-WI) pushed a "union-busting" bill in early 2011, restricting collective bargaining rights of all public employees, including teachers. The bill passed, but large-scale protests led to a recall election in 2012. Gov. Walker survived the recall, and got re-elected in 2014. In July 2014, the Wisconsin Supreme Court upheld the law. Jeb's reference to "unions versus kids" means he takes Gov. Walker's side.*

Hillary Clinton on Employment Policy

Pushed for extension of unemployment insurance

First, Hillary went on the attack, undermining a solemn agreement made with the Republicans on the extension of unemployment insurance, only to eventually relent and settle for an agreement to revisit the expansion of one of her beloved programs.

This formula explains why staid Senate Republicans have such a hard time understanding Hillary. How can she be so nice on the floor and then turn around and say these awful things about us? They do not grasp the purpose of agitprop: To force a compromise in her direction, it is first necessary to disturb the peace.

Source: Madame Hillary, by R. Emmett Tyrrell, p. 51-52, Feb. 25, 2004

Passed 2 planks of 7-plank platform, "New Jobs for New York"

Hillary's "New Jobs for New York" platform included seven measures promising to create 200,000 jobs in NY:

1. Create "technology bonds" to fund interest-free loans to improve Internet access.
2. A "Broadband Expansion Grant Initiative" to provide grants & loan guarantees to fund networks in "under-served rural areas."
3. Fund research on broadband technology in rural areas.
4. Tax credits for small businesses that created jobs in smaller communities.
5. Federal funding for "entrepreneurs who have good ideas but cannot afford lawyers and consultants to help them."
6. Funding for the Commerce Department's Cooperative Extension Service to allow it to subsidize non-agricultural technologies.
7. Create "Regional Skills Alliances" to train technology workers.

She got two of her plan's seven measures signed into law. NY lost 35,800 jobs; Clinton blamed GOP economic policies.

Source: Madame Hillary, by R. Emmett Tyrrell, p. 51-52, Feb. 25, 2004

Jeb Bush on Employment Policy

Cutting taxes on job creators benefits everyone

The biggest tax cut of Jeb's time in office, the intangibles tax, had diminished the state treasury by $1 billion a year. An analysis of that policy starts with two fundamental questions.

1. Given Florida's poor rankings in various quality-of-life measures, were large tax cuts appropriate public policy?

2. Once you have decided that tax cuts were appropriate, was the intangibles tax the most appropriate one to cut?

On the first question, Jeb is part of the wing of the Republican Party that believes as a fundamental truth that taxes are too high. Period. The second question: if you cut taxes on the rich, everyone benefits. There, in a nutshell, is the Bush Family Economic Theory, boiled down to nine words. The emphasis is not to cut taxes for everybody—[but to] cut proportionately more for the wealthy—or, in Bush parlance, the investor class, the risk takers, the job creators.

Source: America's Next Bush, by S.V. Dáte, p.277-278, Feb. 15, 2007

Job growth during Bush terms, but very low wage jobs

In his 2006-2007 Budget Message he cited the lowest unemployment rate in the nation and an "unprecedented" job creation rate. While there was job growth during the Bush term of office it was smaller than in any gubernatorial administration since 1978. In addition, much of the job growth was the product of a growing population rather than the tax cuts the governor generated.

Most of the jobs created during the Bush administration were in the low-paying sectors of the economy. The state's 2004 median hourly wage ($13.10 per hour) was below the national average and the state had an unusually high percentage of very low-wage workers who earned wages at or below the federal minimum wage.

Source: Aggressive Conservatism in Florida, by Robert Crew, p.109-10, Dec. 11, 2009

Hillary Clinton on Affirmative Action

Equal pay is not yet equal

Equal pay is not yet equal. A woman makes $0.77 on a dollar & women of color make $0.67. We feel so passionately about this because we not only are running for office, but we each, in our own way, have lived it. We have seen it. We have understood the pain and the injustice that has come because of race, because of gender. It's imperative that we make it very clear that each of us will address these issues. You don't hear the Republicans talking about any of this. You don't hear them talking about the disgrace of a criminal justice system that incarcerates so many more African-Americans proportionately than whites, and any kind of effort to help Historically Black Colleges and Universities, something that I'm committed to doing. We have a specific set of policies and priorities that are really part of who we are, as well as part of what the Democratic Party stands for.

Source: Congressional Black Caucus Democratic debate, Jan. 21, 2008

We've come a long way on race, but we have a long way to go

Q: Is race still the most intractable issue in America?

A: It is abundantly clear that race and racism are defining challenges not only in the United States but around the world. We have made progress. You can look at this stage and see an African American, a Latino, a woman contesting for the presidency of the United States. But there is so much left to be done. And for anyone to assert that race is not a problem in America is to deny the reality in front of our very eyes. You can look at the thousands of African-Americans left behind by their government with Katrina. You can look at the opportunity gap. So, yes, we have come a long way, but, yes, we have a long way to go. The march is not finished, and I hope that all of us, the Democratic candidates, will demonstrate clearly that the work is yet to be done. And we call on everyone to be foot soldiers in that revolution to finish the job.

Source: Democratic Primary Debate at Howard University, June 28, 2007

Jeb Bush on Affirmative Action

One Florida: equal minority contracts and admissions

The One Florida initiative was actually designed to maintain the status quo—to admit just as many black and Hispanic students to Florida universities and award just as many contracts to black and Hispanic businesses as was possible under affirmative action, except to do this without specifically using race. The college admissions, for example, would be done using a "Talented 20" scheme, in which students in the top 5th of any high school class would be guaranteed entrance to a public university, regardless of their actual grade point average or SAT scores. The net result was to be the same. Students in predominantly minority high schools who scored at the top of their class would have a huge leg up over white students in suburban schools.

This was a program that, had Jeb used some savvy in rolling it out, blacks and Hispanics could easily have embraced. Jeb's problem, as was typical, was that he reached out for their support only when it came time to roll out the proposal.

Source: America's Next Bush, by S.V. Dáte, p.187-188, Feb. 15, 2007

Insisted on more racial and gender diversity in trial judges

Florida's nominating commissions recommend candidates for the Florida Supreme Court, the district courts of appeal, and all midterm vacancies in the circuit and county courts. Since 2001, the governor has appointed not just three but all nine members of each commission. One way in which Governor Jeb Bush used his vastly increased influence was to insist on more racial and gender diversity on the trial bench. But he was criticized for making the process much more partisan, and for appointing several conspicuously ideological attorneys and politicians to the district courts of appeal.

Source: A Most Disorderly Court: Scandal and Reform in the Florida Judiciary, p. 162, by Martin Dyckman, March 30, 2008

Hillary Clinton on College Policy

Establish right to education from pre-school thru college

Let's recommit ourselves to the idea that every young person in America has the right to a high-quality education, from pre-school all the way through college. I have proposed universal pre-kindergarten for every 4-year-old. If we provide that, the evidence is overwhelming, children will stay in school longer, they will do better, and they'll stay out of trouble. Because you know what? There are states in our country who actually plan how many prison beds they will need by looking at third grade reading scores. They look at the failure rates and they extrapolate how many prison spots they're going to need in 10 to 15 years. Well, I think it is time that we had a real debate about that. And I, for one, would much rather pay for pre-kindergarten than for more prison beds. Let's keep kids on the right track and out of the prison system.

Source: Take Back America Conference, June 20, 2007

Transfer tax cuts from rich & corporations to student aid

We were making progress in narrowing the gap between high tuition and costs and what the average student and his or her family could pay. We ought to be making sure every qualified student can go to college and pursue his or her dreams. And you know, there's a very easy way to do that. All we have to do is cut all the tax breaks for oil companies, pharmaceutical companies and billionaires and put it into student aid.

Source: Take Back America Conference, June 14, 2006

Jeb Bush on College Policy

Guarantee college admission for top 20% of high school grads

After discussions failed to convince him to delay his initiative until 2002, Bush stepped in with an executive order banning racial and gender preferences in university admissions and state contracting. Called "One Florida" the governor's program guaranteed college admissions to the top 20% of each high school graduating class, provided that students had taken college preparatory classes. It also required agencies of Florida state government to make special efforts to reach out to minority contractors and to increase state business with such companies without the use of set-asides and price preferences.

Source: Aggressive Conservatism in Florida, by Robert Crew, p. 91, Dec. 11, 2009

Replaced college affirmative action with "One Florida" initiative

An ardent proponent of privatization, Bush helped eliminate nearly 14,000 jobs, and by executive order he replaced affirmative action in university admissions and state contracting with his own "One Florida" initiative, a move that generated lasting ill will with many in the African American community.

Bush was alternately dubbed the "best governor in America" by admirers and "King Jeb" by detractors, but few would dispute that [Bush will] "go down as one of Florida's most consequential governors."

Source: The Rise of Marco Rubio, by Manuel Rogi-Franzia, p.132, June 19, 2012

Hillary Clinton on Common Core

OpEd: Common Core recycled from Clintons in 1980s and 1990s

Common Core recycles a decades-old, top-down approach to education clearly laid out in a letter sent to Hillary Clinton by Marc Tucker, president of the National Center on Education and the Economy (NCEE), immediately after Bill Clinton's 1992 presidential victory. Marc Tucker has and is now advising the Obama Administration's U. S. Department of Education about how to implement the Common Core Standards and Race to the Top programs.

Marc Tucker and Hillary Clinton apparently had plans to have national standards, national tests, national curriculum, and a national database way back in the 1980's.

The "Dear Hillary" letter, written on Nov. 11, 1992 by Marc Tucker, lays out a plan "to remold the entire American system." This is now the blueprint for the Common Core plan. On September 25, 1998, Representative Bob Schaffer placed the 18-page, original "Dear Hillary" letter by Marc Tucker in the Congressional Record.

Tucker's ambitious plan was implemented in three laws passed by Congress and signed by President Bill Clinton in 1994: the Goals 2000: Educate America Act, the School-to-Work Act, and the fifth reauthorization of the Elementary and Secondary Education Act.

These laws establish [using] "national standards" and "national testing" to cement national control of tests, assessments, school honors and rewards, financial aid, and the Certificate of Initial Mastery (CIM), which is designed to replace the high school diploma.

Source: William Taylor Reil in Times-News (Allentown PA), June 8, 2013

Jeb Bush on Common Core

Common Core lets 1,000 different curriculum flowers bloom

Q: How important is it to have national standards?

BUSH: I think higher standards is really the element of this that's most important. So if you dumb down the standards, everybody feels good. Little Johnny's going to get a piece of paper that says he's graduated from high school. But this massive remediation that's necessary to access higher education is evidence that we're not benchmarking ourselves to college readiness. So higher standards matter. The commonality of them—in this case 45 states—voluntarily creating them.

Q: The Common Core?

BUSH: The Common Core standards in language arts and math is important because curriculum is developed in this kind of system where there's common expectations. You'll have one thousand different flowers blooming as it relates to curriculum. It won't be homogenized, it will be diverse and alive which is what we need.

Q: But a lot of conservatives, certainly Tea Party movement, are very suspicious of this process. Standards means testing; you hear a common complaint, "We test too much."

BUSH: I think we do test too much. You could have fewer tests and achieve the desired results of transparency and accountability for sure.

Source: ABC This Week interview, Oct. 20, 2013

NOTE: *The Common Core State Standards Initiative, begun in 2009, has been adopted fully by 32 states and partially adopted by 13 others. The Obama administration provided competitive 'Race to the Top' grants as an incentive for states to adopt the Common Core. The Common Core defines standards for math and English, with standards to come in the future for science and social studies. Because the standards are copyrighted, critics consider them to be a 'one-size-fits-all' model, and a step towards nationalizing America's schools.*

Hillary Clinton on No Child Left Behind

Arkansas Education Reform taught
that there is a place for testing

Q: How do you feel about the testing mania forced upon our children by No Child Left Behind?

A: I believe in accountability. In 1983, I led the effort in Arkansas to improve our schools, and I do think there is a place for testing. But we should not look at our children as though they are little, walking tests, and we've gone way overboard. So I would like to see us do assessments, but understand we need a broad, rich curriculum that honors the spark of learning in every child.

Source: Huffington Post Mash-Up: Democratic on-line debate,
Sept. 13, 2007

1986: HIPPY program empowers parents as kids' first teacher

Home Instruction for Parents and Preschool Youngsters was developed in Israel in 1969 to help new immigrants prepare their young children to succeed in school. HIPPY empowers parents as their children's first teachers by giving them the tools, skills, and confidence to work with their children at home. The program is designed to help those families coping with poverty.

In 1986, Hillary helped establish a HIPPY program in Arkansas. Hillary wrote, "When we brought HIPPY into rural areas a projects in Arkansas, a number of educators and others did not believe that parents who had not finished high school were up to the task of teaching their children. Not only did the program help kids get jump-started in the right direction, it also gave the parents a boost in self-confidence." In 1988, HIPPY USA was established as an independent NGO headquartered in New York City. There are now about 146 HIPPY programs in twenty-five states, serving more than sixteen thousand children and their families.

Source: Giving, by Bill Clinton, p. 71-73, Sept. 4, 2007

Jeb Bush on No Child Left Behind

No Child Left Behind got states to start reforms

Q: "No Child Left Behind" was one of the great bipartisan achievements that your brother had. What's its legacy?

BUSH: I think "No Child Left Behind" pushed states that refused to begin the process of reform into the arena. So now every state is on the journey. Some really slow and some far more advanced. But ultimately this is a state-driven kind of enterprise. But the jump start for a lot of states that refused to use accountability and testing and a focus on early literacy and all the things that began with "No Child Left Behind" wouldn't have happened. So I think it served a useful purpose.

Q: How bad is the current system?

BUSH: If you measure it by outcomes, [only] 25% of kids pass all of the four segments of the ACT test which means that they're college-ready or career-ready. And about 20% don't graduate at all. That's failure.

Source: ABC This Week interview, Oct. 20, 2013

Florida Formula: schools graded A-to-F; extra funding for A

Bush's "Florida formula" rests on the principles of increasing accountability and expanding parental choice. Among its tenets:

- Grade schools on an A-to-F scale, based mostly on student scores and growth on standardized tests. Give students in poorly ranked schools vouchers to attend private and religious schools.

- Hold back 8-year-olds who can't pass a state reading test rather than promote them to fourth grade.

- Expand access to online classes and charter schools, which are publicly funded but privately managed.

Source: Stephanie Simon on Reuters, "Bush Foundation," Nov. 30, 2012

Hillary Clinton on Charter Schools

Charter schools provide choice within public system

I stand behind the charter school/public school movement, because parents do deserve greater choice within the public school system to meet the unique needs of their children. Slowly but surely, we're beginning to create schooling opportunities through the public school charter system-raising academic standards, empowering educators. When we look back on the 1990s, we will see that the charter school movement will be one of the ways we will have turned around the entire public school system.

Source: Remarks to NEA in Orlando, Florida, July 5, 1999

Supports public school choice and charter schools

Some critics of public schools urge greater competition among schools as a way of returning control from bureaucrats to parents and teachers. I find their argument persuasive and I favor promoting choice among public schools, much as the President's Charter Schools Initiative encourages.

Charter schools are public schools created and operated under a charter. They may be organized by parents, teachers, or others. The idea is that they should be freed from regulations that stifle innovation, so they can focus on getting results. By 1995, 19 states had enacted charter school laws about 200 schools have been granted charters.

The Improving America's Schools Act, passed in October 1994 with the President's support, provided federal funds for a wide range of reforms, including launching charter schools. Federal funding is needed to break through bureaucratic attitudes that block change and frustrate students and parents, driving some to leave public schools.

Source: It Takes A Village, by Hillary Clinton, pp.244-5, Sept. 25, 1996

Jeb Bush on Charter Schools

800,000 FL parents selected schools, not district zoning

Starting in 1999, Florida embarked upon a series of reforms designed to improve public schools and broaden educational choices.

All parents should be empowered to choose the best schools for their children, and in Florida school choice is widespread. Last year in Florida, nearly 800,000 students attended schools selected by their parents, not by district zoning laws. More than 200,000 students attend public charter schools. About 25,000 special-needs children attend private schools using scholarships. Almost 50,000 students from low-income families receive scholarships funded by tax credits to attend the schools that best fit them.

Source: Immigration Wars, by Jeb Bush, p.184-185, March 5, 2013

NOTE: *'Charter schools' are publicly-funded and publicly-controlled schools which are privately run. They are usually required to adhere to fewer district rules than regular public schools. The first charter schools started in Minnesota in 1991.*

By 2011, there were 5,600 public charter schools enrolling more than two million students nationwide. More than 400,000 students remain on wait lists to attend charter schools. Over 500 new public charter schools opened their doors in the 2011-12 school year, an estimated increase of 200,000 students.

Hillary Clinton on School Vouchers

Supports public school choice; but not private nor parochial

In 2006, Hillary disparaged vouchers partly on the worry that vouchers enabling parents to send their children to parochial schools could be used to train children to become terrorists. A Cato Institute Education specialist pointed out that "under federal law no one would be permitted to open a school that advocates violence against the country." Thus vouchers could not go to a "School of Jihad."

Years earlier, Hillary tried to play centrist on the school choice debate. In It Takes a Village she said she supported "choice among public schools" but redefined "school choice." Instead of helping provide choice between public and private schools, she uses choice to mean choice among public schools. She wrote "some critics of public schools urge greater competition among schools as a way of returning control from bureaucrats and politicians to parents and teachers. I find their arguments persuasive, and that's why I strongly favor promoting choice among public schools."

Source: Vast Right-Wing Conspiracy, by Amanda Carpenter, pp. 89-90, Oct. 11, 2006

Vouchers would take money from public schools

Q: Why don't you support vouchers for low-income parents?

CLINTON: I could not support vouchers that would take money away from schools where teachers are in partitioned hallways, where the teacher has the only textbook in the classroom. If we can get class size down, if we can provide qualified teachers, we can make a difference. I support adding 100,000 teachers to lower class size. I support the bipartisan school construction funding authority that would permit New York to have school construction without raising taxes.

Source: Senate debate in Manhattan, Oct. 8, 2000

Jeb Bush on School Vouchers

Education savings accounts: Fund students instead of schools

The best way for education policy to catch up with technology advances is to fund students rather than schools. After the Arizona Supreme Court struck down a voucher program for foster and disabled children under the state's Blaine Amendment, the Goldwater Institute proposed an innovative idea called education savings accounts. For any eligible student who leaves the public schools, the state each year deposits the student's share of state education spending in an account owned by the student's family. The accounts can be used for any educational expense, from private school tuition to distance learning, computer software, tutors, community college classes, and discrete public school services. Any money remaining can be saved for college.

Source: Immigration Wars, by Jeb Bush, p.193, March 5, 2013

School choice is about unions versus kids

There are many people who say they support strong schools but draw the line at school choice. "Sorry, kid. Giving you equal opportunity would be too risky. And it will upset powerful political forces that we need to win elections."

I have a simple message for these masters of delay and deferral: Choose. You can either help the politically powerful unions. Or you can help the kids. Now, I know it's hard to take on the unions. They fund campaigns. But you and I know who deserves a choice.

Source: Republican National Convention speech, Aug. 29, 2012

NOTE: *'vouchers' are a means of implementing school choice—parents are given a 'voucher' by the school district, which entitles them to, say, $4,000 applicable to either public school or private school tuition. The value of the voucher is generally lower than the cost of one year of public education (which averages $5,200), so private schools (where tuition averages $8,500) may require cash payment in addition to the voucher.*

Hillary Clinton on Social Security Privatization

Privatization off the table; but maybe payroll cap increase

During her 2008 presidential bid, Clinton was relatively non-committal about reforms to the Social Security program. She said in 2007 that certain reforms such as cutting benefits, privatizing the program or raising the retirement age were "off the table." There were some articles at the time that gave mixed signals on whether she would be willing to increase payroll taxes.

One account from the Associated Press featured a conversation between a campaigning Clinton and an Iowa voter in which the candidate said she might consider committing more of workers' income to Social Security. "She told him she didn't want to put an additional tax burden on the middle class but would consider a 'gap,' with no Social Security taxes on income from $97,500 to around $200,000. Anything above that could be taxed," according to the article.

Ultimately, Clinton officially shied away from the increase in taxes, and stuck with official comments that revolved around improving the economy overall.

Source: Megan R. Wilson in TheHill.com weblog, "Clinton vs. Warren,"
Aug. 24, 2014

1997: Hillary warned against privatizing Social Security

Following two and a half years of study, members of Bill's Advisory Co until on Social Security offered proposals for investing a portion of Social Security retirement funds in the stock market. Hillary reacted emphatically to the report, telling her husband, "We mustn't let Social Security be privatized."

Source: For Love of Politics, by Sally Bedell Smith, p.269, Oct. 23, 2007

Jeb Bush on Social Security Privatization

Privatization became administration's fundamental philosophy

The governor sought to extend the use of privatization, and adopted the theory as the fundamental philosophical principle of his administration. He declared, "I would look at any outsource opportunity."

The governor was extraordinarily successful in achieving his legislative goals regarding privatization: Florida hired private sector companies to administer programs that other states had also privatized: managing state prisons, collecting fees on the state's tollways, and cleaning state buildings. But Bush expanded privatization into uncharted territory and contracted out state personnel services (payroll, benefits, training, recruitment, etc.), the management of Medicaid billing.

Like other officials throughout the nation, Bush argued that he was privatizing Florida state government in order to bring about cost savings and efficiency. However, the speed and manner in which he initiated and carried out his plans led some to suggest that political philosophy was the driving force.

Source: Aggressive Conservatism in Florida, by Robert Crew, p.116-7, Dec. 11, 2009

Wrong to scare seniors about not protecting Social Security

A statement from former Florida governor Jeb Bush on Charlie Crist's dishonest Social Security attack on Marco Rubio: "Charlie Crist should be ashamed of his false attack against Marco Rubio on Social Security. Charlie Crist is purposely trying to scare seniors in order to win votes. "The fact is, Marco Rubio will protect Social Security. His own mother relies on Social Security and he has repeatedly stated that he would not support or propose any benefit reductions for current retirees or people who are close to retirement."

Source: John McCormack, The Weekly Standard, "Jeb Rips Crist," Oct. 5, 2010

Hillary Clinton on Welfare Reform

1990s welfare work requirement
was critical step despite flaws

Bill & I, along with members of Congress who wanted productive reform, believed that people able to work should work. But we recognize that assistance & incentives were necessary to help people move permanently from welfare to employment & that successful reform would require large investment in education and training, subsidies for child care and transportation, transitional health care, tax incentives to encourage employers to hire welfare recipients, and tougher child support collection efforts.

The third bill passed by Congress had the support of the majority of the Democrats in the House & Senate. It contained more financial support for moving people to work, offered new money for child care and restored the federal guarantees of food stamps & medical benefits.

The President eventually signed this third bill into law. Even with its flaws, it was a critical first step to reforming our nation's welfare system. I agreed that he should sign it and worked hard to round up votes for its passage.

Source: Living History, by Hillary Rodham Clinton, p.366-368,
Nov. 1, 2003

NOTE: *The welfare reform bill, signed by President Clinton in 1996, ended the federal entitlement to welfare, imposed strict work requirements on recipients, and set a five-year lifetime limit for aid. In 1995, 88% of poor children received food stamps. By 1998 the figure had dropped to 70%. The welfare load currently stands at about 2 million recipients, which has dropped by about 1/3 since the welfare reform bill was enacted.*

Jeb Bush on Welfare Reform

Taking welfare should be more shameful than working

Aristotle created a special category of virtue, which he called "quasi virtues." In it he placed shame. Shame has always been an important mechanism for exercising self-control.

An example of how we have come to devalue shame in our society is in our welfare system. In the mid-1960s, only half of those eligible for welfare payments were taking them and many enrolled would refuse to take the maximum allowance. People shined shoes and found other ways to bring in money that by today's standards would be considered shameful. However, by the early 1970s, the stigma of receiving welfare had been lost by an administration that encouraged receipt of welfare. The rolls exploded as a much higher percentage of those who were eligible suddenly thought it less shameful to take advantage of the benefits rather than employ themselves in a job requiring hard work, such as shining shoes or sweeping floors. For many it is more shameful to work than to take public assistance-that is how backward shame has become!

Source: Profiles in Character, by Jeb Bush , p. 52-55, Nov. 1, 1995

Vision for a right-to-rise society

Jeb Bush outlined his vision for a "right to rise society," tying it to Detroit's emergence from financial crisis and bankruptcy. In remarks designed to show it's possible for conservative Republicans to care about urban centers, Bush brought to mind the "compassionate conservatism" espoused by his brother, ex-President George W. Bush.

Bush told listeners at the Detroit Economic Club that they "are part of a great story—the revival of a city that means so much to all Americans." Bush continued, "In these past few years, when confronted with grave challenges, you have seized the opportunity to reform the city you love. And you have begun to repair the damage done by decades of mismanagement and empty promises."

Source: Detroit News, "Right-to-rise society," Feb. 4, 2015

Hillary Clinton on Faith-Based Organizations

Partner with faith based community in empowerment zones

Q: What leadership would you take to ensure that young people and Latino and Black communities not only have access to capital but to ensure that economic development is more inclusive of black and brown youth?

A: In New York City we have seen the transformation of Harlem from a combination of government action creating an empowerment zone, the private sector coming in to take advantage of that and an explosion of entrepreneurial dynamism. We've also seen the faith based community like Abyssinians & others that have been partners with it and of course we've seen a lot of hip hop participants and leaders taking advantage of that. So we need this partnership. We need this partnership between the public and private sector and the not-for-profit and faith-based sector. And we need to make sure that young people have a particular stake in what we are going to present. That's what I've worked on in NYC and in upstate NY and I intend to put that to work when I'm president.

Source: Iowa Brown & Black Presidential Forum, Dec. 1, 2007

NOTE: *President George W. Bush initiated the White House Office of Faith-based and Neighborhood Partnerships to institute his Charitable Choice proposal. Churches are tax-exempt, and donations to churches and other charities are tax-deductible; Pres. Bush's policy was intended to encourage churches to perform more social services. Proponents focus on removing restrictions on religious organizations' activities, so that churches can bid on government block grants for performing welfare services. Opponents claim that lessens restrictions on separation of church and state.*

Jeb Bush on Faith-Based Organizations

Welcome community and faith based organizations as partners

Last year, I asked you to join me in an unshakable commitment to educating our children, diversifying our economy, and strengthening the bonds that hold our families together. Today, I thank you for honoring that commitment and ask that we continue on the path of progress for the people we serve.

We are stronger because we recognize that government isn't the sole answer to the most important questions, and we welcome community and faith based organizations as partners to serve the needs of Florida families. Florida is in a better position to serve our people and face our future, and I thank the members of the Legislature for creating that opportunity.

Source: State of the State speech to the Florida Legislature, March 2, 2004

Created Governor's Faith-Based Advisory Board

Governor Bush embraced with greater enthusiasm the use of religious organizations to take over activities traditionally provided by governmental agencies. Florida has a long history of working with religious based organizations to provide social services.

To pursue his strategy, Bush created in the Office of the Governor a Faith-Based Advisory Board designed to mobilize additional religious organizations and to encourage their participation in his efforts to make nongovernmental organizations the primary mechanism for delivering public services in Florida. The board also provided direction to state agencies in their use of religious organizations in their work and technical assistance to the organizations in securing grant funds from both the federal and state governments. Bush also required state agencies to create official positions—called faith-based liaisons—to help eliminate internal obstacles to the receipt of funding for religious groups.

Source: Aggressive Conservatism in Florida, by Robert Crew, p. 34, Dec. 11, 2009

Hillary vs. Jeb on Social Issues

Social issues focus on matters which are based primarily on moral values. Jeb and Hillary are both moderates on social issues, who would prefer that most of these issues just weren't issues. These are the issues that the religious conservatives on the right, and the progressives on the left, care deeply about (the Tea Party on the right generally stays silent on social issues). Jeb agrees with the religious conservatives on social issues, more or less, but wants to compromise. Hillary agrees with the progressives on social issues, more or less, but wants to compromise. If you are a religious conservative or a progressive and want a firebrand on social issues, that firebrand is neither Jeb nor Hillary. This chapter including the following sections:

- **Abortion (pp. 110-115):** including embryonic stem cell research, contraception, adoption, and state-level restrictions. This topic has always been the most viewed topic on our website www.OnTheIssues.org, so we explore several aspects. Jeb opposes abortion and embryonic stem cell research on moral grounds; Hillary supports abortion on women's rights grounds, and supports embryonic stem cell research on medical grounds. Abortion-related issues will likely be more relevant in the primaries than in the general election, because Jeb and Hillary are both less-than-extreme on this most extreme of issues.

- **Gay Rights (pp. 116-119):** including same-sex marriage at both the state and federal levels. Hillary has "evolved" on gay marriage to become a supporter ("evolved" is the latest euphemism for "changed her mind"; Hillary supported DOMA when Pres. Bill Clinton signed it into law in the 1990s, but now she is fully pro-gay marriage). Jeb has "evolved" a little bit too: from fully anti-gay marriage in the 1990s to accepting some recognition of some basic rights (but not marriage) now. To be fair, America has "evolved" on gay marriage too: at the beginning of 2004, same-sex couple could not get legally married anywhere in America; at the end of 2014, same-sex marriage is legal in 35 states.

- *Families and Children (pp. 120-123):* This section would include father's rights and how the candidates apply family values to issues like abortion; but Jeb and Hillary don't talk about those issues. Jeb and Hillary both wrote books that focused on family values: Jeb's book *Profiles in Character* (reviewed on pp. 225-226) tells parents to teach virtue to their kids (excerpt below, p. 121). Hillary's book *It Takes a Village* (reviewed on p. 217) encourages "character education." But as elected officials, both Jeb and Hillary applied family values to family issues (like adoption), but not to anything controversial beyond that.

- *Religion and Patriotism (pp. 124-129):* Jeb and Hillary differ only in degree on issues like school prayer (both support restrictions) and on flag-related issues (both are moderate). But more surprisingly, Jeb and Hillary agree on the role of faith in their personal lives. Most voters would readily agree that Jeb relies on his faith as the basis for much of his political philosophy; but most voters do not realize that Hillary does the same. See our book review of *God and Hillary Clinton* (pp.212-3) for evidence that Hillary really is a member of the "religious left."

- *Principles and Values (pp. 130-135):* This section includes some possible campaign themes for 2016, and excerpts one local issue, casino gambling, in which both Jeb and Hillary both participated in their home states. The mainstream media will be most interested in Jeb's and Hillary's views on partisanship (they both play up bipartisan cooperation), since they each embody the most partisan aspects of the American politics, according to their opponents.

Hillary Clinton on Social Issues

Jeb Bush on Social Issues

Hillary Clinton on Abortion

Make abortion rare by supporting adoption & foster care

I think abortion should remain legal, but it needs to be safe and rare. And I have spent many years now, as a private citizen, as first lady, and now as senator, trying to make it rare, trying to create the conditions where women had other choices.

I have supported adoption, foster care. I helped to create the campaign against teenage pregnancy, which fulfilled our original goal 10 years ago of reducing teenage pregnancies by about a third. And I am committed to do even more.

Source: Democratic Compassion Forum at Messiah College,
April 13, 2008

Long-held moderate stance focuses on reducing abortions

When Clinton said that pro-choice and pro-life people could find common ground by trying to reduce the number of abortions through increased access to birth control, it was called "an attempt to move to the center as she contemplates a presidential run in 2008." The Wall Street Journal described her alleged changes in position as a "makeover and move to the center that she's now attempting." NPR saw Clinton spinning in circles: "She is doing what her husband did. Which was not so much move to the center or the right, but figure out a way to bridge the left-wing base of the Democratic Party. And move to the center at the same time."

Yet she was not changing her position on anything. For her entire time in public life, Clinton has been pro-choice and has supported access to birth control. Pointing out that such access would reduce the number of abortions, something anti-abortion forces ought to favor, cannot fairly be described as a shift in any direction.

Source: Free Ride, by David Brock and Paul Waldman, p.134-135,
March 25, 2008

Jeb Bush on Abortion

No need to teach about abortion if we have moral absolutes

Virtues are standards of behavior that are fixed & firm in any civilized society. Who would argue that fortitude, prudence, justice, temperance, discipline, work, responsibility, honesty, honor & compassion are not good things? Listen to William Bennett:

> Forming good character in young people does not mean having to instruct them on thorny issues like abortion, creationism, homosexuality, or euthanasia, to name just a few. People of character can be conservative and good people can be liberal.

Virtues are agreed-upon standards of right and wrong. Values, on the other hand, refer to a system of beliefs possessed by certain groups. Even Nazis and the worst street gangs have values. Since values focus on a position, they tend to accentuate our differences. Modern values often trump traditional values such as accountability, moderation, and deferred gratification. We have all seen the value of personal choice warring against the value of commitment to the family and children.

Source: Profiles in Character, by Jeb Bush, pp. 36-37 ,Nov 1, 1995

OpEd: Jeb avoids extremism on women's issues

The 2012 election cycle has been characterized by an almost obsessive focus on women's reproductive rights. But, amid the chaos, there is still more than one party heavyweight that believes the party's position on women's medical decisions needs to catch up to the modern age. Jeb Bush acknowledged that some conservatives' rather extreme rhetoric on some issues relating to women and minorities is understandably repelling those two groups from the Republican Party.

"I'm concerned about it over the long haul for sure. Our demographics are changing and we have to change not necessarily our core beliefs, but the tone of our message and the intensity of it, for sure," Bush said.

Source: Ashley Portero in International Business Times, Aug. 28, 2012

Hillary Clinton on Family Planning

Advocates birth control
but OK with faith-based disagreement

Mother Teresa had just delivered a speech against abortion, and she wanted to talk to me. Mother Teresa was unerringly direct. She disagreed with my views on a woman's right to choose and told me so. I had the greatest respect for her opposition to abortion, but I believe that it is dangerous to give any state the power to enforce criminal penalties against women & doctors. I consider that a slippery slope to state control [like] in China & Communist Romania. I also disagreed with her opposition—and that of the Catholic Church—to birth control. However, I support the right of people of faith to speak out against abortion and try to dissuade women, without coercion or criminalization, from choosing abortion instead of adoption. Mother Teresa and I found much common ground in many other areas including the importance of adoption.

Source: Living History, by Hillary Rodham Clinton, pp.417-8 , Nov. 1, 2003

Prevention First Act: federal funds for contraception

In 2006 Hillary pushed to increase federal funding to abortion providers such as Planned Parenthood. Senator Clinton co-wrote an editorial with Sen. Harry Reid titled, "Abortion Debate Shuns Prevention." The piece said, "As two senators on opposite sides of the abortion debate, we recognize that one side will not suddenly convince the other to drop its deeply held beliefs. And we believe that, while disagreeing, we can work together to find common ground."

The "common ground" was government programs to promote contraception. The Prevention First Act, as they named it, would increase accessibility and "awareness and understanding" of emergency contraception. They aimed to ensure that sex education programs have medically accurate information about contraception and "end insurance discrimination against women."

Source: Vast Right-Wing Conspiracy, by Amanda Carpenter, pp. 96-97, Oct. 11, 2006

Jeb Bush on Family Planning

Funded adoption counseling, but not abortion counseling

As governor, his entry into this arena came in his first year in office when he was called upon to support legislation permitting the state of Florida to offer a specialty license plate promoting the right-to-life side of the abortion controversy. The plate, containing the message "Choose Life," was available for $20 and the proceeds went to organizations that provided counseling and support to pregnant women "who are committed to placing their children up for adoption" but not to "any agency that is involved in or associated with abortion activities including counseling." Not surprisingly, the pro-choice advocates opposed the legislation. Bush's predecessor, Lawton Chiles, had vetoed the same measure on the grounds that it unnecessarily interjected religion into a public issue. Jeb sided with the pro-life side of this debate and signed the bill into law when it came to his desk.

Source: Aggressive Conservatism in Florida, by Robert Crew, p. 74, Dec. 11, 2009

NOTE: *"Roe v. Wade" refers to the 1973 Supreme Court decision legalizing abortion. The essence of the Roe decision is that Constitutional rights apply only after birth; hence abortion does not breach a person's right to life. States cannot regulate 1st trimester abortions; states can regulate but not ban 2nd trimester abortions; and states can ban 3rd trimester abortions (as many have). In 2014 and 2016, abortion opponents focus on peripheral issues like contraception and parental notification, rather than attempting to overturn Roe directly.*

Hillary Clinton on Stem Cells

Expand embryonic stem cell research

Clinton signed a letter from 58 Senators to the President:

Dear Mr. President:

We write to urge you to expand the current federal policy concerning embryonic stem cell research. We appreciate your words of support for the enormous potential of this research, and we know that you intended your policy to help promote this research to its fullest. As you know, the Administration's policy limits federal funding only to embryonic stem cells that were derived by August 9, 2001.

However, scientists have told us that since the policy went into effect more than two years ago, we have learned that the embryonic stem cell lines eligible for federal funding will not be suitable to effectively promote this research. We therefore feel it is essential to relax the restrictions in the current policy for this research to be fully explored. Among the difficult challenges with the current policy are the following:

- While it originally appeared that 78 embryonic stem cell lines would be available for research, only 19 are available to researchers.

- All available stem cell lines are contaminated with mouse feeder cells, making their therapeutic use for humans uncertain.

- It is increasingly difficult to attract new scientists to this area of research because of concerns that funding restrictions will keep this research from being successful.

- Despite the fact that U.S. scientists were the first to derive human embryonic stem cells, leadership in this area of research is shifting to other countries.

We would very much like to work with you to modify the current embryonic stem cell policy so that it provides this area of research the greatest opportunity to lead to treatments and cures.

Source: Letter from 58 Senators to Pres. George W. Bush on Jun 4, 2004

Jeb Bush on Stem Cells

Prevent use of public funds for stem cell research

Governor Bush took the side of the right-to-life constituency in a battle to prevent the use of public funds in support of stem cell research. While this stance put him at odds with his economic development supporters, he argued that this technology "takes a life to give a life," and opposed a ballot initiative that would have amended the state's constitution to provide $200 million over 10 years for this purpose. He also opposed actions to permit the Scripps Medical Institute to conduct research on this topic, even though he had committed $310 million of state-controlled federal funds to attract Scripps to Florida. At the same time he was attempting to lure the Burnham Institute of La Jolla, California, to build a lab in Florida, he also attached a condition that the Florida labs of this company, which was a leader in embryonic stem cell research, could work only on the noncontroversial stem cells from adults or umbilical cords.

Source: Aggressive Conservatism in Florida, by Robert Crew, p. 75, Dec. 11, 2009

Notes: *Stem cells are undifferentiated cells, which are useful in disease research. Stem cells are best taken from human fetuses; hence the pro-life opposition. Many pro-life advocates support fetal stem cell research because of the medical potential. In 2001, Pres. George W. Bush announced that the federal policy would be to allow fetal stem cell research on existing stem cell lines but not on new ones.*

In March 2009, Pres. Obama ended the ban on funding embryonic stem cell research. In signing the executive order, Obama said: "When it comes to stem cell research, rather than furthering discovery, our government has forced into what I believe is a false choice between sound science and moral values. In this case, I believe the two are not inconsistent."

Hillary Clinton on Gay Rights

GLBT progress since 2000, when I marched in gay pride parade

Q: When your husband was elected president, it was a very hopeful time for the gay community. But in the years that followed, our hearts were broken. A year from now, are we going to be left behind like we were before?

A: Well, obviously, I don't see it quite the way that you describe, but I respect your feeling about it. You know, we certainly didn't get as much done as I would have liked, but I believe that there was a lot of honest effort going on by the president, the vice president and the rest of us who were trying to keep the momentum going. You know, I remember when I was running for the Senate as first lady marching in the gay pride parade in New York City, and to a lot of people that was just an unbelievable act.

Q: Why not be the leader now?

A: I think I am a leader now. But as president, I think I have an opportunity to reverse the concerted assault on people. It wasn't just on people's rights; it was on people. It was demeaning; it was mean-spirited. And that will end.

Source: HRC/LOGO debate on gay issues, Aug. 9, 2007

NOTE: *Pres. Bill Clinton implemented two policies on gay rights as President: "don't ask, don't tell" (DADT) and DOMA (see next page). The policy banning open homosexuals serving in the military was repealed on Sept. 20, 2011. Hence gay and lesbian people may now openly serve in the US military. Since 1993, the DADT policy held that homosexuals may serve as long as they do not announce their homosexuality ("Don't Tell"), but also that the military may not investigate their homosexuality ("Don't Ask"). The policy banning open homosexuals serving in the military was repealed on Sept. 20, 2011. Hence gay and lesbian people may now openly serve in the US military. Jeb has not made his policy clear on DADT or its overturn.*

Jeb Bush on Gay Rights

Gay rights & feminism are "modern victim movements"

Since the 1960s, the politics of victimization has steadily intensified. Being a victim gives rise to certain entitlements, benefits, and preferences in society. The surest way to get something in today's society is to elevate one's status to that of the oppressed. Many of the modern victim movements-the gay rights movement, the feminist movement, the black empowerment movement-have attempted to get people to view themselves as part of a smaller group deserving of something from society.

It is a major deviation from the society envisioned by Martin Luther King, who would have had people judged by the content of their character and not by the color of their skin—or sexual preference or gender or ethnicity. Eventually there will come a time when everybody will be able to claim some status as a victim of society, leaving few in society who will actually be considered the victimizers. Who, then, will be left to blame in a world in which it is victim against victim?

Source: Profiles in Character, by Jeb Bush, pp. 59-60, Nov. 1, 1995

1994: LGBT protections are tantamount to elevating sodomy

A sharply conservative tone came to characterize Bush's entire 1994 gubernatorial campaign. In July, Bush published a now-infamous op-ed arguing against anti-discrimination protections for LGBT people, which he said were tantamount to elevating "sodomy." Bush's team has since sought to distance him from that piece, with a spokeswoman telling BuzzFeed that it "does not reflect Gov. Bush's views now."

Source: New York Times interview, "Evolving Views", Jun. 11, 2015

Hillary Clinton on Defense of Marriage Act

I support gay marriage personally and as law

Hillary Clinton endorsed gay marriage in a new video saying "that her views on the issue have evolved as a result of her experiences personally and as secretary of state," Politico reports.

Said Clinton: "I support it personally and as a matter of policy and law. Marriage is a fundamental building block of our society—a great joy and, yes, a great responsibility. To deny the opportunity to any of our daughters and sons solely on the basis of who they are and who they love is to deny them the chance to live up to their own God-given abilities."

Source: PoliticalWire.com, "Clinton backs same-sex marriage," March 18, 2013

2007: Supported DOMA, which Bill Clinton signed

Hillary stated categorically that she opposed legalizing same-sex marriage. She provided a clear explanation that to this day is the most quoted statement enunciating her position. "Marriage has historic, religious, and moral content that goes back to the beginning of time, and I think a marriage is as a marriage has always been, between a man and a woman. But I also believe that people in committed gay marriages, as they believe them to be, should be given rights under the law that recognize and respect their relationship."

Hillary said she backed her husband's signing of the Defense of Marriage Act. She said what everyone wanted to know: Yes, if she had been in the Senate in 1996, she would have supported the law.

Source: God and Hillary Clinton, by Paul Kengor, pp.189-90, July 18, 2007

NOTE: *As of the 2012 election, 13 states allowed same-sex civil unions or had some similar legislation, and 29 states had laws defining marriage as one-man-one-woman. By the 2014 election, the number of states allowing same-sex marriage had risen to 34 states. Several more states have legalized same-sex marriage but it has not yet taken effect (but will by the 2016 election). With a majority of states having legalized same-sex marriage, at issue now is federal law, which includes numerous aspects of federal benefits.*

Jeb Bush on Defense of Marriage Act

Traditional marriage best; but recognize gay couples

Bush believes in traditional marriage, but he supports recognition for gay couples: "I don't think people need to be discriminated against because they don't share my belief on this, and if [gay] people love their children with all their heart and soul, that should be held up as examples for others to follow because we need it," he told Charlie Rose last June. Likewise, he told the conservative CPAC conference earlier this month that "way too many people believe Republicans are anti-everything," including "anti-gay."

Back in 2006 Bush said he was leaning towards support for a constitutional ban on gay marriage in Florida, after previously holding that the ban was unnecessary. (Same-sex marriages were already illegal under state law). But in the gay marriage debate, six years is a long time. Bush seems positioned to move toward gay marriage support if he so chose.

Source: Rachel Weiner in Washington Post, March 26, 2013

No hate-crimes status for gays; no gay marriage

Q: Do you believe that the Florida government should include sexual orientation in Florida's anti-discrimination laws?

A: No.

Q: Do you believe that the Florida government should recognize same-sex marriages?

A: No.

Source: Florida National Political Awareness Test, July 2, 1998

NOTE: *"DOMA" refers to the Defense of Marriage Act, passed by Congress in 1996, which defined marriage as consisting of one man and one woman (in other words, barring same-sex marriage). DOMA applies to all federal benefits and taxes, but not necessarily to state benefits and taxes. On March 27, 2013, the Supreme Court heard US v. Windsor on overturning DOMA.*

Hillary Clinton on Families & Children

"It Takes a Village" implies family as part of society

Bob Dole, in his acceptance speech at the Republican Convention, had attacked the premise of my book *It Takes a Village*. He mistakenly used my notion of the village as a metaphor for "the state" and implied that I, and by extension Democrats, favor government intrusions into every aspect of American life. "After the virtual devastation of the American family, we are told that it takes a village, and thus the state, to raise a child," he said. "I am here to tell you it does not take a village to raise a child. It takes a family to raise a child."

Dole missed the point of the book, which is that families are the first line of responsibility for children, but that the village—a metaphor for society as a whole—shares responsibility for the culture, economy and environment in which our children grow up. The policeman walking the beat, the teacher in the classroom, the legislator passing laws—all have influence over America's children.

Source: Living History, by Hillary Rodham Clinton, p.375, Nov. 1, 2003

Critics misinterpret 70s article on "Children Under the Law"

In Hillary's 1970s Harvard Educational Review article "Children Under the Law," she gave lawyers the go-ahead to "remodel" the family. As Senator, she complains about the "misinterpretation" of her article in *Living History*: "Conservative Republicans twist my words to portray me as 'anti-family.' Some claimed that I wanted children to be able to sue their parents if they were told to take out the garbage."

In the original piece, Hillary says, "Ascribing rights to children will force from the judiciary and the legislature institutional support for the child's point of view." In the essay, Hillary reveals her view that the family and marriage are just artificial constructs—policies, really—that can be altered at will: "The basic rationale for depriving people of rights in a dependency relationship is that certain individuals are incapable of the right to take care of themselves. Examples of such arrangements include marriage, slavery, and the Indian reservation system."

Source: Madame Hillary, by R. Emmett Tyrrell, p.129-130, Feb. 25, 2004

Jeb Bush on Families & Children

Pass moral judgment & teach virtue to our children

Correcting our social pathologies will take time. Foremost, it will require a renewal of virtue and character and a rejuvenation of those institutions that teach virtue and character. We need to teach our children that there are universal rights and wrongs, that you can't spend your life explaining away or justifying deviant conduct. This means, then, that we must regain confidence in passing moral judgments, using the language of virtue and teaching virtue to our children.

It is important that we begin to discuss virtue and character in the context of those who exhibit true virtue and character on a routine basis. We must elevate the people who are redefining our culture every day for the better for they are the profiles in character from whom we must learn. Following their lead, we must make a conscious effort to practice even small acts of character and virtue. If we roll up our sleeves and do our part, the answer to our cultural problems will come.

Source: Profiles in Character, by Jeb Bush, pp. 41-42, Nov. 1, 1995

Conservatives and Hispanics share family values

Certainly the most important characteristics most conservatives and Hispanics share are religious and family values. What is most striking about Hispanic religious beliefs is their attachment to "renewalist" faiths—Pentecostal, evangelical, and charismatic: 2/3 of Hispanics say their religious beliefs are an important influence on their political thinking.

But conservatism among religious Hispanics has not translated into Republican partisan affiliation. Democrats outnumber Republicans by 55 to 18% among Hispanic Catholics, compared to a 39 to 32% Republican edge among non-Hispanic Catholics. Republicans should make an effort to connect with Hispanics on religious faith and moral values.

Source: Immigration Wars, by Jeb Bush, p.219-220, March 5, 2013

Hillary Clinton on Foster Care Policy

Even welfare children are better off with their parents

Minor controversy erupted over remarks Newt Gingrich made about welfare reform and orphanages. Some Republicans had suggested that the nation could reduce welfare rolls by placing the children of unwed welfare mothers in orphanages.

I thought this was horrible idea. All the work I have done on behalf of children convinced me that they are almost always best off with their families, that poverty is not a disqualification from good parenting, that financial and social support for families with special problems, including poverty, should be a first step before we give up on them and take away their children. Only when children are endangered by abuse and neglect should the government intervene on their behalf.

In a speech on Nov. 30, 1994, I criticized Gingrich for promoting legislation that punished children for circumstances over which they had no control. Gingrich swung back: "I'd ask her to go to Blockbuster and rent the movie Boys Town [an orphanage]."

Source: Living History, by Hillary Clinton, pp.262-3, Nov. 1, 2003

Supported foster care adoptions as First Lady & as Senator

Many of the ideas from the first edition of this book about how to refocus the foster care system on the best interests of the child were later included in the Adoption and Safe Families Act of 1997. After the passage of that legislation, foster adoptions increased 64% nationwide from 31,000 the year the law passed to 51,000 last year. As First Lady, I met many young people aging out of foster care who had little of the emotional, social, and financial support families provide. I worked on the Foster Care Independence Act of 1999, which provides young people aging out of foster care with support services, including access to health care, educational opportunities, job training, housing assistance, and counseling. In the Senate, we passed a law that provides financial incentives to people who adopt older children.

Source: Intro to It Takes A Village, by H. Clinton, pp.299-300,
Dec. 12, 2006

Jeb Bush on Foster Care Policy

No Place Like Home initiative: find families for DCF kids

We must do our part to find families for children who need them, by finding permanent homes for the children in state care. There are more than 4,000 children in Department of Children & Families care today. In November, we launched the *No Place Like Home* initiative to find Florida families who will open their hearts and homes to them.

We're actively looking for the right families, and streamlining the adoption process to remove the obstacles and frustrations that have been part of the process for far too long. We are committed to supporting Florida's families, but government will never be the full answer to their needs. Our state is blessed with an incredibly strong network of community and faith-based partners that offer a helping hand, provide counseling, and teach skills required to build strong families and hold them together.

Source: State of the State speech to the Florida Legislature,
March 2, 2004

Parental consent over government intrusions into families

While I support the idea of providing comprehensive services for the early identification and intervention of learning disabilities, I have a number of concerns with Senate Bill 1018, grounded on the potential for excessive intrusiveness of government in the lives of Florida's families.

- The bill is silent on the issue of parental consent for referral, assessment and intervention services for identified children and their families. Referrals of "high risk children" are automatic and may be interpreted to be without parental consent.

- The absence of a public records exemption to protect the privacy of families and children impacted is also problematic.

- The Florida State Laboratory will be required to purchase an expensive piece of equipment to process required Tandem Mass Spectrometry tests of all newborns.

- And finally, this program is to be provided at an enormous cost to taxpayers, despite services already provided by the state.

Source: Veto notification on Senate Bill 1018, May 31, 2001

Hillary Clinton on School Prayer

Allow student prayer, but no religious instruction

To bring reason & clarity to this often contentious issue, my husband's administration developed a statement of principles concerning permissible religious activities in the public schools. The complete guidelines include:

- Students may participate in prayer during the school day, as long as they do so in a non-disruptive manner and when they are not engaged in school activities.

- Schools should open their facilities to student religious organizations on the same terms as other groups.

- Students should be free to express their beliefs about religion in school assignments.

- Schools may not provide religious instruction, but they may teach about the Bible, civic values and virtue, and moral codes, as long as they remain neutral with respect to the promotion of any particular religion.

This last point is particularly important, [because religious institutions, parents, and schools share] the responsibility of helping children to develop moral values and a social conscience.

Source: It Takes A Village, by Hillary Clinton, p.162-163, Sept. 25, 1996

NOTE: *Current law is that schools allow religious groups to organize on school grounds as if they are any club. Schools are not allowed to conduct prayers at the beginning of school, but neither are they allowed to stop a student from praying.*

Jeb Bush on School Prayer

School prayer OK if prayers are voluntary and student-led

No longer faced with a sure-fire veto by the governor, a Republican-heavy group of lawmakers is resurrecting a controversial school-prayer bill for the first time in three years. "Children should be allowed to pray if they choose to so long as all religions are respected and it's not during class time," said one state Representative. State law permits public schools to offer secular Bible or religion study as an extracurricular activity, but the House measure would allow students to lead a public, nonsectarian prayer at graduations, school athletic events and some assemblies.

The measure is virtually identical to a bill that made it through the Legislature in 1996 but was killed by then-Gov. Lawton Chiles, a Democrat who vowed to veto any future school-prayer legislation that crossed his desk. In Gov. Jeb Bush, though, the Legislature now at least has a willing ear. Bush has said he would consider school-prayer legislation if the prayers were voluntary and student-led.

Source: Orlando Sentinel, "School Prayer," March 20, 1999

Let businesses express religious freedom

Bush opened up a bit about his Catholic faith and religious freedom laws. He embraced Indiana Gov. Mike Pence's recent signing of a controversial religious-freedom law calling it "the right thing" to do. The legislation has sparked intense backlash from Democrats and gay-rights groups, but Bush noted that President Clinton had signed a similar measure two decades ago. "This is simply allowing people of faith space to be able to express their beliefs, to be able to be people of conscience," Bush said. "I just think, once the facts are established, people aren't going to see this as discriminatory at all."

In recent weeks, some of Bush's biggest skeptics in the faith community had specifically mentioned wanting to hear from Bush on the issue of religious liberties. His comments put him publicly in line with the conservative evangelical right that he is quietly wooing.

Source: National Journal, "Jeb Bush Interview," March 30, 2015

Hillary Clinton on Flag Issues

Voted NO on recommending
Constitutional ban on flag desecration

The Senate voted on a resolution which would recommend a Constitutional Amendment banning flag desecration:

- the flag of the US is a unique symbol of national unity...

- the Bill of Rights should not be amended in a manner that could be interpreted to restrict freedom...

- abuse of the flag causes more than pain and distress... and may amount to fighting words...

- destruction of the flag of the US can be intended to incite a violent response rather than make a political statement and such conduct is outside the protections afforded by the first amendment to the Constitution.

Opponents of the Resolution said:

I am deeply offended when people burn or otherwise abuse this precious national symbol. I oppose this amendment not because I condone desecration of our flag, but because I celebrate the values our flag represents. Flag burning is despicable. However, the issue is whether we should amend the Constitution to proscribe it.

Source: Flag Desecration Amendment; Bill S.J.Res.12; Jun 27, 2006

Co-sponsored bill to criminalize flag-burning

Q: Is Hillary Clinton somebody who can reach the moderates?

A: She's a paradox. No one has been more diligent in trying to re-create her image as a centrist, even to the point of sponsoring legislation to make flag-burning illegal [but opposing a Constitutional Amendment], which is a naked play for a kind of voter who is not attracted to her.

Source: Jeffrey Goldberg in the New Yorker, May 29, 2006

Jeb Bush on Flag Issues

Removed Confederate battle flag from Florida Capitol

Jeb unceremoniously banished the "Stainless Banner"—a small Confederate battle flag on an otherwise white field—from the grounds of the Florida Capitol. Previously it had flown along with all the others flags that Florida had flown under in the five centuries since Europeans arrived.

There was no announcement, no nothing. The official reasoning, released after the fact, was that the flagpoles had all been taken down anyway for some renovation work on that side of the building, and, when it was over, it was decided that the Confederate flag would not go back up. Simple as that. Passive voice construction—"it was decided"—and that was the end of it.

No one really noticed, in fact, until the local papers got a complaint from the head of the Sons of the Confederacy, the self-described nonracist group that is merely interested in preserving Southern heritage. To his credit, Jeb did not back down. He didn't even waste much breath defending his decision. The action spoke for itself.

Source: America's Next Bush, by S.V. Dáte, p.195, Feb. 15, 2007

NOTE: *The flag desecration amendment is considered a proxy issue for free speech (if you oppose the amendment) or a proxy issue for patriotism (if you support the amendment). A flag-desecration law was introduced in every Congress from 1995 to 2006; it passed the House in each session, and failed to pass the Senate by only one vote in 2005. A flag-desecration bill has been sponsored in both the House and Senate (without a vote) in every Congress from 2007 to 2013.*

Hillary Clinton on Personal Faith

I have always felt the presence of God in my life

Q: You said in an interview last year that you believe in the Father, Son and the Holy Spirit. And you have actually felt the presence of the Holy Spirit on many occasions. Share some of those occasions with us.

A: You know, I have, ever since I've been a little girl, felt the presence of God in my life. And it has been a gift of grace that has, for me, been incredibly sustaining.

But, really, ever since I was a child, I have felt the enveloping support and love of God and I have had the experiences on many, many occasions where I felt like the Holy Spirit was there with me as I made a journey. It didn't have to be a hard time. You know, it could be taking a walk in the woods. It could be watching a sunset.

I don't think that I could have made my life's journey without being anchored in God's grace and without having that sense of forgiveness and unconditional love. My faith has given me the confidence to make decisions that were right for me, whether anybody else agreed with me or not.

Source: Democratic Compassion Forum at Messiah College, April 13, 2008

Sincere Christian & lifelong member of religious left

Some things regarding Hillary Clinton and her faith are clear: Although no one can profess to know any individual's heart and soul, there seems no question that Hillary is a sincere, committed Christian and has been since childhood. The same applies to her husband. Surely not even the most cynical rightwinger would insist that Hillary and Bill were playing politics when they eagerly attended Sunday school as eight-year olds. Hillary is a very liberal Christian, and would be categorized as part of the religious left, along with millions of Christian Americans, a designation that seems to have disappeared from the media's lexicon now that the secular press is obsessed with fears over the religious right.

Source: God and Hillary Clinton, by Paul Kengor, p. xii, July 18, 2007

Jeb Bush on Personal Faith

9/11/2001: after emergency meeting, went to church to pray

On Sep. 11, 2001, Jeb answered the expected questions about what the state would be doing to guard against new attacks. And finally someone asked where Jeb was going next. With the familiar, pinched grin, Jeb told us: "I'm going to Mass."

Something like that, on a day like that, there should have been absolutely no reason for it not to ring true. And yet...it was somehow off, just a little bit. He knew that whatever he said was likely to be widely reported. He was going to Mass. He was a good Catholic, and in a time of trouble, he was seeking solace in prayer.

Why the need to get this message out? Because unlike his brother, Jeb had never been a particularly public Christian. It was more important to be a Christian, in the immediate aftermath of September 11, in the high-contrast, Christianity-versus-Islam worldview that set in.

Source: America's Next Bush, by S.V. Dáte, p.303-304, Feb. 15, 2007

Focus on virtue & character, not values

We must do a better job of instilling character and virtue in our children and helping those institutions charged with this task. It means not getting bogged down in the current and unwinnable debate over values. That debate must be redefined in the context of virtues.

Values have replaced virtues as our moral lighthouses, and there are many different value systems present in our culture. Our character-building institutions have bought into the idea that we have to recognize all kinds of value systems and, instead of providing us guidance, now provide us with tools to justify a wide variety of deviant behaviors. In other words, they do not teach our children right from wrong, but rather how to make informed choices.

Our children need direction, not choices. If we give them the proper direction, the principles by which to live their lives, then in the long run they will be more likely to make the right choices. We must become more virtue oriented and less value oriented.

Source: Profiles in Character, by Jeb Bush, p. 21 & 35, Nov. 1, 1995

Hillary Clinton on Principles & Values

Make a pact not to give in to cynicism or hate

"Life can have some transcendent meaning," Hillary Rodham Clinton said to the graduation class of 1992 in an address at Hendrix College, a Methodist College in Conway, Arkansas. "Make a pact not to give in to selfishness or cynicism or hate. Cling to the enduring values you have been exposed to. Cling especially to the value that is given to all people and that is premised on their equal worth. Respect and trust individuals of all races, creeds, and colors. Work toward the achievement of a universal human dignity, not just your own personal security."

It was one of the most stirring speeches she's ever given. It might just as well have been a personal prayer. Delivered as it was in the heart of the campaign year, uttered, as it were, between the bullets of press and public attack, it was like a statement of faith.

Such statements, such faith, are what carried Hillary Clinton through the 1992 campaign year.

Source: The Inside Story, by Judith Warner, p. 229, Aug. 1, 1993

Lives by Wesleyan credo: Do all the good you can

We once asked Ann Lewis, Hillary Clinton's friend and adviser, to describe Clinton's political philosophy. She pointed to the words of John Wesley: "Do all the good you can, By all the means you can, In all the ways you can, In all the places you can, At all the times you can, To all the people you can, As long as ever you can." By that, Lewis sought to explain Clinton's devotion to issues like health care, children's well-being, and education. In New Hampshire that John Wesley credo defined her entire candidacy. She would wrest every opportunity out of every minute of every day until the polls had closed and she could no longer affect the outcome.

Source: The Battle for America 2008, by Balz & Johnson, p.140,
Aug. 4, 2009

Jeb Bush on Principles & Values

America is different because identity derives from ideals

American is different from any other country on earth in many ways, but most significant is that our national identity derives not from a common ethnicity but from a set of ideals—not just life, liberty, and the pursuit of happiness, but individualism, faith, family, community, democracy, tolerance, equal opportunity, individual responsibility, and freedom of enterprise. Those ideals are set forth in our nation's founding documents and enmeshed in its institutions.

But though our nation was founded on those ideals and continues largely to hold fast to them, America does not hold a monopoly over them. Quite to the contrary, millions of people around the world cherish those ideals and strive toward becoming Americans.

Source: Immigration Wars, by Jeb Bush, p. 69, March 5, 2013

1994 and 1998 campaign theme: Think outside the box

With Jeb, Floridians in 1994 & 1998 were told they were getting a Bush who, despite his family, was his own man. He was a thinker, a "searcher," Jeb told us. Someone who would think outside the box. Should he run for the presidency, this idea will become a main theme for his campaign, the number one talking point, at least at first, to open as much space as possible between the Jeb the Serious and Curious Grown-up and George the Perpetual Frat-boy Adolescent.

A decade and a half after his first appearance in statewide politics, it became clear that there was some truth to the original sales pitch. Jeb does seem more thoughtful and analytical than his father had been, and is obviously much more so than his older brother. But to focus on these differences downplays a far more important truth: that Jeb's agenda and his views on most major topics are virtually identical to that of his father and brother, with at best minor refinements.

Source: America's Next Bush, by S.V. Dáte, p. 27, Feb. 15, 2007

Hillary Clinton on Casino Gambling

Supports Niagara casino, but prefers job creation strategy

Q: Americans spend millions at the local casino in Niagara Falls, Canada. Why not have a casino built on this side of the border to help our economy?

LAZIO: I don't believe that it's a good idea for us to be building casinos. I would allow the state of New York to make these decisions. But in the end, I'm not a big fan of gambling. Economic development in the area is an important issue, but I would not focus on the quick hit, the cheap hit in gambling. I'd focus on the kind of jobs where our children can afford to stay here, raise a family, buy their own home.

CLINTON: I know how hard the people in Niagara are working to try to turn their economy around, and if they believe that a casino would help attract more tourists back, I would support that. I leave that to their judgment. But there has to be more of a strategy about the upstate economy —tax credits to help jobs be created, creating the regional skills, alliances, commitment to work force development, etc.

Source: Clinton-Lazio Senate debate, Buffalo NY, Sept. 13, 2000

NOTE: *Casino regulations are made by states, not by the federal government. Casino gambling is an interesting issue because politicians determine their issue stances on any of several different grounds:*

- *Morality: casinos are wrong because they prey on poorer people.*
- *Economic: casinos earn tax revenue for the state and the gambling would take place anyway, somewhere else.*
- *Employment: casinos create jobs during their construction, and create permanent jobs to operate the casino.*
- *Local development: Often a state will seek a casino because a neighboring state has one, with revenues lost to the home state,*

Jeb Bush on Casino Gambling

Gambling is emblematic of "something for nothing" culture

Jeb worked against a slot-machine gambling amendment in 2004. Jeb, as a good Christian conservative, has long opposed gambling as emblematic of the "something for nothing" culture that afflicts America. And so when the gambling interests put on the ballot an initiative to allow slot machines at pari-mutuels in Miami-Dade and Broward counties by local referendum, one would have expected Jeb to fight it tooth and nail, right?

Wrong. In fact, Jeb barely lifted a finger. The consequence: the pro-slots initiative passed. Jeb mobilized his people to defeat it in Miami-Dade, but could not stop it in Broward.

But why so little effort? [Jeb might say], "My brother was facing a tight race again, and I needed every Republican and independent vote I could get, including the libertarians who have no problem with gambling." And so, Florida in 2006, with a conservative Republican governor, finally got casino-style gambling that Democratic governors had successfully staved off in 1978, 1986, and 1994.

Source: America's Next Bush, by S.V. Dáte, p. 14-15, Feb. 15, 2007

Hillary Clinton on Partisanship

Triangulation replaces partisanship with a dynamic center

Dick Morris helped Bill develop a strategy to break through the wall of obstructionist Republicans.

When opposing camps are in two polar positions, they can decide to move toward a third position—like the apex of the triangle—what came to be called "triangulation." This was essentially a restatement of the philosophy Bill had developed as Governor and as Chairman of the Democratic Leadership Council. In the 1992 campaign, he championed moving beyond the "brain-dead" politics of both parties to craft a "dynamic center." More than old-fashioned compromise of splitting the difference, triangulation reflected the approach Bill had promised to bring to Washington.

When, for example, the Republicans tried to claim ownership of welfare reform, an issue Bill had been working on since 1980, Bill would avoid saying no. Instead, he would support the objectives of reform but insist on changes that would improve the legislation and attract enough moderate support to defeat the extreme Republican position.

Source: Living History, by Hillary Rodham Clinton, p.290, Nov. 1, 2003

NOTE: *Both Jeb and Hillary would prefer non-partisanship, but their opponents consider both of them the embodiment of partisanship. From the Republican side, the partisan anger expressed at Bill Clinton in his impeachment has transferred to Hillary. From the Democratic side, partisan anger directed at George W. Bush about the Iraq War has transferred to Jeb. Neither Jeb nor Hillary are as partisan as their opponents believe; but partisan attacks will be a major part of the 2016 campaigns for either candidate. That is the reason they both seek to downplay partisanship: to prepare for the inevitable partisan attacks.*

Jeb Bush on Partisanship

GOP isn't about orthodoxy & disallowing disagreement

I asked Jeb there about the Republican Party. "Ronald Reagan would have, based on his record of finding accommodation, finding some degree of common ground, as would my dad—they would have a hard time if you define the Republican Party—and I don't—as having an orthodoxy that doesn't allow for disagreement, doesn't allow for finding some common ground," Bush said, adding that he views the hyper-partisan moment as "temporary."

"Back to my dad's time and Ronald Reagan's time—they got a lot of stuff done with a lot of bipartisan support," he said. Reagan "would be criticized for doing the things that he did."

In the 12 years(!) since he last ran for office, Bush missed the rise of the tea party, and the ascendancy of a new generation of politicians—Marco Rubio, Paul Ryan, Scott Walker, Ted Cruz, among them. Those men occasionally, carefully, respectfully break with the movement. Scorning today's Republican Party is, by contrast, the core of Jeb's political identity.

Source: Ben Smith on BuzzFeed.com, "Terrible Candidate," April 7, 2014

OpEd on 2016 Hillary: Which family dynasty do you want?

In the summer of 2005, Jeb restarted his dormant Foundation for Florida's Future, putting on its board some of his most reliable political fundraisers. Maybe he could transmogrify his Foundation for Florida's Future into something with a more national-sounding sweep—Foundation for America's Future, say.

Ultimately, if indeed Jeb is hobbled by the myth or reality of Americans' "Bush fatigue," there is one certain cure. Hillary. She would immediately provide Jeb a ready answer to those who argue against a Bush dynasty. "We're going to have a dynasty," he could say. "The question is which one do you want? My family's? Or hers?"

Source: America's Next Bush, by S.V. Date, p.367-368, Feb. 15, 2007

Hillary vs. Jeb
on National Security Issues

This chapter focuses on issues of war policy and defense spending, and issues involving foreign nations that may lead to U. S. military action in the future (the following chapter focuses on non-military foreign policy). Hillary, as Secretary of State and in her recent book, has a well-established record on national security issues, while Jeb has expressed only limited views.

Jeb's lack of a full set of policy stances in this topic area must be addressed before Jeb hits the hustings in 2016, lest he appear unknowledgeable like Sarah Palin or Herman Cain when they were suddenly confronted with questions on foreign policy topics they had not previously been asked. Jeb has had more time to prepare than did Palin or Cain, so presumably he will surround himself with foreign policy advisors who will ensure that Jeb knows his stuff. Jeb has already begun this process, which we capture in his excerpts below.

Jeb does have some long-standing policy stances in this area, for issues that relate to Florida, such as Cuba and National Guard deployments. And he published a book in 2013 discussing numerous aspects of immigration, including cross-border issues with Mexico (see pp. 191-199). But other than immigration and Florida issues, Jeb's foreign policy stances are still "thin."

When Jeb finally does make a major speech on the missing topics in national security and foreign policy, you can infer two certain outcomes: (1) We will edit this book to produce a new revision with his more complete stances on national security; and (2) Jeb is most certainly running for president.

This chapter includes the following sections:

- ***Global War on Terror (pp. 140-147):*** This category addresses how Hillary and Jeb would take action against terrorism. Jeb blames President Obama for the rise of the Islamic State, and blames Hillary for Benghazi. Hillary would like to blame President George W. Bush for every world problem, because as Secretary of State, she inherited the problems left over from the Bush administration and dealt with them.

- *Middle East (pp. 148-155):* Jeb has made clear that he supports the Iraq War and Afghan War, and takes a hard line against Iran and supporting Israel. Voters might be surprised to learn that Hillary is as much of a hawk on these issues as is Jeb: She voted for the Iraq War (but now regrets it); she encouraged Obama to be tougher on Iran; she failed to get Obama to take action in Syria, but succeeded in guiding Obama to decisive action in Afghanistan. Jeb may draw a primary challenger who opposes his hawkishness (an anti-war libertarian like Sen. Rand Paul, R-KY) and Hillary may draw a Democratic dove who opposes her (an anti-war veteran like Sen. Jim Webb, D-VA). In the general election, the Republican nominee would likely follow Jeb's model of questioning Hillary's "resolve" by reneging on her vote for war in Iraq.

- *Military Budget (pp. 156-159):* This section concerns defense policy, not war policy: defense spending issues and defense strategy goals. We have to infer Jeb's views on federal defense spending from how he handled Florida's defense spending (pushing to keep military bases open). Hillary's Senate votes were, again, hawkish: but she may follow President Obama's policy of reducing the growth rate of the Pentagon (details on p. 157).

- *Political Hotspots (pp. 160-167):* including the current ongoing international disputes in Russia and North Korea. Jeb has far fewer opinions that does Hillary in these issues, but Jeb is studying, as described in his views on Russia and North Korea below. Jeb's views on Cuba are well-established from his Florida governorship; and also a historical record on the Vietnam war; we compare those views to Hillary's below. Jeb's views will expand to a fuller description on many political hotspots as he forms his views during 2015; but this chapter contains a comprehensive record of Jeb's views as of the end of 2014.

Hillary Clinton on
National Security Issues

Jeb Bush on National Security Issues

Hillary Clinton on Terrorism Policy

Called war on terror "Bush's war" but has played active role

[After 9/11], Clinton called for punishment for those responsible, the hijackers, and their ilk and vowed that any country that chose to harbor terrorists and "in any way aid or comfort them whatsoever will now face the wrath of our country."

On the campaign trail, and especially in television debates, Clinton is at pains to frame the so-called war on terror as "Bush's war," but she's had an active part in it. It isn't as if her 9/11 speech was an exception. Clinton supported Bush's invasion and bombardment of Afghanistan. She voted for the USA PATRIOT Act, which gave the government new unconstitutional tools of search and seizure even as federal agents were sweeping thousands of innocent civilians off the streets of US cities, notably in New York.

Source: The Contenders, by Laura Flanders, p. 18-19, Nov. 11, 2007

Consistently supported tough anti-terrorism measures

The only exception to Hillary's party-line voting were her support for the Iraq War & her votes for appropriations to fund it, her uniform support for tough anti-terrorism measures, and—in an attempt to curry favor with the media—her opposition to nullification of the FCC rules making media consolidation easier.

Hillary has amassed a good legislative record on fighting terrorism. She has pushed hard for threat assessments on bioterrorism, to protect the food supply, promote benefits to children of terror victims, increase homeland security grants, investigate securing radioactive materials, require annual inspections of high-risk sites, identify potential terror sites, encourage bomb-scanning technology, and improve protection at our embassies. But none of these bills has passed.

[On spending bills], Hillary has proposed additional spending to improve military housing, keep open facilities on closed defense bases, upgrade armed forces medical readiness, and increase aid to blind veterans.

Source: Condi vs. Hillary, by Dick Morris, p. 86-88, Oct. 11, 2005

Jeb Bush on Terrorism Policy

$17M for new programs for terrorism response

Immediately following the terrorist attacks on September 11th, we acted quickly. By executive order, I put in place new programs that bolstered law enforcement's ability to deal with the terrorist threat and authorized specialized training for domestic security personnel.

I am proud of the rapid response of the Legislature in aggressively addressing this new threat. A few weeks ago, in special session, you dedicated more than $17 million in new programs to bolster homeland security, put into place harsher criminal penalties for terrorist acts, and created a new, coordinated system for law enforcement's response to terrorism.

But we must do more. I am proposing this session that we spend $45 million to further strengthen domestic security, including $6 million to continue the efforts begun in the current year.

Source: State of the State address to 2002 Florida Legislature,
Jan. 22, 2002

NOTE: ISIS ("Islamic State in Iraq and Syria", next page) began taking territory from the Iraqi government control in early 2014. The United States sent 300 "advisers" to help the Iraqi army fight ISIS, in June 2014, after ISIS had captured substantial territory.

ISIS is more accurately known as ISIL, "Islamic State in Iraq and the Levant"; the Levant is the Eastern Mediterranean area that includes Syria, Lebanon, Israel, and Palestine.

ISIL had been fighting in Syria alongside Al-Qaeda, but broke ties with Al Qaeda in Iraq.

Hillary Clinton on ISIL (Islamic State)

Not helping Free Syrian Army left vacuum for ISIS to fill

Q: You go out of your way in Hard Choices to praise the U.S. ambassador to Syria who quit in protest of the inadequacies of Obama administration policy. Are we at fault for not doing enough to build up a credible Syrian opposition when we could have?

A: I'm the one who convinced the administration to send an ambassador to Syria; and this is why I called the chapter on Syria "A Wicked Problem." I can't sit here today and say that if we had done what the Ambassador and I recommended, that we'd be in a demonstrably different place.

Q: That's the president's argument, that we wouldn't be in a different place.

A: Well, if we were to carefully vet, train, and equip early on a core group of the developing Free Syrian Army, we would, number one, have some better insight into what was going on on the ground. Two, we would have been helped in standing up a credible political opposition.

Q: Do you think we'd be where we are with ISIS right now if the U.S. had done more three years ago to build up a moderate Syrian opposition?

A: Well, I don't know the answer to that. I know that the failure to help build up a credible fighting force of the people who were the originators of the protests against Assad—-there were Islamists, there were secularists, there was everything in the middle—-the failure to do that left a big vacuum, which the jihadists have now filled.

Source: Jeffrey Goldberg in The Atlantic, Aug. 10, 2014

Jeb Bush on ISIL (Islamic State)

ISIL's rise is because world has no clue where US will be

Jeb Bush directly blamed the rise of the Islamic State (ISIS) forces and other crises in the Middle East on a widespread lack of trust in President Barack Obama's statements. "A president's word matters," Bush said. "Language matters. The use of their bully pulpit matters. So when you say things like, 'We're gonna have a red line,' you need to mean it. You can't just say that and then say, 'Well, I was talking about the world's red line,'" Bush said, adding, "Give me a break."

Bush was referring to Obama's declaration in August 2012 that Syria's use of chemical weapons would cross "a red line for us," necessitating U.S. military intervention. Obama reneged on that commitment following Syria's apparent actual use of such weapons a year later, claiming "I didn't set a red line; the world set a red line."

"Presidents need to accept responsibility for their language," Bush said. "It needs to be taken to the bank. The problem in America today is that our friends have no clue where we will be, and so they change their behavior." By contrast, he said, "our enemies have a clue where we will be and they change their behaviors as well. And so these voids are created and bad things happen."

Source: Theodore Kettle on Newsmax.com, "Obama's Untrustworthiness Led to Rise of ISIS" Oct. 31, 2014

NOTE: *The groups fighting in the Syrian civil war can be entirely divided along Shia-Sunni lines: Assad is supported by Iran (a Shi'ite country), and by Hezbollah (a Shi'ite terrorist group); the Syrian rebels are supported by the Saudi Arabia and the Emirates (Sunni countries), and by Al-Qaeda, a Sunni terrorist group.*

That list of groups is confusing, and President Obama had trouble figuring out in June 2013 which groups to help and which to attack. Or more specifically, how to explain to Americans that we should help some groups and attack others. Obama did try to enforce the "red line," by planning aid to some groups and attacks on others, but the American public soundly rejected any support for Obama's policy, and the policy was abandoned.

Hillary Clinton on Benghazi

Benghazi: Figure out what happened to prevent repeating

The NATO intervention in Libya was the most important foreign intervention of her tenure, and a seemingly successful one, but the lack of security in Benghazi and the confusion over how the incident occurred set off a heated Republican attack on Clinton's handling of the disaster. In January, she took responsibility for the deaths of the four Americans before Congress—while also questioning her inquisition, snapping at a Republican congressman, "What difference at this point does it make? It is our job to figure out what happened and do everything we can to prevent it from ever happening again."

Benghazi will be the go-to bludgeon for Republicans if and when Clinton tries using her experience at State to run for president. Republicans are liable to use Benghazi as a wedge to pry back her stately exterior, goading her into an outburst, once again revealing the polarizing figure who saw vast right-wing conspiracies.

Source: New York Magazine interview, "Hillary in Midair," Sep 22, 2013

Benghazi was a tragedy, but we get it right 99% of the time

Any clear-eyed examination of this matter must begin with this sobering fact: Since 1988, there have been 19 Accountability Review Boards investigating attacks on American diplomats and their facilities. Benghazi joins a long list of tragedies. Of course, the list of attacks foiled, crises averted, and lives saved is even longer. We should never forget that our security professionals get it right 99% of the time. That's why, like my predecessors, I trust them with my life.

Let's also remember that administrations of both parties, in partnership with Congress, have made concerted and good faith efforts to learn from the tragedies that have occurred, to implement recommendations from the Review Boards, to seek necessary resources, and to better protect our people from constantly evolving threats. And it's what we are doing again now. I take responsibility. Nobody is more committed to getting this right. I am determined to leave the State Department and our country safer, stronger, & more secure.

Source: Benghazi Hearing, Senate Foreign Relations Committee, Jan. 23, 2013

Jeb Bush on Benghazi

Conflicting accounts of Benghazi emboldens terrorists

Jeb Bush said that the administration's conflicting accounts of the tragic murders of four Americans in the Benghazi terrorist attack has "emboldened" America's enemies and puts the United States "in a more perilous position." Bush added that the Obama administration's handling of the tragedy "has created a cloud that doesn't serve us well."

Bush indicated the administration's mixed messaging makes America look weak. "When the world sees us as uncertain and not surefooted, they act," he said. "Our friends act by pulling away and nervously kind of not being assured that the United States is there to support them. And our enemies are emboldened. So the tragedy of this is that four people lost their lives; great public servants. And then, because of the politics of this, the Obama administration sent such a confusing signal out that they did themselves no good," he added.

[Benghazi was] the first deadly assault on a U.S. diplomat since 1979. [It was recently revealed that] special ops soldiers made at least three requests for permission to respond to the developing firefight in Benghazi, which were denied.

Source: David Patten and Kathleen Walter, Newsmax TV , Oct. 28, 2012

NOTE: *There have been many fatal attacks on US overseas diplomatic facilities, including ambassadors killed, other than Benghazi. Following is the list of fatalities from such attacks during the George W. Bush presidency, excluding many attacks on the US Embassy in Baghdad:*
- *1/22/2002. U.S. Consulate in Calcutta, India: 5 killed.*
- *6/14/2002. U.S. Consulate in Karachi, Pakistan: 12 killed.*
- *2/28/2003. U.S. Embassy in Islamabad, Pakistan: 2 killed.*
- *5/12/2003. U.S. Compound in Riyadh, Arabia: 36 killed (9 Americans).*
- *7/30/2004. U.S. Embassy in Tashkent, Uzbekistan: 2 killed.*
- *12/6/2004. U.S. Consulate in Jeddah, Saudi Arabia: 9 killed.*
- *3/2/2006. U.S.Consulate Karachi,Pakistan (again):4 killed(one Diplomat).*
- *9/12/2006. U.S. Embassy in Damascus, Syria: 4 killed.*
- *3/18/2008. U.S. Embassy in Sana'a, Yemen: 2 killed.*
- *7/9/2008. U.S. Consulate in Istanbul, Turkey: 6 killed.*
- *9/17/2008. U.S. Embassy Sana'a, Yemen (again): 16 killed.*

Hillary Clinton on September 11th

2001: Called for wrath
on those who attacked America on 9/11

Within hours of two planes crashing into two New York towers on 9/11/2001, Hillary Clinton's closest advisor, Bill, urged her to come out strong. It was he who encouraged her to show that she had the requisite boldness and guts to lead the nation and protect her people. The very next day, Hillary delivered a call to arms that hailed "wrath" on those who harbored terrorists. While others were modeling a different style of leadership by holding firm for global cooperation, criminal prosecution, and a reassertion, rather than a shedding of international jurisprudence, Clinton channeled Thatcher, Britain's "Iron Lady," and delivered a bombastic speech in which she described the attacks on the World Trade Center and Pentagon as an "attack on America." Clinton called for punishment for those responsible, the hijackers, and their ilk and vowed that any country that chose to harbor terrorists and "in any way aid or comfort them whatsoever will now face the wrath of our country."

Source: The Contenders, by Laura Flanders, p. 18-19, Nov. 11, 2007

9/11: Got $20B to rebuild lower Manhattan

After the 9/11 memorial service in Washington, Hillary went to New York, as did Bush. At Ground Zero, Bush made his iconic appearance, rallying rescue workers and telling the crowd through a bullhorn, "I can hear you. The rest of the world hears you. And the people who knocked these buildings down will hear all of us soon." Hillary stood nearby and cheered the president's vow.

With each passing day that week, Hillary seemed to grow more comfortable in her role as an energized street fighter for a shattered city. She was inevitably overshadowed by Mayor Giuliani, who would be acclaimed as "America's Mayor" for his resolve in lower Manhattan. And yet, for many New Yorkers, the images of Hillary fighting for the $20 billion in federal assistance for lower Manhattan dispelled any lingering doubts that she was a carpetbagger celebrity politician with few authentic ties to her new home state.

Source: Her Way, by Jeff Gerth & Don Van Natta, p.235, June 8, 2007

*Jeb Bush on September 11*th

Threat from 9/11 is unprecedented for our generation

In most years, we mark change by the passing of foreseeable events. But since I spoke here last, a new rhythm has been violently layered over the old. We awoke one morning in September, and we confronted a threat that is unprecedented for our generation.

As I have come to expect from Floridians, we have been extraordinary in our response to that threat. As a state, we will meet, and soon overcome, the obstacles that evil has devised. We will understand, and soon eliminate, any barrier that would keep this state from realizing its destiny. And when we do, we will be stronger and better for it. Floridians are united as never before, and when the current crisis has passed, we will remain bound to one another in a spirit of caring and community that will endure. Stronger, wiser, with an unshakable determination: that is the state of our state.

We must continue to thwart those who would harm us. We must renew our commitment to ensure the security of our citizens and our guests.

Source: State of the State address to Florida Legislature,
Jan. 22, 2002

NOTE: *On September 11, 2001, Jeb Bush was serving as Governor of Florida. The State of the State speech above was his first after the terrorist attack. Jeb's brother was president of the United States at that time.*

Hillary Clinton at that time was serving as Senator from New York. The twin towers of the World Trade Center were part of her constituency; hence the money she requests to rebuild lower Manhattan was partly a constituent service.

Hillary Clinton on Iranian Sanctions

Political restraint against Iran's Ahmadinejad was a mistake

Clinton said the Obama administration's decision to offer a muted response to the political demonstrations that broke out against former President Mahmoud Ahmadinejad's re-election in 2009 was a mistake:

"In retrospect, I'm not sure our restraint was the right choice. It did not stop the regime from ruthlessly crushing the Green Movement, which was exceedingly painful to watch. More strident messages from the United States would probably not have prevented the outcome and might even have hastened it, but there's no way of knowing now if we could have made a difference." (Page 423)

Source: Wall Street Journal on Hard Choices, by Hillary Clinton, June 17, 2014

Rushing to war with Iran vs. doing nothing is a false choice

Q: Would you pledge to the American people that Iran will not develop a nuclear bomb while you are president?

A: I have pledged that I will do everything I can to prevent Iran from developing a nuclear bomb.

Q: Why did you vote for the Kyl-Lieberman amendment which calls upon the president to structure our military forces in Iraq with regard to the capability of Iran?

A: I am against a rush to war. I was the first person on this stage and one of the very first in the Congress to go to the floor of the Senate back in February and say President Bush had no authority to take any military action in Iran. Secondly, I am not in favor of this rush for war, but I'm also not in favor of doing nothing. Iran is seeking nuclear weapons. And the Iranian Revolutionary Guard is in the forefront of that, as they are in the sponsorship of terrorism. So some may want a false choice between rushing to war, which is the way the Republicans sound—it's not even a question of whether, it's a question of when and what weapons to use— and doing nothing. I prefer vigorous diplomacy. And I happen to think economic sanctions are part of vigorous diplomacy.

Source: Democratic debate at Drexel University, Oct. 30, 2007

Jeb Bush on Iranian Sanctions

Encourage regime change in Iran; keep military option open

Military options must be left on the table to force Iran's leaders to abandon their nuclear ambitions, according to Jeb Bush. The US should be much more assertive in encouraging regime change there as well, he said.

Bush said that not maintaining the viable prospect of US military action "empowers bad behavior in Tehran amongst its leaders." Bush criticized the Obama administration for failing to encourage internal resistance to Iran's mullahs. Iran's theocrats have subjected the "green movement" protesters to a series of brutal crackdowns.

"I think we need to be much more aggressive in supporting civil opposition to the regime in Iran," Bush said. "I was saddened to see how the Obama administration handled the post-election revolution on the streets. It seemed like we were very tepid, at a time when we should forcefully support freedom. It's part of who we are as a nation, and I think we should embrace this noble notion: If not for the United States, who? Who will be there to help?"

Source: David A. Patten and Kathleen Walter on Newsmax.com,
Nov. 29, 2010

NOTE: *In November 2011, the International Atomic Energy Agency (IAEA) Board of Governors criticized Iran after an IAEA report concluded that before 2003 Iran likely had undertaken research and experiments geared to developing a nuclear weapons capability. A number of Western nuclear experts have stated there was very little new in the report, that it primarily concerned Iranian activities prior to 2003.*

Iran rejected the details of the report and accused the IAEA of pro-Western bias. The IAEA Board of Governors has found Iran in non-compliance with its Nuclear Non-Proliferation Treaty safeguards agreement. Iran says its nuclear program is peaceful. Iran also claims that it was forced to resort to secrecy after US pressure caused several of its nuclear contracts with foreign governments to fall through.

Hillary Clinton on Iraq War

I got it wrong on 2002 Iraq War vote

Many Senators came to wish they had voted against the resolution [authorizing the Iraq War in 2002]. I was one of them. As the war dragged on, with every letter I sent to a family in New York who had lost a son or daughter, a father or mother, my mistake became more painful.

I thought I had acted in good faith and made the best decision I could with the information I had. And I wasn't alone in getting it wrong. But I still got it wrong. Plain and simple.

Source: Hard Choices, by Hillary Clinton, CBS pre-release excerpts, June 6, 2014

Iraq war authorization was not authority for preemption

I warned at the time the Iraq war authorization was not authority for a preemptive war. Nevertheless, he went ahead and waged one, which has led to the position we find ourselves in today. Now we have to look at how we go forward. There will be a great debate between us and the Republicans, because the Republicans are still committed to Bush's policy, and some are more committed than others, with McCain's recent comments. He's now accusing me of surrendering because I believe we should withdraw starting within 60 days of my becoming president. Well, that is a debate I welcome, because the Democrats have a much better grasp of the reality of the situation that we are confronting. We have to continue to press that case. It will be important, however, that our nominee be able to present both a reasoned argument against continuing our presence in Iraq and the necessary credentials and gravitas for commander-in-chief. That has to cross that threshold in the mind of every American voter.

Source: Democratic debate in Los Angeles, Jan. 31, 2008

Jeb Bush on Iraq War

Keep US forces in Iraq, like we did after WWII

Bush compared keeping forces in Iraq to the post-World War II missions involving U.S. troops in Japan, Korea, and Europe, which "created a security for the world and allowed people to rise up from poverty." According to Bush, those missions "should be something that we are really proud of," and not doing something similar in Iraq "created a void that has allowed ISIS to emerge in Iraq as a force to be reckoned with."

According to Bush, "there is a consistent foreign policy for our country that has worked" since World War II under Democrats and Republicans alike, "and it starts with saying that we lead the world. We're not part of the 'community of nations,'" a term Bush said gave him nausea.

Source: Theodore Kettle on Newsmax.com, Oct. 31, 2014

Over time, people will respect our resolve in Iraq

Q: We're coming up on the ten-year anniversary of the war in Iraq which is widely seen in public opinion polls as a mistake. Do you think that will ever change?

BUSH: Yes. You know, a lot of things in history change over time. I think people will respect the resolve that my brother showed, both in defending the country and the war in Iraq. But history will judge that in a more objective way than today. The war has wound down now and it's still way too early to judge what success it had in providing some degree of stability in the region.

Source: CNN State of the Union interview, March 10, 2013

NOTE: *The Iraq War formally ended on Dec. 15, 2011. Approximately 5,000 "security contractors" will remain to guard the US Embassy in Baghdad, plus several thousand more "general support contractors." Another 9,000 US troops are just over the border in Kuwait.*

Hillary Clinton on Israel/Palestine

We are invested in Israel: negotiate a ceasefire in Gaza

Clinton devotes many pages to her fealty to Israel, and to her understanding of Israeli Prime Minister Benjamin Netanyahu, who fell from power then rose to it again: "I am not alone in feeling so personally invested in Israel's security and success," she writes. "Many Americans admire Israel as a homeland for a people long oppressed and a democracy that has had to defend itself at every turn. In Israel's story we see our own, and the story of all people who struggle for freedom and the right to chart their own destinies."

Clinton has long paid heed to her standing among Jewish supporters, and she was clear in public comments in the last several months she remains "skeptical" about Iran's commitment to a true nuclear freeze deal. The many sections on Israel—and on her role in negotiating a ceasefire in Gaza—serve a political purpose. But they also reflect the significance of Israel for any secretary of State, especially as the Arab Spring protests were unfolding.

Source: Politico.com on Hard Choices, June 7, 2014

Allegedly pro-PLO in 1960; but pro-Israel by 1981

In 1981, while the Clintons campaigned to win back the governorship, their pastor, Vaught approached them about a trip to Israel. As Bill and Hillary found themselves struggling spiritually and politically to put Bill back in the governor's mansion, the couple decided to go.

In contrast to the anti-Israel version of Hillary portrayed during parts of the 1970s, some sources claim this trip gave Hillary an inspired appreciation for the state of Israel, and if so, it may have mitigated her alleged pro-PLO sympathies, giving more balance in her perspective. A friend of the Clintons says: "Bill and Hillary understood the profound effect that Israel has on American Jews and around the world and share a feeling for the security and stability of the State of Israel."

Source: God and Hillary Clinton, by Paul Kengor, p. 70-71, July 18, 2007

Jeb Bush on Israel/Palestine

Israel will make no sacrifices when she feels threatened

Conducting the foreign policy of a great nation requires maturity and a strategic sense of America's long-term interests. With Israel, those interests lie in a firm alliance. Israel and America must work together to build a more prosperous and hopeful future for the region.

A state for the Palestinian people, side by side with Israel, will be possible only if the Palestinian people are represented by leaders committed to delivering on the promises made at the negotiating table. Ultimately, the most fruitful efforts for peace come in moments when America's word is trusted and America's commitment is certain. Anyone who claims to pursue peace in the region—especially between Israel and her neighbors—must know that Israel will make no sacrifices for peace when she feels threatened.

The future success of American foreign policy in the Middle East—and the world—will require a fresh approach. One that takes to heart the realities of the region. One that rebuilds the friendships we once enjoyed. One that reminds our enemies of our determination. And one that fundamentally believes that when America leads, the world is more stable and America's security is more certain.

Source: Jeb Bush opinion piece in National Review, March 25, 2015

NOTE: *Israel made peace with the PLO in 1993, and granted autonomy to the Palestinian Authority. That entity split in 2007 into Fatah governing the West Bank (at peace with Israel) and Hamas governing the Gaza Strip (with regular rocket fire into Israel through 2014).*

AIPAC is the American Israel Public Affairs Committee, founded in 1951. The pro-Israel group, with 100,000 grassroots members nationally, is currently considered one of the most powerful lobbying groups in Washington. Detractors claim that AIPAC support causes politicians to support Israel, as Jeb and Hillary both do. Supporters claim that supporting Israel makes sense since it is the only stable democracy in the Middle East.

Hillary Clinton on Afghanistan War

Clinton-Gates combo won push for Afghan surge

Just as the Obama administration was beginning to hold meetings to decide [whether to send a troop surge to] Afghanistan, Gen. Stanley McChrystal's report leaked out [recommending 30,000 to 40,000 more US troops in Afghanistan].

[Secretary of Defense] Robert Gates gradually came around to supporting the McChrystal request, and Hillary Clinton did, too. During that period, the two often sided with each other in administration debates; they were happy to show that the secretaries of state and defense could work smoothly together, unlike their immediate predecessors, Donald Rumsfeld with Colin Powell & Condi Rice. The Clinton-Gates combine helped to win over the president to sending more troops, despite the skepticism of other senior administration officials such as Biden; the president was not prepared to override the recommendations of the two departments primarily responsible for foreign affairs. Obama approved the deployment of 30,000 more American troops for Afghanistan, bringing the total to about 100,000.

Source: The Obamians, by James Mann, p.134-136, June 14, 2012

Would have never diverted attention from Afghanistan

It's clear that if I had been president, we would have never diverted our attention from Afghanistan. When I went to Afghanistan the first time and was met by a young soldier from New York, who told me that I was welcomed to the forgotten front lines in the war against terror, that just struck me so forcefully. We have so many problems that we are going to have to untangle. Day after day, what I spend my time working on is trying to help pick up the pieces for families and for injured soldiers trying to make sure that they get the help that they need, trying to give the resources that are required. We had to fight to get body armor. Bush sent people to war without body armor. We need a president who will be sensitive to the implications of the use of force and understand that force should be a last resort, not a first resort.

Source: Democratic debate in Los Angeles, Jan. 31, 2008

Jeb Bush on Afghanistan War

OpEd: Not willing to distance himself from brother's Afghan policy

On five talk shows Sunday morning, Jeb Bush reminded America why he'll never be president: it's hard to distance yourself from your own last name. "I don't think there's any Bush baggage at all," the former Florida governor said on Fox News Sunday. "I love my brother. I'm proud of his accomplishments." On Meet the Press, he added that "history will be kind to George W. Bush."

To seriously challenge for the presidency, a Republican will have to pointedly distance himself from Jeb's older brother. No Republican will enjoy credibility as a deficit hawk unless he or she acknowledges that George W. Bush squandered the budget surplus he inherited. No Republican will be able to promise foreign-policy competence unless he or she acknowledges the Bush administration's disastrous mismanagement in Afghanistan and Iraq. It won't be enough for a candidate merely to keep his or her distance from W. John McCain and Mitt Romney tried that, and they failed because the Obama campaign hung Bush around their neck every chance it got. To seriously compete, the next Republican candidate for president will have to preempt that Democratic line of attack by repudiating key aspects of Bush's legacy. Jeb Bush would find that excruciatingly hard even if he wanted to. And as his interviews Sunday make clear, he doesn't event want to try.

Source: Peter Beinart in The Daily Beast, March 11, 2013

Hillary Clinton on Defense Spending

Our troops are stretched; so increase size of military

Recommends a bigger Army in 2004: "We have to face the fact we need a larger active-duty military. We cannot continue to stretch our troops, both active-duty, Guard and Reserve, to the breaking point, which is what we're doing now... I'm supporting an effort to increase the end strength of the Army, increase the size of the military. This is a big decision for our country to make. It is expensive, but I don't think we have any alternatives."

Muscle, not rhetoric, leads to strong homeland security: "We have relied on a myth of homeland security—a myth written in rhetoric, inadequate resources, and a new bureaucracy instead of relying on good, old-fashioned American ingenuity, might, and muscle."

Source: What Every American Should Know, by the ACU, pp. 74-76, Sept. 30, 2005

Served on Armed Services Committee & was always prepared

She came into the Senate under the most intensive scrutiny of any senator in recent history, McCain said, and "she has conducted herself very admirably." McCain added that Hillary was "always well prepared" at hearings on the Armed Services Committee.

Hillary landed her most important post, a slot on the Armed Services Committee, after the 2002 midterm elections. It was a conscious decision to burnish her national-security resume after September 11.

Hillary had previously impressed the army's vice chief of staff, Gen. John Keene, one of the architects of the invasion of Iraq, with her grasp of military culture. Hillary learned how to fit into a community that had long harbored hostility toward her husband. Hillary's service on the Armed Services Committee enabled her to reach out to the military. It also allowed her to travel on official business to war zones.

Source: Her Way, by Jeff Gerth & Don Van Natta, p.254-256, June 8, 2007

Jeb Bush on Defense Spending

Weakness invites war: our military should equal any threat

The President's word needs to be backed by the greatest military power in the world. The president should show leadership—and commitment to solving the problem. Having a military that is equal to any threat is not only essential for the commander-in-chief—it also makes it less likely that we will need to put our men and women in uniform in harm's way. Because I believe, fundamentally, that weakness invites war—and strength encourages peace.

The threats of the 21st century will not be the same as the threats of the 20th—and it is critical that we adapt to meet this challenge. We have no reason to apologize for our leadership and our interest in serving the cause of global security, global peace and human freedom.

Source: Speech to the Chicago Council on Global Affairs, Feb. 18, 2015

Make Florida the most military-friendly state in the nation

We must protect our military bases and the $44 billion defense industry by aggressively defending our military installations in the 2005 base closure (BRAC) process. We must also find more ways to support the military men and women who serve their country from our state. I support the legislation proposed to help military families transition into our communities and our schools, as part of our effort to make Florida the most military friendly state in the nation.

Source: State of the State speech to the Florida Legislature, March 2, 2004

NOTE: *President Obama proposes slowing the growth of defense spending in future years. Obama would increase the defense budget by 2% per year, while the CBO projects GDP to grow at about 3% per year. In 2017, Obama proposes $568 billion for the defense budget.*

Defense spending does not include $221 billion in defense-related spending: The Department of Homeland Security's 2013 budget is $55 billion; the Department of Veterans Affairs' 2013 budget is $60 billion plus $89 billion in mandated spending; and part of the Department of Energy's 2013 budget of $35 billion goes toward maintaining our nuclear weapons.

Hillary Clinton on Military Bases

No permanent bases, but continuing residual force in Iraq

Q: You say you envision a continuing presence in Iraq to protect vital American interests?

A: My goal is to end the war when I'm President & to bring our troops home. But as has been stated in [April 2007 legislation], we do envision a vastly reduced residual force to remain for some limited period of time to train Iraqi troops, to provide logistical support, for counter-terrorism missions, to protect the Kurds if necessary. That does not mean we would have a permanent force. I am absolutely clear: we do not plan a permanent occupation or permanent bases, but there may be a continuing mission to protect America's vital interests, and to support an Iraqi government that we hope to be an ally going forward, assuming they are acting responsibly. So, the bottom line for me is that we will begin re-deploying our troops as soon as I am President, and we will do so in as expeditious a manner as possible, [leaving] as few troops as necessary with no permanent occupation, and no permanent bases.

Source: Virtual Town Hall on Iraq, sponsored by MoveOn.org, April 10, 2007

NOTE: *The United States Armed Forces maintain 395 military bases abroad. These bases cost billions of dollars and have not been subject to periodic BRAC-style closures since 1965. Bases by country:*

U.S. Bases in Europe		Bases in the Mideast		Bases elsewhere	
4	Bulgaria	16	Afghanistan	2	Australia
62	Germany	3	Bahrain	1	Brazil
1	Greece	1	Diego Garcia	1	Cuba
1	Greenland	1	Djibouti	2	Guam
120	Italy	2	Israel	1	Honduras
1	Kosovo	4	Kuwait	103	Japan
1	Netherlands	2	Oman	1	Singapore
1	Portugal	3	Pakistan	48	South Korea
2	Spain	1	Qatar		
1	Turkey	1	Saudi Arabia		
5	United Kingdom	3	U.A.E.		

Jeb Bush on Military Bases

Save Florida's 21 military bases from closure or downsizing

Gov. Jeb Bush led a delegation of business and retired military leaders in meetings with top Pentagon officials and members of Florida's congressional delegation as part of a mission to save the state's military bases from possible closure or downsizing. Protecting the 21 installations and three unified commands during the 2005 Base Realignment and Closure, or BRAC, round is a one of Bush's core priorities.

Source: Bradenton (FL) Herald, Feb. 9, 2005

NOTE: *The 2005 BRAC report (Base Realignment and Closure Commission) recommended the following occur by 2011:*

- *9 bases for closure (originally 14 bases, but 5 later removed)*

- *13 bases for realignment*

- *12 joint bases created by merging two adjacent bases.*

Another BRAC commission is scheduled for 2015, and then every 8 years thereafter. The five bases originally slated for closure had their status reversed by political action (like Jeb describes above); the purpose of having an independent BRAC commission is to avoid such political interference.

Hillary Clinton on Cuba Policy

Architect of ending Cuban travel & trade restrictions

Although President Barack Obama is taking the credit for the historic deal to reverse decades of US policy toward Cuba, when Hillary Clinton was secretary of state, she was the main architect of the new policy. Clinton and her top aides took the lead on the sometimes public, often private interactions with the Cuban government. Clinton was also the top advocate inside the government for ending travel and trade restrictions on Cuba and reversing 50 years of U.S. policy to isolate the Communist island nation. Repeatedly, she pressed the White House to move faster and faced opposition from cautious high-ranking White House officials.

After Obama announced the deal, which included the release of aid contractor Alan Gross, Clinton issued a supportive statement: "As Secretary of State, I pushed for his release, and called for a new direction in Cuba," she said. "Despite good intentions, our decades-long policy of isolation has only strengthened the Castro regime's grip on power."

Source: Bloomberg News, "Clinton secretly pushed Cuba deal"
Dec. 18, 2014

Meet with Cuban leaders only after evidence of change

Q: Would you be willing to sit down with Raul Castro?

A: The people of Cuba deserve to have a democracy. And this gives the Cuban government, under Raul Castro, a chance to change direction from the one that was set for 50 years by his brother. I'm going to be looking for some of those changes: releasing political prisoner, ending some of the oppressive practices on the press, opening up the economy.

Q: Very simply, would you meet with Raul Castro or not?

A: I would not meet with him until there was evidence that change was happening. A presidential visit should not be offered without some evidence that it will demonstrate the kind of progress that is in our interest, and in this case, in the interests of the Cuban people.

Source: Democratic debate at University of Texas in Austin, Feb. 21, 2008

Jeb Bush on Cuba Policy

Strengthen the Cuban embargo instead of lifting it

Jeb Bush's call for strengthening the US embargo of Cuba signals a get-tough approach to foreign policy sure to please his political base of Cuban-American conservatives. Bush's stance sets up a clear contrast to Hillary Clinton, who wants to lift the embargo: "I would argue that instead of lifting the embargo we should consider strengthening it again to put pressure on the Cuban regime," Bush told cheering supporters at a gathering of the US Cuba Democracy PAC, a pro-embargo advocacy group.

Bush did not spell out proposals for strengthening the embargo. But he implied that he wanted to reverse travel rules made by President Obama that allow Cuban-Americans to make unlimited trips to visit relatives. "Thousands of people travel to Cuba from the US , spending billions of dollars," Bush said. "Would lifting the embargo change the fact that the government receives almost all of the money that comes from these well-intended people that travel to the island?"

Source: Sun-Sentinel, "Jeb Bush gets tough on Cuba," Dec. 3, 2014

1990: Defended anti-Castro terrorist as patriot in exile

Jeb petitioned the Justice Department in 1990 on behalf of Orlando Bosch. The anti-Castro terrorist was implicated in a car-bombing assassination and was notorious for having masterminded the bombing of ·a Cubana Airlines Flight in Oct. 1976, which killed all 73 on board.

At the time George H. W. Bush was CIA director. The US sanctioned terrorism against Cuba and routinely trained commandos to infiltrate the island. Jeb, who planned to run for governor of Florida, represented a rabid anti-Castro constituency, a voting bloc that held his father's anti-Castro actions at the CIA in the highest esteem. Jeb's public support for paroling Bosch further enhanced his standing in the Cuban community, which considered Bosch a patriot in exile and honored him for his murderous bombings around the globe. At this son's behest, George Bush intervened to obtain the release of the Cuban terrorist from prison and later granted Bosch US residency.

Source: The Family, by Kitty Kelley, p.407-408, Sept. 14, 2004

Hillary Clinton on Vietnam

Vietnam converted her from conservative to liberal

On college campuses, the war in Vietnam helped turn the children of conservative Republicans, like Hillary Rodham, into liberal Democrats. It also fostered a dark view of America's role in the world. Vietnam taught the lesson that even a supposedly small and limited war could eventually consume the US and divert it from all other objectives. It demonstrated that military force could lead to disastrous results. Opponents of the war argued that there should be new limits on American power and the defense and intelligence agencies that wield it. The main lesson was that if American resorts to force at all, it had better do so carefully.

Vietnam had social and political ramifications that were not foreseen at the time. The war led to the abolition of the draft, and that in turn had sweeping consequences for many other aspects of American life.

Source: The Obamians, by James Mann, p. 14, June 14, 2012

NOTE: In 1975, after North Vietnam won the Vietnam War, President Gerald Ford extended the 1964 trade embargo on North Vietnam to unified Vietnam. In 1994, President Bill Clinton ordered an end to the U.S. trade embargo. In 2001, the U.S.-Vietnam Bilateral Trade Agreement granted Vietnam permanent normal trade relations (PNTR). In 2007, Vietnam joined the World Trade Organization (WTO). In 2011, bilateral trade reached $21.8 billion, compared to $220 million in 1994.

For the 2016 race, the key issues are how to conduct trade with a non-market economy (Vietnam is socialist). Vietnam with six other countries are now in the ongoing Trans-Pacific Partnership (TPP) negotiations with the U.S. (see p. 188)

Jeb Bush on Vietnam

1971: Troubled by LBJ's Vietnam, but registered to serve

The flames of 1968 seemingly had no effect on George W. Jeb wasn't so sure.

The fact of it was, Jeb was deeply troubled by Vietnam and Johnson's handling of it. So troubled, in fact, that in the coming years, not only did he not sign right up to join the infantry but instead he was seriously considering filing for conscientious objector status, and wanted to run it past his dad.

To George H. W. Bush's credit, and notwithstanding his later, withering criticism of those who did not fight, he told Jeb that he would support whatever decision he made. George said, 'Whatever you decide, I will back you 100%.'"

In late 1971, Jeb, a lanky 18-year-old with hair longer than his parents might have liked, decided to back his father's political career. He went to Houston to get his physical. Had Nixon & Congress not wound down the draft, Jeb would likely have been called up. So he can argue that although he wrestled with the prospects of fighting in a war, in the end he did the right thing by his country.

Source: America's Next Bush, by S.V. Dáte, p.332-334, Feb. 15, 2007

Hillary Clinton on Korea Policy

Get China involved with North Korea diplomacy

South Korea [is] a wealthy, advanced democracy and key ally living in the shadow of a repressive and bellicose neighbor to the north. Many of North Korea's 25 million people live in abject poverty. Yet the regime devotes most of its limited resources to supporting its military, developing nuclear weapons, and antagonizing its neighbors.

In my public remarks [in Feb. 2009] in Seoul I extended an invitation to the North Koreans. If they would completely and verifiably eliminate their nuclear weapons program, the Obama Administration would be willing to normalize relations, and assist in meeting the economic and humanitarian needs of the North Korean people. If not, the regime's isolation would continue. It was an opening gambit that was not one I thought likely to succeed. But, as with Iran, we started off with the offer of engagement knowing it would be easier to get other nations to pressure North Korea if and when the offer was rejected. It was particularly important for China, a longtime patron and protector of the regime in Pyongyang, to be part of a united international front. [The opening failed, as have numerous others since then].

Source: Hard Choices, by Hillary Clinton, p.53-4, June 10, 2014

Balance American interests between China & Korea

I decided to use my first trip as Secretary to accomplish three goals: visit our key Asian allies, Japan and South Korea; reach out to Indonesia; an emerging regional power and the home of ASEAN; and begin our crucial engagement with China.

We talked about how to balance America's interests in Asia, which sometimes seemed in competition. For example, how hard could we push the Chinese on human rights or climate change and still gain their support on security issues like Iran and North Korea?

Source: Hard Choices, by Hillary Clinton, p.46, June 10, 2014

Jeb Bush on Korea Policy

South Korea success: 1952 devastation to 2014 first-world

I want to tell a story about a country that was the poorest country on the planet in 1952. The country was Korea: a country that had been ravaged by war; a country that had the highest illiteracy rate in the world; a country with no natural resources; devastated in every possible way.

Fast forward. Over 62 years, not that long in historical terms, Korea now is a first-world country. Korea has the highest literacy rate of all the countries in the world. Korean moms and dads, some of them, save everything they have, to assure that their children get tutorial help. When President Obama was in Korea a year ago, he asked, "What is the big challenge that you face in Korea today?" it's that parents want to start English in 4th grade instead of 5th grade, and it's creating enormous political pressure on the system. But If you make a command-focused commitment to education, you can change the course of a country's future.

Source: Speech at PPF 2013 Empower SC Conference, June 27, 2013

NOTE: *North Korea never signed the Nuclear Test Ban Treaty, but was criticized internationally anyway for its first nuclear test in 2006. It is estimated that North Korea possesses 10 nuclear warheads, compared to 8,500 possessed by the United States.*

As many as two million North Koreans have died from starvation since 1995. Drought and famine continue today, and South Korea is concerned that the North will attack if facing imminent political collapse.

Kim Jong-Il, the "Dear Leader" of North Korea, died in Dec. 2011, and was succeeded by his son, Kim Jong-un, now dubbed the "Great Successor." Besides his idiosyncratic personality, the new North Korean leader has been criticized for human rights violations, as well as grandstanding on nuclear weapons.

Hillary Clinton on Russia Policy

Take a harder line with Russia's Putin

Clinton said she urged Obama to take a tougher line with Russian President Vladimir Putin shortly before she left office in 2012: "With all this in mind, I suggested we set a new course. The reset had allowed us to pick off the low-hanging fruit in terms of bilateral cooperation. And there was no need to blow up our collaboration on Iran or Afghanistan. But we should hit the pause button on new efforts. Don't appear too eager to work together. Don't flatter Putin with high-level attention." (Page 244)

Source: Wall Street Journal excerpts of Hard Choices, June 17, 2014

Putin's annexing Crimea plays outdated zero-sum game

Putin's worldview is shaped by Russia's long-standing interest in controlling the nations on its borders, and his personal determination that his country never again appear weak or at the mercy of the West, as he believes it was after the collapse of the Soviet Union. He wants to reassert Russia's power by dominating its neighbors and controlling their access to energy. To achieve these goals, he seeks to reduce the influence of the US in Central and Eastern Europe and other areas that he considers part of Russia's sphere.

All of that helps explain why Putin first pressured Ukraine to walk away from closer ties with the European Union in late 2013, and why Putin invaded and annexed Crimea.

Putin sees geopolitics as a zero-sum game in which, if someone is winning, then someone else has to be losing. That's an outdated but still dangerous concept, one that requires the US to show both strength and patience. To manage our relationship with the Russians, we should work with them on specific issues when possible, and rally other nations to work with us to prevent or limit their negative behavior when needed. That's a difficult but essential balance to strike.

Source: Hard Choices, by Hillary Clinton, p.227-8, June 10, 2014

Jeb Bush on Russia Policy

Passivity hasn't worked on Russia and Ukraine

Bush has joined Chris Christie and other center-right Republicans in criticizing President Obama for alleged "passivity." In a private speech in March to Sheldon Adelson and the Republican Jewish Coalition, Bush slammed Obama on Russia and Ukraine: "He was very rough on the president in terms of his handling of foreign policy, referring to the dangers of 'American passivity.'"

Back in 2012, [one pundit wrote in] Foreign Policy: "The next Republican nominee will need distance both from George W. Bush's foreign policy and from Mitt Romney's campaign. Even Jeb Bush—particularly Jeb Bush—would have to look like he was taking a very different approach to foreign policy than his brother."

But can Jeb Bush so easily make a "clean break," so to speak, with W.? According to the website On the Issues, Bush was a founding member of the Project for a New American Century, the neoconservative outfit formed in the 1990s that played a leading role in generating support for war in Iraq and whose members took up key positions in the administration of George W. Bush, Jeb's brother.

Lately, Bush hasn't said much about either PNAC, his brother or foreign policy generally. According to Defense News, Jeb Bush's views on foreign policy and defense are closer to those of his father—i.e., more centrist, more realist, more diplomacy-minded, in other words, Obama-like—than they are to the views of his militarist brother.

Chris Christie, Jeb Bush, a handful of other GOP governors: none of them have fully developed views on foreign policy.

Source: Bob and Barbara Dreyfuss, The Nation, May 30, 2014

NOTE: *In March 2014, Crimea held a referendum vote on whether to declare independence from Ukraine; the vote passed with 96% in favor. Russia recognized the independent Crimean Republic the next day; and the day after that, signed a treaty with Crimea's leaders annexing it to Russia. Russia then invaded and annexed the Crimea. A 1954 Soviet Decree was hence undone, which had transferred Crimea from Russia to Ukraine.*

Hillary vs. Jeb
on International Issues

International issues focus on foreign relations and anything involving foreign nations, except the military issues covered in the previous chapter. In our national security chapter above, Jeb is just forming his views; in this chapter, that applies to the foreign relations section as well. Jeb's views are more fully formed on issues of global warming and global trade, and he has written a book on immigration issues. Hillary has a long record on all of the issues in this chapter, and are often the opposite of Jeb's views in this chapter.

The key question to be addressed by 2016: Is Jeb a neocon? That means a "neo-Conservative," the group that dominated the international policymakers of the George W. Bush administration. We conclude: No, not quite, Jeb is not a neocon like his brother George. Jeb may be advised by neocons in a Bush Administration, but he is much more of a multilateralist, and much more cautious in his foreign policy, than the second President Bush. At issue with the George Bush presidency is that George allowed the neocons to determine policy, especially with the Iraq War (which was a major neocon goal). Jeb starts off much more knowledgeable and involved about international affairs than was George at this phase of his campaign, and although Jeb will likely have neocon advisers, Jeb does not seem as likely to follow neocon policies. On the other hand, Jeb was a founding member of Project for a New American Century (PNAC, the organization that defined the neocon movement, see p. 167). So Jeb's statements in 2015 will have to determine the answer.

The corresponding key question to be addressed in 2016 on the Democratic side: Is Hillary a progressive? The answer is unambiguously no; Hillary is a liberal centrist, and that difference is highlighted in this chapter. Progressives support "fair trade," which means that free trade agreements should include environmental and labor clauses; Hillary is an ardent free-trader. Progressives ardently oppose military intervention abroad; Hillary is a hawk, as detailed in the previous chapter. And progressives are ardently anti-corporate, while Hillary is pro-corporate, as discussed in the economic chapter. In fact, Hillary has anti-progressive views in *every* chapter in this book; we point out in each chapter the issue on which she might draw a progressive primary challenger. But while

Hillary is not a progressive, the progressives accept the inevitability of her nomination (at least that is true as 2015 begins!). Progressives were thrilled to vote for the first African-American president, and will be similarly thrilled to vote for the first female president. In other words, the progressives *accept* Hillary; in contrast, the Tea Party and the libertarians may not as readily accept Jeb.

This chapter includes the following topics:

- *Global Warming (pp. 172-177):* including climate change, domestic drilling and alternative energy sources. On this issue, Jeb and Hillary are polar opposites; Hillary would fight global warming, while Jeb is a "skeptic." Jeb opposes offshore oil drilling, but on environmental grounds, not on global warming grounds.

- *Foreign Relations (pp. 178-185):* Hillary is a multilateralist who supports engaging America with the world; Jeb seems to be following the multilateral path also. Mostly Jeb defines himself as not Obama (whom he considers too passive) and not Rand Paul (whom he considers an isolationist). We attempt to define the "Hillary Doctrine" and the "Jeb Doctrine" on pp. 182-183.

- *Global Trade (pp. 186-191):* including NAFTA (the North American Free trade Agreement) and other bilateral agreements. At issue for 2016 are expanding NAFTA to all of the Americas, and an equivalent trans-Pacific trade pact. Both Jeb and Hillary are free-traders; Hillary will likely hedge her advocacy if faced with a progressive fair-trader in the primary.

- *Immigration (pp. 192-199):* including border security; the border fence; and dealing with the current 12 million illegal immigrants in the US. Both Jeb and Hillary support a path to citizenship, which opponents call "amnesty." Immigration, which is one of Jeb's core issues, is the most likely issue to draw an anti-immigration opponent in the Republican primary: especially the Tea Party opposes Jeb on immigration.

Hillary Clinton on International Issues

Jeb Bush on International Issues

Hillary Clinton on Climate Change

$100B per year by 2020 for climate change mitigation

I told the crowd that the US was prepared to lead a collective effort by developed countries to mobilize $100 billion annually by 2020 from a combination of public and private sources to help the poorest and most vulnerable nations mitigate the damage from climate change – if we could also reach a broad agreement on limiting emissions.

The idea began with the Europeans, particularly British Prime Minister Gordon Brown, who had proposed a similar deal in the summer. By offering a concrete commitment, I hoped to breathe new life into the talks, put pressure on China and the other "emerging emitters" to respond, and win support from developing countries who would welcome this new assistance.

In the end, after lots of cajoling, debating, and compromising, the leaders in that room fashioned a deal that, while far from perfect, saved the summit from failure and put us on the road to future progress. For the first time all major economies, developed and developing alike, agreed to make national commitments to curb carbon emissions through 2020 and report transparently on their mitigation efforts.

Source: Hard Choices, by Hillary Clinton, p.498-500, June 10, 2014

$50B strategic energy fund from taxing oil companies

In May 2006, Clinton unveiled a proposal for a "virtual revolution" in energy, to decrease the use of foreign oil by 8 million barrels a day by 2025. The plan called for the creation of a $50 billion "strategic energy fund" by increasing taxes on oil companies. Clinton also suggested the government force oil firms to invest in renewable fuels like ethanol.

Clinton, in short, sought to reallocate money from fuel that consumers do buy (oil) to fuel that they don't buy (renewables). Clinton's plan was consistent with her tenacious opposition to any measure allowing oil companies to increase domestic drilling [both in ANWR and off the US coast].

Source: Vast Right-Wing Conspiracy, by A. Carpenter, p. 62-63, Oct. 11, 2006

Jeb Bush on Climate Change

I'm a skeptic about global warming

Q: Do you believe global warming is primarily man-made?

A: I'm a skeptic. I'm not a scientist. I think the science has been politicized. I would be very wary of hollowing out our industrial base even further. It may be only partially man-made. It may not be warming; the last six years we've actually had mean temperatures that are cooler. I think we need to be very cautious before we dramatically alter who we are as a nation because of it.

Source: Tucker Carlson interview of Jeb Bush in Esquire, Aug. 1, 2009

A "patriotic energy policy" will yield far more revenue

What I would do is advocate policies that would create high growth because the revenue collected by government when you're growing at 3.5% instead of 1.5% is exponentially more. And high growth over a sustained period of time by having a patriotic energy policy, bringing regulation to the 21st Century, immigration reform would be a good one, reforming our education system, tax policy – all those things would yield, I think, far more revenue. That should be where there's the common ground. And in return, there should be some give and take as it relates to entitlement reform. You could get to a place where our fiscal house would be in order if we achieved that. The president has not been willing to discuss that but in the last week, he's begun to at least reach out to Republicans which is quite encouraging.

Source: CBS Face the Nation, March 10, 2013

__NOTE:__ In 2016, the phrase "all-of-the-above" has come to mean support of investing in alternative energy while simultaneously supporting nuclear power and more oil and gas drilling. The focus of an "all-of-the-above" stance is to decrease America's dependence on imported oil, by increasing domestic supplies of oil plus other energy sources, rather than a focus on replacing oil with renewable energy sources. Jeb's phrase "patriotic energy policy" implies the same focus on domestic sources.

Hillary Clinton on Kyoto Treaty

Ratify Kyoto; more mass transit

As Senator, I will work for New York to get its fair share of federal mass transit funds and to increase the amount of money that goes to transit funds. And, I will vote to ratify the Kyoto Protocol to bring all nations together to address global warming and build a better future for us all.

Source: www.hillary2000.org, "Environment," Sept. 9, 2000

Led delegation, with McCain, to see effects of polar warming

Virtually the entire Senate voted for a resolution opposing the Kyoto Climate Change Treaty even before [Pres. Bill Clinton in 1997] could submit it for ratification.

All that changed after 9/11 and the Iraqi War. With oil prices soaring and mounting evidence of the destructive impacts of climate change, everyone began to take the issue more seriously. Sen. John McCain and Hillary led delegations of more skeptical senators to northern Norway and Alaska to see the already clear impact of warming for themselves. Other countries proved that clean efficient energy use could be profitable. While the US government was condemning Kyoto as a threat to growth, the United Kingdom determined to beat its Kyoto reduction target by 25% to 50%, and in so doing created enough good jobs to enjoy something we Americans didn't—rising wages and declining inequality. Germany is now the number one producer of wind energy, and Japan leads the world in the production and installation of solar panels.

Source: Giving, by Bill Clinton, p.154-155, Sept. 4, 2007

NOTE: *"Kyoto" refers to a Climate Change Treaty which sets carbon dioxide reduction targets for the US and other developed countries, via a policy that has become known as "cap-and-trade." Completed in 1998, the US has not yet signed. This is politically controversial because it would require the US to cut CO_2 emissions, which is potentially costly. "Cap-and-trade" is intended to minimize the cost, but has become a buzzword for the opposition.*

Jeb Bush on Kyoto Treaty

Kyoto Treaty must include reductions by all countries

Bush adopted the National Governors Association policy:

The Governors recommend that the federal government continue to seek the advice of state and local officials and nongovernmental organizations with expertise in economic, trade, jobs, public health, and environmental issues and assess the potential economic and environmental consequences of proposed policies and measures, including a thorough and broadly accepted analysis of costs and benefits. The Governors recommend that the US:

- not sign or ratify any agreement that mandates new commitments to limit or reduce greenhouse gas emissions for the US, unless such an agreement mandates new specific scheduled commitments to limit or reduce greenhouse gas emissions for developing countries within the same compliance period;

- aggressively undertake strategies for including emissions-reduction commitments from developing countries;

- not sign or ratify any agreement that would result in serious harm to the US economy;

- support flexible policies and measures in continuing negotiations that provide an opportunity for the US to meet global environmental goals without jeopardizing US jobs, trade, or economic competitiveness;

- insist on flexible implementation timetables in continuing negotiations that permit affected parties adequate time to plan strategies for meeting commitments; and

- ensure that no single sector, state, or nation is disproportionately disadvantaged by the implementation of international policies.

Source: NGA policy NR-11, Climate Change International Policy on Aug 15, 2000

Hillary Clinton on International Treaties

Regrets US not part of International Criminal Court

The Obama administration has broader ambitions including an ill-conceived desire to join the International Criminal Court (ICC). The Clinton administration initially signed the ICC's founding document, the Rome Statute, in June 1998, but there was no prospect that the Senate would ratify it.

To date, the ICC has proceeded slowly, partly in the hope of enticing the US to cooperate with it, and the Bush administration succumbed to it in its final years. The ICC's friends under President Obama want to go even further. Secretary of State Hillary Clinton said in 2009, for example, that it was "a great regret but it is a fact we are not yet a signatory" to the Rome Statute, signaling unmistakably what she hopes to do.

The Obama administration's willingness to submit US conduct to international judicial review also extends to the concept of "universal jurisdiction," which permits even countries utterly unrelated to an event to initiate criminal prosecutions regarding it.

Source: Obama is Endangering our Sovereignty,
by Ambassador John Bolton, pp. 25-6, May 18, 2010

NOTE: *The ICC was founded by the United Nations General Assembly in 1998, by a vote of 120-7. The United States voted against the Rome Statute, the founding treaty, along with China, Iraq, Israel, Libya, Qatar, and Yemen. The U.S. never ratified the treaty, and hence is not legally bound by the ICC. President George W. Bush opposed the ICC on grounds that U.S. service members could be prosecuted. President Barack Obama stated in 2009 that the U.S. would cooperate with the ICC, but has not attempted to ratify the Rome Statute in the Senate.*

Jeb Bush on International Treaties

We are leader among equals in community of nations

Bush said relatively little about his brother or his father in [his foreign policy speech to the U.S.-Cuba Democracy PAC]. He spent far more time talking about President Obama. Bush said the current president violated his first foreign-policy precept: to lead both the United States and the world. "We are not an equal partner in this so-called community of nations. We are a leader among equals," Bush said. "First, I think the United States needs to lead. Lead with humility. Lead with respect. But lead."

In calling for a foreign policy laced with "humility," Bush echoed his brother's call in 2000 to have a "humble" foreign policy. A year later, the US became far more interventionist after the 9/11 attacks, which ultimately helped lead the nation into invading Afghanistan and Iraq.

One of Bush's precepts was more of a slogan: "Words matter." He said that time and again, Obama has made threats or promises and then failed to act: "Presidents need to set United States aspirations and intentions where there is little gap between words and deeds," Bush said. "Think of the 'Russian reset.' Think of the 'Syrian red line.' Think of the 'pivot to Asia.' Think of taking out ISIS."

Bush said Obama failed to accomplish any of these goals: "It undermines our credibility in the world. Our allies don't trust us. And our enemies don't fear us. There is no situation worse for stability and peace than that," Bush said. "The iron rule of superpower deterrent is 'mean it when you say it.' And it has been broken by this president."

Source: Miami Herald, "The 'Jeb Bush Doctrine' makes debut,"
Dec. 2, 2014

Hillary Clinton on International Diplomacy

New American Moment: new ways of global leadership

She didn't want Obama's speech to be misinterpreted overseas as a sign that America was in retreat, that it would bring its troops home and turn inward.

Clinton began by saying that the world's problems required bringing people together "as only America can." Foreign leaders and ordinary people overseas "look to America not just to engage, but to lead," she said. Then she quickly came to the heart of her speech: "Let me say it clearly: The US can, must and will lead in this new century."

This was a "New American Moment," Clinton said, the words capitalized in the transcript of the speech to indicate a special phrase meant to be highlighted. It was "a moment when our global leadership is essential, even if we must often lead in new ways." When she extolled the virtues of diplomacy, she immediately added, "Of course, this administration is also committed to maintaining the greatest military in the history of the world, and, if needed, to vigorously defend ourselves and our friends."

Source: The Obamians, by James Mann, p.249, June 14, 2012

Dems believe in fighting terror with cooperation

We believe in fighting terror and other threats to our security by cooperating with others whenever we can and acting alone only when we are forced to. Republicans believe just the reverse — in acting alone whenever they can, and cooperating only when there is no alternative. So for five and a half years, they have controlled the White House and the Congress, and they have succeeded in concentrating wealth and power, in resisting accountability, in ignoring evidence, and going it alone in the world.

Source: Annual 2006 Take Back America Conference, June 14, 2006

Jeb Bush on International Diplomacy

God grants liberty only to ready to defend it

Last month, we welcomed home almost 2,000 soldiers of the Florida National Guard from the war on terror. Some won't make it home. It has been said, "God grants liberty only to those who love it and are always ready to defend it." Because of the thousands who continue the fight, America will always be free.

We must acknowledge the great debt we owe patriots like [our lost soldiers]. We should honor their service by ensuring that our actions, both in and out of this chamber, are worthy of their sacrifice. We must serve this state as honorably and effectively as they serve this country. I believe we are on the right path.

Source: State of the State speech to the Florida Legislature,
March 2, 2004

NOTE: *"American exceptionalism" means that America has a unique status in the world today. The interest in American exceptionalism counters Obama's rejection of the concept, when Obama said, "Sure, I believe in American exceptionalism in the same way the British believe in British exceptionalism." Republicans generally interpret that as meaning, "No, I don't believe in your version of American exceptionalism at all." Jeb has avoided the phrase "American exceptionalism," and Hillary will certainly avoid it.*

Hillary Clinton on International Alliances

NATO essential for evolving threats of the 21st century

The long war in Afghanistan had taxed NATO's capacities and exposed gaps in its preparedness. Some allies were slashing their defense budgets, leavings others (mostly the Unites States) to pick up the slack. Everyone was suffering from the economic crisis. There were voices on both sides of the Atlantic asking whether NATO was still relevant twenty years after the end of the Cold War.

I thought NATO remained essential for meeting the evolving threats of the 21st century. America can't and shouldn't do everything by ourselves; that's why building partnerships around common interests and goals was so important. NATO was still our most capable partner.

In 2011 we were able to show what a relevant 21st-century NATO looks like as the Alliance took the lead in military intervention to protect civilians in Libya, working in concert for the first time with the Arab League. The US provided unique capabilities but our allies—not us—flew 75% of the sorties. That was a reversal of the distribution of labor a decade before, during NATO's intervention in Kosovo, when the US was responsible for 90% of the bombing.

Source: Hard Choices, by Hillary Clinton, p.213, June 10, 2014

Voted YES on enlarging NATO to include Eastern Europe

H.R. 3167; Gerald B. H. Solomon Freedom Consolidation Act of 2001, To endorse the vision of further enlargement of the NATO Alliance. Vote to pass a bill that would support further expansion of the North Atlantic Treaty Organization, authorize military assistance to several eastern European countries and lift assistance restrictions on Slovakia.

Reference: Bill H.R.3167 ; vote number 116 on May 17, 2002

NOTE: *NATO, the North Atlantic Treaty Organization was, during the Cold War, the main counterbalance to the Soviet Union. Now it includes 28 countries, including some of the former Soviet bloc. At issue in 2015 is which former Soviet allies to include in NATO: the most recent additions were Albania and Croatia in 2009.*

Jeb Bush on International Alliances

Nourish our existing alliances: that means NATO & Israel

Bush outlined a series of principles as necessary for an effective U.S. foreign policy: "The appropriate traditional foreign policy," Bush said, "requires you to nourish the alliances that exist in the world and have kept us safe. That means NATO. That means our relationship with Israel. These alliances have been built by American leadership and we need to nourish them so that they're real rather than just paper tigers."

Bush also blamed Obama for "gutting the military and our intelligence capabilities in a world where these asymmetric threats are real." Bush concluded that "in every one of those 4 or 5 principles of foreign policy I would say that the president's let us down." Bush explained Obama's failures: "you need to lead, and reacting is not leadership."

Source: Theodore Kettle on Newsmax.com, "Obama's Untrustworthiness Led to Rise of ISIS" Oct. 31, 2014

US should shape events and build alliances of free people

My goal today is to explore how America can regain its leadership in the world. And why that leadership is more necessary than ever. American leadership projected consistently and grounded in principle has been a benefit to the world.

I have doubts whether this administration believes American power is such a force. Under this administration, we are inconsistent and indecisive. We have lost the trust & the confidence of our friends. We definitely no longer inspire fear in our enemies.

The great irony of the Obama Presidency is this: Someone who came to office promising greater engagement with the world has left America less influential in the world.

The United States has an undiminished ability to shape events and build alliances of free people. We can project power and enforce peaceful stability in far-off areas of the globe. To do so, I believe we need to root our foreign policy in a set of priorities and principles.

Source: Speech at Chicago Council on Global Affairs, Feb. 18, 2015

Hillary Clinton on Foreign Policy Doctrine

Idealistic realism: embody hybrid rather than categorizing

[In the] running debate between so-called realists and idealists, the former, it is argued, place national security ahead of human rights, while the latter do the opposite. Those are categories that I find overly simplistic. No one should have any illusions about the gravity of the security threats America faces, and as Secretary I had no higher responsibility than to protect our citizens and our country. But at the same time, upholding universal values and human rights is at the core of what it means to be American. If we sacrifice those values or let our policies diverge too far from our ideals, our influence will wane.

There are times when we do have to make difficult compromises. Our challenge is to be clear-eyed about the world as it is while never losing sight of the world as we want it to become. That's why I don't mind that I've been called both an idealist and a realist over the years. I prefer being considered a hybrid, perhaps an idealistic realist. Because I, like our country, embody both tendencies.

Source: Hard Choices, by Hillary Clinton, p.566, June 10, 2014

NOTE: *The "Clinton Doctrine" from the Bill Clinton presidency is usually defined as intervening to prevent genocide or other internationally-agreed upon crimes, and only intervening otherwise when both humanitarian and national interests converged.*

What will the "Hillary Doctrine" be? At this stage, Hillary mostly focuses on distancing herself from some of the "Obama Doctrine" while embracing other parts. Obama is a cautious participant in fighting terrorism and is accused of "leading from behind"; Hillary would take a more active role and a more traditional leadership role. Obama sought to rebuild and strengthen American alliances while recognizing a multipolar world; as Obama's Secretary of State, Hillary was the instrument to accomplish that, and would certainly continue this policy.

We chose the phrase "idealistic realism" as our best guess for the core of the "Hillary Doctrine." Her reference to "human rights" above hints at her long-standing dictum that "women's rights are human rights" (see p. 224), which she first said in reference to China. And her reference to "universal values" harkens back to the 1990s "Clinton Doctrine."

Jeb Bush on Foreign Policy Doctrine

Neo-isolationism and American passivity both have dangers

Jeb Bush attacked the White House's approach to foreign policy in a speech given to the Republican Jewish Coalition. Bush focused on economic policy in his remarks but also impressed the pro-Israel group with his defense of muscular American foreign policy.

"He showed a lot of knowledge about foreign policy that he must have been working hard to acquire," said Ari Fleischer, the former White House Press Secretary and a board member of the RJC, noting Bush discussed diplomatic challenges presented by countries like Ukraine, Russia and Moldova. "He was very rough on the president in terms of his handling of foreign policy, referring to the dangers of 'American passivity.'"

The son and brother of presidents, Bush cautioned the Republican party against "neo-isolationism," a line universally understood as a shot at Rand Paul. Bush also pushed back on Democratic attacks that whenever a Republican calls for a more activist foreign policy that they are "warmongering."

Source: Time Magazine, "American Passivity," March 28, 2014

NOTE: *The "Bush Doctrine" from the George W. Bush presidency is usually defined as taking a hard line against terrorism and defending American interests abroad, and doing both pre-emptively.*

What will the "Jeb Doctrine" be? At this stage, Jeb focuses on differentiating himself. Certainly he recognizes a more multi-polar world (like Hillary) than a bipolar world (like his brother). The excerpt above, which we posit as a first pass of a "Jeb Doctrine," differentiates Jeb from Obama's "passivity" and from Sen. Rand Paul's "neo-isolationism."

Jeb's focus on immigration policy and on free trade perhaps indicates that his focus would be on the Americas, but we cite his comments on China, Israel, and NATO elsewhere in this chapter. Mostly, it's too early to define a "Jeb Doctrine," other than what it is not.

Hillary Clinton on Ebola Policy

Ebola won't stay confined; put resources into Africa

Former Secretary of State Hillary Clinton claimed Ebola is "not going to stay confined" in a speech she gave to the UNLV Foundation in Las Vegas. "Ebola, as we're seeing very painfully, is not going to stay confined unless we put in a lot more resources to try to begin to tailor down the epidemic and contain it and end it the way we have previously by putting in a lot of resources. So, it's not either/or.

"We can't say we're not going to be involved because these things are somebody else's problems because in the world of inter-dependence that we currently live in, a lot of those problems end up eventually on our doorstep," Clinton said.

Source: Ian Schwartz on RealClearPolitics.com, "Not Stay Confined,"
Oct 14, 2014

NOTE: *The largest Ebola outbreak in history began in West Africa in December 2013. The disease was first identified in 1976, but the 2014 outbreak was the first to infect cities rather than rural areas. After one year, about 6,000 people have died from 17,000 cases, mostly in Guinea, Sierra Leone, and Liberia. The infection rate is still increasing in those three countries.*

Unlike most viruses, Ebola is infectious even after its host has died; hence many people get infected while preparing the dead for burial (until special Ebola-safe burial practices took effect). At greatest risk are the doctors and nurses treating the ill, since the virus spreads though contact with bodily fluids, which are commonly exposed during treatment.

President Obama's response has been to send U.S. military personnel to assist with constructing more hospital beds and other needed infrastructure. The medical infrastructure of the affected countries has been severely damaged, with the deaths of many doctors and nurses.

Jeb Bush on Ebola Policy

Handle Ebola crisis like I handled anthrax in Florida

Former Florida Gov. Jeb Bush criticized President Barack Obama's initial handling of the Ebola crisis as "incompetent," saying it gave rise to unneeded fears among the American public about the virus. Bush also said in a wide-ranging discussion at Vanderbilt University that he supports travel restrictions for people who have been to the most severely affected countries in Africa.

Bush said Obama should have been more "clear and concise" about his plans, and lent more credibility to health officials leading the response. "It looked very incompetent to begin with, and that fueled fears that may not be justified," Bush said. "And now you have states that are legitimately acting on their concerns, creating a lot more confusion than is necessary."

Bush contrasted what he characterized as the president's indecisive approach on Ebola to his own actions as governor when anthrax was mailed to a supermarket tabloid in Florida after the 9/11 terrorist attacks in 2001. "We gave people a sense of calm, what the plan was," Bush said. "We talked in plainspoken English. We were totally engaged."

Source: Erik Schelzig on Associated Press, Oct. 28, 2014

NOTE: *President Obama has stated that he will not impose travel restrictions on West Africa, an action which has been demanded by many Americans, except to screen incoming air passengers. Obama states that restricting air travel would hinder the medical response because fewer doctors and nurses could fly into the affected area. Hillary above agrees with that approach, Jeb disagrees.*

Hillary Clinton on China Policy

Focus on BRICs: Brazil, Russia, India, China, & South Africa

Early on, the Obama administration seemed to embrace a new concept: Its diplomacy would emphasize 4 emerging economic powers called the BRICs, or Brazil, Russia, India & China. (Later on, South Africa was sometimes added as a 5th country, conveniently taking up the letter S.) The idea originally came from Wall Street: In 2001, a Goldman-Sachs economist invented the concept of the BRICs to describe the 4 emerging economies that he believed would play an increasingly important role in the world markets. By 2009, the term had become an addition to the jargon of foreign policy, and the Obama team began to talk about the importance of the BRICs in their speeches. In her first major speech as secretary of state, Clinton said that the Obama administration, while reinvigorating its traditional alliances, "will also put special emphasis on encouraging major emerging global powers—China, India, Russia & Brazil, as well as Turkey, Indonesia & South Africa—to be full partners in tackling the global agenda."

Source: The Obamians, by James Mann, p.174, June 14, 2012

Operate from a position of strength, but not confrontation

Q: Should we believe that the U.S. relationship with China under a Hillary Clinton administration would be less one of cooperation and engagement and one more akin to confrontation?

A: No, absolutely not. It would be a position where we would operate from strength with a coherent policy about what our interests were and what we hope to achieve.

Source: Democratic radio debate on NPR, Dec. 4, 2007

Jeb Bush on China Policy

Supports economic cooperation between US and China

Chinese Vice President Xi Jinping met with former Governor of Florida Jeb Bush Tuesday at the Great Hall of the People in Beijing, calling for closer cooperation between China and the United States.

For his part, Bush said that he will continue making contributions to the development of bilateral ties and economic cooperation between the two nations.

Source: Xinhua News (China), "Xi meets Jeb Bush," Jan. 17, 2012

Four visits to Taiwan to increase trade exchange

Vice President Annette Lu asked Florida Governor Jeb Bush, brother of US President George W. Bush, to convey greetings to the US president. Lu, who sat beside the governor at a national banquet given by El Salvador's new President, asked the governor to convey her appreciation to the US leader for his long-term support for Taiwan.

Knowing of Jeb Bush's friendship with Therese Shaheen, the former chairperson of the American Institute in Taiwan, Lu also asked him to convey her greetings to Shaheen. They also talked about increasing trade exchanges between Taiwan and Florida. The governor said that he has visited Taiwan four times, with the last visit in 1991. Lu invited him to visit again, and he said he would consider this. In turn, the governor invited Lu to visit his state.

Source: Xinhua Taipei Times(Taiwan), page 5, June 3, 2004

NOTE: China, the world's largest Communist country, will soon become the world's largest economy (estimated to pass the U.S. in 2024). In 2014, China's economy grew at an annual rate of 7.4%, despite the lingering Great Recession (which only slowed China's growth slightly). U.S. trade with China totaled $562 billion in 2013, but with a $319 billion trade deficit. The U.S. has issues with China on currency manipulation, export dumping, and labor conditions within China. Those trade-related issues will dominate U.S.-China relations in the 2016 campaign and afterwards.

Hillary Clinton on Free Trade

Supported NAFTA in 1998; opposed CAFTA since 2005

Obama released a radio ad saying, "Hillary Clinton championed NAFTA even though it has cost thousands of jobs. It's what's wrong with politics today. Hillary Clinton will say anything to get elected."

The ad's claim that Clinton "championed NAFTA" is misleading. It is true that Clinton once praised NAFTA. As recently as 1998, she praised business leaders for mounting "a very effective business effort in the U.S. on behalf of NAFTA." But her position on trade shifted before her presidential run: In 2005, for example, she voted against the Central America Free Trade Agreement (CAFTA), and she told Time in 2007 that "I believe in the general principles [NAFTA] represented, but what we have learned is that we have to drive a tougher bargain."

Source: FactCheck's AdWatch on radio ads on Free Trade, Jan. 24, 2008

Chief advocate for Trans-Pacific Partnership (TPP)

Clinton has been involved with many of the pacts from her time as first lady, in the Senate and finally, as part of the Obama administration. Clinton saw herself in the middle of NAFTA during her husband's presidency. She supported deals with Oman, Chile and Singapore during her tenure in the Senate. As secretary of State, she was a chief advocate as talks commenced surrounding the Trans-Pacific Partnership (TPP), one of the largest worldwide deals in recent history.

Critics have said that the agreement would ease regulations protecting both laborers and the environment, despite claims from Clinton to the contrary: "Our goal for TPP is to create not just more growth, but better growth. We believe the TPP needs to include strong protections for workers, the environment, intellectual property, and innovation," Clinton said in 2011. "It should also promote the free flow of information technology and the spread of green technology, as well as the coherence of our regulatory system and the efficiency of supply chains."

Source: M. R. Wilson on TheHill.com, "Clinton vs. Warren," Aug. 24, 2014

Jeb Bush on Free Trade

Advocated Miami as HQ for Free Trade Area of the Americas

An international summit this month could move the Western Hemisphere toward becoming a free trade zone. Florida expects to be at the heart of the Free Trade Area of the Americas, the proposed $13 trillion market that would serve 800 million consumers in 34 countries. Local business leaders, backed by Gov. Jeb Bush, want Miami to become home to the FTAA's headquarters and reap the benefits of enhanced trade and commerce. But Florida's sugar and citrus growers fear the trade talks could lead to the elimination of tariffs, opening them up to competition from cheaper produce from Brazil and potentially dooming their industries.

Jeb Bush has aggressively courted support for the headquarters. The governor says his brother's decision on backing a U.S. city for the headquarters—either Atlanta or Miami—"will be based on the merits of the location." The eventual winner must be approved by the 34 nations that comprise the trade group.

Source: 7 News WSVN coverage of FTAA, Nov. 12, 2003

NOTE: *The Trans-Pacific Partnership is a proposed free trade agreement between the U.S. and Australia, Brunei, Canada, Chile, Japan, Malaysia, Mexico, New Zealand, Peru, Singapore, and Vietnam. Negotiations began in 2005; China, Mexico, and South Korea may also join.*

The TPP is potentially the largest free trade agreement in the world, laying the framework for a "free trade area of the Pacific," analogous to the "free trade area of the Americas" (FTAA). Negotiations have been mostly held in secret, a source of some controversy. Other controversial topics include trade barriers and currency manipulation (by the Asian nations) and labor and environmental issues (by China).

The FTAA is an extension of NAFTA to include the entire North American continent; negotiations began in 2001. It was scheduled to take effect by 2005, but has been met by strong anti-corporate protests.

Hillary Clinton on Latin American Policy

Integrate with Latin America but focus on income inequality

[In 2009], economic inequality in Latin America was still among the worst in the world. I argued that a key challenge for Latin America in the years ahead would be to make sure that the benefits of economic growth were broadly shared and that the region's democracies delivered concrete results for their citizens. "Rather than defining economic progress simply by profit margins and GDP, our yardstick must be the quality of human lives," I suggested, so we should be measuring "whether families have enough food on the table, whether young people have access to schooling, whether workers have safe conditions on the job."

A number of Latin American countries, notably Brazil, Mexico, and Chile, had already found success in reducing inequality and lifting people out of poverty. [Some successful policies include] "conditional cash transfer" programs; cooperation on energy and climate change; and on linking different national and regional electrical grids from northern Canada all the way down to the tip of Chile.

Source: Hard Choices, by Hillary Clinton, p.254-55, June 10, 2014

NOTE: *President Hugo Chavez of Venezuela was a nationalist and a Marxist. Because of his connection to Communism, he was considered an enemy of America; but because of Venezuela's oil wealth and drug pipeline, Venezuela was important for American policy. In 2006, President Chavez spoke at the United Nations the day after President George W. Bush had spoken there, and said, "Yesterday, the devil came here. And it smells of sulfur still today. From this rostrum, the president of the United States, the gentleman to whom I refer as the devil, came here, talking as if he owned the world. Truly. As the owner of the world." Chavez died in office in 2013; relations have still not thawed.*

Jeb Bush on Latin American Policy

2010: Ineptitude will bring down Chavez regime in Venezuela

Bush has appeared particularly unwilling to push back against the neoconservatives who supported his brother's administration, at times echoing their complaints about the Obama administration's foreign policy.

Bush mused that "sheer ineptitude and incompetency and corruption will bring down the [Hugo] Chavez regime" in Venezuela, "but we can't sit back passively and let this happen naturally." Instead, Bush advocated offering U.S. support to "elements of Venezuelan society that are fighting back against" the democratically elected Chavez, who eventually died of cancer in early 2013 after being resoundingly reelected.

Source: International Relations Center "RightWeb," April 1, 2014

Two years in Venezuela; majored in Latin American studies

In at least one way, a Jeb-directed foreign policy would be different from that of his brother, if only because Jeb would take personal interest in it. George is not a details guy. Jeb is. George also was open about his lack of interest in countries other than our own.

Jeb, in contrast, not only majored in Latin American studies but actually lived for the better part of two years in Venezuela without the accoutrements of officialdom. Whether this results in a different overall direction or merely a more competent version of the same old story cannot be known.

Overall, though, it is hard to imagine that the basic thrust of American diplomacy would be terribly different. Jeb would have far more knowledge of this hemisphere, but countries in South and Central America need to understand that this is not necessarily a good thing. It's not enough, for example, to be a democratic nation. You must also then vote for pro-capitalist leaders.

Source: America's Next Bush, by S.V. Dáte, p. 344, Feb. 15, 2007

Hillary Clinton on Mexico Policy

More border patrolling
on both Mexican *AND* Canadian borders

Q: None of the 9/11 terrorists entered the US through the Mexican border. Why build a wall there in the name of national security? You voted in favor of the border wall. Why on the Mexican border and not on the Canadian border?

A: I do favor much more border patrolling and much more technology on both of our borders, and in certain areas, even a physical barrier, because I think we've got to secure our borders. That has to be part of comprehensive immigration reform. I have championed comprehensive immigration reform, and it includes starting with securing our borders in order to give people the support they need to come over and support us when it comes to having a pathway to legalization. We all know that this has become a contentious political issue. We want to work in a bipartisan way to have comprehensive reform—employer verification, more help for local communities so that they can pay for schooling and hospital and other expenses that they have to bear because of the immigration crisis.

Source: Democratic primary debate on Univision in Spanish, Sept. 9, 2007

Voted YES on building a fence along the Mexican border

Within 18 months, achieves operational control over U.S. land and maritime borders, including:

1. systematic border surveillance through more effective use of personnel and technology; and
2. physical infrastructure enhancements to prevent unlawful border entry

Defines "operational control" as the prevention of all unlawful U.S. entries, including entries by terrorists, other unlawful aliens, narcotics, and other contraband.

Source: Secure Fence Act; Bill H.R.6061 ; vote #262 on Sept. 29, 2006

Jeb Bush on Mexico Policy

Deploy military on both sides of the US-Mexican border

Fighting the drug cartels at the border may present a threat of potentially epic proportions, calling for a strong response. The cartels are paramilitary organizations with dangerous and sophisticated weaponry. Our Border Patrol officers are neither trained nor equipped to blunt the cartels' firepower if it comes to that. As a result, the president should be authorized to deploy military or National Guard forces if necessary to counter the cartels' threat and secure the US border.

Preferable to US military deployment would be efforts to increase the effectiveness of Mexican authorities in dealing with the cartels on their side of the border. US officials have worked closely with their Mexican counterparts, including the deployment of unmanned aerial surveillance vehicles and the opening of a compound to gather intelligence in northern Mexico.

Source: Immigration Wars, by Jeb Bush, p. 53, March 5, 2013

Married high school sweetheart, exchange student from Mexico

Jeb met Columba Garnica in Mexico in 1971, when he was an exchange student from Andover. He never dated anyone else, and he married her in 1974. He introduced Columba to his parents for the first time the day of the wedding.

"I'm not going to lie to you and say we were thrilled," Barbara told one writer. In fact, Barbara was so worried about her son's marriage to a Mexican that she sought advice from her friend the society columnist Ymelda (nee Chavez) Dixon: "I told Barbara, 'As long as the girl hangs a sign around her neck that says "Bush," she'll be fine.'"

Jeb, who spoke with his wife in fluent Spanish, was spared her further social discomfort in Houston when the Texas Commerce Bank transferred him to Venezuela in 1977 for two years to handle international loans.

Source: The Family, by Kitty Kelley, p.354-355, Sept. 14, 2004

Hillary Clinton on Path to Citizenship

Introduce a path to earn citizenship in the first 100 days

I, as president, would work with our neighbors to the south, to help them create more jobs for their own people. We need to bring the immigrants out of the shadows, give them the conditions that we expect them to meet, paying a fine for coming here illegally, trying to pay back taxes, over time, and learning English. If they had committed a crime, then they should be deported. But for everyone else, there must be a path to legalization. I would introduce that in the first 100 days of my presidency.

Source: Democratic debate at University of Texas in Austin, Feb. 21, 2008

Guest workers only for farms, to address labor shortage

Q: You oppose guest worker program saying that it exploits workers, but you would carve out a special program for agricultural workers. Why single out agriculture and not other industries, like the hotel & hospitality industry here?

A: For one, there is a shortage of farm workers. This is a sector of the economy that over decades has been demonstrated to be very difficult to attract legal workers. That is not true yet in the hotel industry and the hospitality industry. So I would like to solve what is clearly a shortage-of-labor problem in the agricultural sector. I'd like to see it be a part of comprehensive immigration reform. In the absence of that, what's happening is that farmers in California are starting to move their production facilities to Mexico and Latin American. It's going to be a lose-lose for us if we don't get that agricultural problem fixed.

Source: Politico pre-Potomac Primary interview, Feb. 11, 2008

NOTE: *Anti-immigration advocates often seek Official English status (the US has no official language), which would enforce assimilation of non-English speaking immigrants. Clinton would require immigrants to learn English, but not establish English as the official language.*

Jeb Bush on Path to Citizenship

There is no realistic pathway to citizenship for most people

Of the many serious and legitimate criticisms that can be leveled against our current immigration system, two in particular stand out in terms of hugely detrimental impact:

- We are not bringing in highly skilled immigrants in sufficient numbers to meet our needs and to maximize future American prosperity.

- There is no realistic pathway for most people who simply wish to become American citizens.

There is a single major explanation for both problems: our immigration policy is driven by an overriding preference for family reunification, which in turn is very broadly defined.

Source: Immigration Wars, by Jeb Bush, p. 17-19, March 5, 2013

Path to legal resident status: pay fines & no criminals

It is in no one's interest for illegal immigrants and their families to live in the shadows. We need everyone to participate in the mainstream economy, to pay taxes, to participate openly in their communities, to be willing to report crimes—that is to say, to be accountable, responsible members of society. That cannot occur when people fear they will be arrested if their immigration status is known.

We propose a path to permanent legal resident status for those who entered our country illegally as adults and who have committed no additional crimes of significance. The first step in obtaining that status would be to plead guilty to having committed the crime of illegal entry, and to receive an appropriate punishment consisting of fines and/or community service. Anyone who does not come forward under this process will be subject to automatic deportation, unless they choose to return voluntarily to their native countries.

Source: Immigration Wars, by Jeb Bush, p. 42-43, March 5, 2013

Hillary Clinton on Sources of Immigration

Immigrants keep America young and dynamic

In 2009, more than 55 million Americans were immigrants or the children of immigrants. These first- or second-generation Americans were valuable links back tot heir home countries and also significant contributors to our own country's economic, cultural, and political life. Immigration helped keep the US population young and dynamic at a time when many of our partners and competitors were aging. Russia, in particular, faced what President Putin himself has called a "demographic crisis." Even China, because of its "One Child Policy," was headed toward a demographic cliff. I only wish that the bipartisan bill passed the Senate in 2013 reforming our immigration laws could pass the House.

Source: Hard Choices, by Hillary Clinton, p.550, June 10, 2014

NOTE: *Talking about immigrants means talking about Latinos: half of all immigrants today are from Latin America. And talking about immigrants means talking about the Latino vote: 70% of Latino voters supported Obama in the last election. The most important demographic is that Latinos make up 17% of the voting population now, but that will rise to 29% by 2050.*

Latinos support immigration reform (and in particular, amnesty) with the same lopsided support with which they support Democrats: over 70% favor amnesty. The Latino vote will become increasingly determinative of future election results, which is why Republicans are so actively recruiting Latino candidates (for example, Sen. Ted Cruz, R-TX, and Sen. Marco Rubio, R-FL), to try to switch the current party loyalty.

We focus heavily in this chapter on immigration issues for two reasons: (1) because these issues will likely be a decisive issue in 2016; and (2) because Jeb has stated his views extensively on these issues (while on other issues his record is more sparse).

Jeb Bush on Sources of Immigration

Immigration is 'not a felony' but 'an act of love'

Jeb Bush said the debate over immigration reform needs to move past derisive rhetoric describing illegal immigrants. The former Florida governor said that people who come to the US illegally are often looking for opportunities to provide for their families that are not available in their home countries.

"Yes, they broke the law, but it's not a felony. It's an act of love, it's an act of commitment to your family," Bush said. "I honestly think that is a different kind of crime, that there should be a price paid, but it shouldn't rile people up that people are actually coming to this country to provide for their families," he said.

"I think we need to kind of get beyond the harsh political rhetoric to a better place." Bush acknowledged that his comments would be recorded. "So be it," he said before discussing immigration reform, an area where he splits from many in the Republican Party in lobbying for a comprehensive overhaul.

Source: Dana Davidsen on CNN Politicker, "Act of love," April 7, 2014

Immigrants are committed to family, even if illegally here

"Immigrants create far more businesses than native-born Americans, over the last 20 years," Jeb said at the Faith and Freedom Coalition Conference in June 2013. "Immigrants are more fertile, and they love families, and they have more intact families, and they bring a younger population. Immigrants create an engine of economic prosperity."

Source: Ben Smith on BuzzFeed.com, "Terrible Candidate," April 7, 2014

Hillary Clinton on Comprehensive Immigration Reform

Focus on comprehensive reform, not driver's licenses

[At the Drexel U. debate on Oct. 30, 2007, Hillary was asked if] she supported the idea of giving driver's licenses to illegal immigrants, as NY's Gov. Eliot Spitzer had proposed.

Clinton said she sympathized with Spitzer, then pivoted to stress the need for comprehensive immigration reform. But when Dodd declared his opposition to the plan, Clinton jumped back in: "I did not say that it should be done, but I certainly recognize why Gov. Spitzer is trying to do it."

"Wait a minute!" interjected Dodd. "You said yes, you thought it made sense to do it." The moderator asked Clinton to clarify her position: Did she support Spitzer's plan or not?

Clinton said, "What is the governor supposed to do? He is dealing with a serious problem. We have failed and George Bush has failed. Do I think this is the right thing for any governor to do? No. But do I understand the sense of real desperation, trying to get a handle on this? He's making an honest effort to do it."

Source: Game Change, by Heilemann & Halpern, p.147-148, Jan. 11, 2010

NOTE: *"Comprehensive reform" is a politicized buzzword that means "provide amnesty and citizenship benefits for illegal immigrants already here, while securing the border and prosecuting illegal employers against new illegal immigration." Opponents of comprehensive reform would prefer a piecemeal approach: their buzzword is "secure the border first," before dealing with any benefits or any other issues.*

President Obama in late 2014 issued an Executive Order deferring deportation of five million illegal immigrants who came to America as minors (known as DREAMers, for the DREAM Act). Opponents claim Obama unconstitutionally bypassed Congress. Supporters claim that Congress failed to pass comprehensive reforms for years, so Obama had to act unilaterally.

Jeb Bush on Comprehensive Immigration Reform

6-part proposal for comprehensive immigration reform

1. *Fundamental Reform:* Comprehensive interrelated approach because system is broken, and to achieve bipartisan consensus.

2. *A Demand-Driven Immigration System:* Replace overriding preference for family reunification with work-based immigration.

3. *An Increased Role for the States:* Share federal authority over immigration policy [such as] social services and providing benefits.

4. *Dealing With Current Illegal Immigrants:* We propose a path to permanent legal resident status for those who plead guilty to having entered our country illegally as adults and who have committed no additional crimes of significance.

5. *Border Security:* Broader immigration reform is an essential component of border security; we can't do one without the other.

6. *Toward a More Vibrant Future:* Getting immigration policy right will allow us to reclaim the prosperity that in recent years has eluded our grasp.

Source: Immigration Wars, by Jeb Bush, p. 12-62, March 5, 2013

Reform must make it easier to come legally than illegally

Q: For years you supported a path to citizenship for illegal immigrants. Now, according to your book, you no longer support that, but support a path to legal residency. Why have you changed?

BUSH: I haven't changed. The book was written to try to create a blueprint for conservatives that were reluctant to embrace comprehensive reform, to give them, perhaps, a set of views that they could embrace. I support a path to legalization or citizenship so long as the path for people that have been waiting patiently is easier and costs less, the legal entrance to our country, than illegal entrance. The worst thing that we could do is to pass a set of laws and have the exact same problem we had in the late 1980s, where there was not the enforcement and it was easier to come legally than illegally.

Source: CBS Face the Nation interview, March 10, 2013

Book Reviews

OnTheIssues excerpts political books and debates as the primary source of the materials in this book. Following are several book reviews, plus links online to additional books and debates cited in this book. These book reviews (and the books themselves) tell a lot about the priorities of the candidates (for memoirs) and about the image of the candidates (both positive and negative, for biographies written by others).

Book reviews:

Additional book / debate excerpts online:

- *The Party's Over*, by Gov. Charlie Crist, (2014)
  www.ontheissues.org/Party_Over.htm

- Speeches to Conservative Political Action Conference (2013)
  www.ontheissues.org/2013_CPAC.htm

- *The Rise of Marco Rubio,* by Manuel Rogi-Franzia, (2012)
  www.ontheissues.org/Rise_of_Rubio.htm

- Republican National Convention speeches (2012)
  www.ontheissues.org/2012_RNC.htm

- *Game Change*, by Heilemann and Halperin (2010)
  www.OnTheIssues.org/Game_Change.htm

- *The Battle for America*, by Balz & Johnson, (2009)
  www.ontheissues.org/Battle_2008.htm

- *Free Ride: John McCain and the Media,*
  by David Brock and Paul Waldman (2008);
  www.ontheissues.org/Free_Ride.htm

- *Her Way*, by Jeff Gerth & Don Van Natta Jr. (2007)
  www.ontheissues.org/Her_Way.htm

- *Giving*, by Bill Clinton, (2007)
  www.ontheissues.org/Giving.htm

- *The Contenders*, by Laura Flanders, (2007)
  www.ontheissues.org/Contenders_2008.htm

- *Vast Right-Wing Conspiracy*, by Amanda Carpenter (2006)
  www.ontheissues.org/vrwc.htm

- *Madame Hillary*, by R. Emmett Tyrell (2004)
  www.ontheissues.org/Madame_Hillary.htm

- Florida State of the State speech (2004)
  www.ontheissues.org/2004_State.htm

- *The Inside Story*, by Judith Warner (1993)
  www.ontheissues.org/Inside_Story.htm

Book Review: Hard Choices,
by Hillary Clinton (June 2014)

Hillary's book came out in June 2014, just in time for a book tour to get completed before the country became embroiled in the 2014 election. The key question most pundits addressed was whether the book indicates that Hillary will announce for president either after her book tour, or after the 2014 elections, or sometime in 2015. Hillary didn't say one word in the book about running for president, but the pundits spent a lot of energy reading between the lines, especially the closing line of the book: "The time for another hard choice will come soon enough" (p. 596), meaning her decision to run for president is an upcoming "hard choice".

The pundits all enjoy reading between the lines, but we at OnTheIssues prefer to "read between the pictures" and "read outside the lines" as well: all three methods concur that, yes, Hillary will soon announce for president, probably in early 2015. The read-outside-the-lines part goes like this: If you were helping to plan Hillary's announcement for 2015, beginning with Obama's re-election in 2012, what would you do to prepare? Here is a checklist:

- Retire as Secretary of State in early 2013 so there's time to physically recuperate *(check, done, Feb. 2013).*

- Sign up to write a book about her experiences as Secretary of State, getting a big enough advance to pay off all past presidential campaign debts *(check, done, April 2013, the advance rumored to be $14 million).*

- Spend enough time working at the Clinton Foundation to look like more than a figurehead (check, done, beginning in May 2013).

- Get onto the speechmaker circuit, to build up a war-chest for 2016 and not have money worries like in 2008 *(check, done, beginning in July 2013, with a fee of $200,000 per speech).*

- Announce the upcoming birth of her first grandchild, to remind us of her humanity and avoid charges of being an over-obsessed policy wonk *(check, done, April 2014, baby born Sept. 2014).*

- Release her book and go on a book tour across America and Europe *(check, done, June 2014 through July 2014).*

- Spend the 2014 campaign season endorsing gubernatorial and congressional candidates, to gather chits for 2016 *(check, ongoing, since Sept. 2014).*

- Announce campaign for president *(The only unchecked item left on the list).*

The content of the book hardly matters to that two-year timeline, but of course the book focuses almost entirely on foreign affairs (to contrast her earlier memoir's focus: *Living History* focused on Hillary's personal background and her domestic policies). The book provides Hillary an opportunity to get the Benghazi issue out of the way (chapter 17, pp. 382-415), although her detractors will still try to use that as the main ammunition against her. The book also provides details of how her policy stances differ from Obama's — basically, Hillary is more of a hawk than Obama, and more for international engagement than Obama. But mostly the book establishes that Hillary is entirely ready to become the most powerful leader in the world — which might not be an explicit attack by her opponents, but she will still be the first woman nominated by a major party for president.

We will close by applying the pundit game of read-between-the-lines to read-between-the-pictures: the photo selections in this book, we think, shout that the book is "campaign prep." There are 101 photos in the book, arranged in roughly chronological order, from photo #1 of Hillary's campaign concession speech on June 7, 2008, to photo #101 of Hillary's farewell speech as Secretary of State on Feb. 1, 2013. There is one glaring outlier in that chronological list: photo #40 is a picture of Hillary at Ground Zero in New York City, taken on Sept. 12, 2001. Why is that photo there, between photos of Hillary with Afghanistan's President Karzai in May 2010, and a Pakistani protest of Hillary's visit in Oct. 2009? We read-between-the-lines as some campaign advisor looked over the 100 photos to be published, and asserted, "Hillary, you have to include a 101st photo of yourself on 9/11, so that voters are reminded that the World Trade Center was your constituency." And so she did, sticking in a photo entirely out of place — unless one reads the photo as evidence of a campaign-in-the-making.

Book review written Oct. 2014;
full excerpts available online at:
www.ontheissues.org/Hard_Choices.htm

Book Review: Immigration Wars:
Forging an American Solution
by Jeb Bush and Clint Bolick (March 5, 2013)

Immigration Wars is Jeb Bush's opening salvo in the battle for the 2016 presidential nomination. It addresses what Jeb sees as a key issue for the 2016 race, and a key issue for the Republican Party. If the Republicans get immigration right, they stand to gain a substantial electoral benefit; this book attempts to position Jeb to be the primary beneficiary of that electoral benefit.

"Getting immigration right" means accomplishing the following (all of which Jeb addresses):

- Addressing the 12 million illegal immigrants presently in the US so that the number gets reduced over time;

- Addressing the needs of businesses for cheap labor, which is the driving force for illegal immigration;

- Addressing those issues in a manner which is affordable under the current tight budget; and

- Doing all of the above in a manner that Hispanics consider fair and acceptable.

That last one is where the electoral benefit comes from. The illegal immigration issue, although it affects immigrants from all countries, is most important to the Hispanic community. That community compromises 16.7% of the current US population, and in 2012 voted 71% for Obama for president.

The electoral benefit comes from shifting enough of those Hispanic votes to win states which would otherwise vote for the Democratic nominee in 2016. The five states most likely to swing on the immigration issue are NM, AZ, NV, FL, and CO. Mitt Romney won only Arizona out of those five swing states in 2012. Romney winning those other four swing states in 2012, totaling 49 electoral votes, would have closed the electoral gap substantially (Romney would have won the presidency with a shift of 64 electoral votes). For the GOP nominee to win those four swing states in 2016...:

State	Electoral Votes	Percent Hispanic Population	2012 votes for Obama	2012 votes for Romney	Hispanics needed for 2016
New Mexico	5	46.3%	415,000 (53%)	336,000 (43%)	79,000 (61%)
Nevada	6	26.5%	531,000 (52%)	464,000 (46%)	68,000 (65%)
Florida	29	22.5%	4,238,000 (50%)	4,163,000 (49%)	74,300 (35%)
Colorado	9	20.7%	1,323,000 (52%)	1,185,000 (46%)	138,000 (66%)

To win those states requires that the 2016 nominee get 35% to 65% of the Hispanic vote instead of the 19% that Romney got. Those figures indicate why this issue is critical to the 2016 presidential election, and why Jeb has written this book.

Jeb Bush is uniquely well-positioned to benefit from a voting shift to Republican line in 2016. He is married to a Mexican woman, Columba, and their three children are who George Bush Sr. referred to as "the little brown ones." Jeb is fluent at Spanish and spent several years teaching English in Mexico (where he met his wife). The only other serious presidential contender positioned to benefit as much is Senator Marco Rubio—who has also proposed major immigration reform—this book is, in effect, Jeb's answer to Rubio's proposal.

That begs the question, "Wouldn't the Republican Party be wise to nominate Marco Rubio instead of Jeb Bush?" Well, maybe so on the immigration issue, but there are other issues as well. Let's summarize those issues into acceptability to the major factions of the Republican Party, and score some of the possible major candidates according to each faction. We'll score the recent GOP nominees for comparison, too:

	Mainstream GOP	Tea Party	Christian Right	Neocons	Libertarians
Jeb Bush	A+	B-	B	A-	B-
Marco Rubio	B	A	B	C	B-
Chris Christie	A-	B-	C	C	B-
Nikki Haley	B	A+	A	B	B-
Rand Paul	C-	A	C	D	A+
Mitt Romney	A	C	C	B-	C
Paul Ryan	B	A	B	B	C
John McCain	A	C	C	A	C
Sarah Palin	C	A	A+	A	C
G.W. Bush	A	B	A	A+	D

Jeb is acceptable to all factions of the Republican Party; no other major 2016 candidate is. Rubio is unacceptable to the neoconservatives (the faction led by Dick Cheney and Karl Rove, who mostly like Jeb because he is George's brother; Jeb's actual foreign policy stances are largely unknown). Some pundits predict that the neocons will become irrelevant by 2016, but it is more likely that they will be a major source of fundraising, as they have been in past elections, and that Jeb will win the "money primary" accordingly. Unlike the other 2016 contenders, Jeb can unite the Republican Party; all of the others will force the GOP to choose one faction over another. Gov. Nikki Haley (R, SC) also is acceptable to all factions, and we include her for that reason; but she has not yet achieved national name recognition like the others in the list.

Reaction to this book was mixed, at least from the perspective of the pundits. Many pundits pointed out that Jeb formerly stated that a pathway to citizenship was important; in this book he says it would encourage more illegal immigration, and prefers a pathway to legal residency status instead. In his book tour following this book's publication, Jeb stated that a pathway to citizenship should be available but with conditions; and that the book outlines a proposal without citizenship as a model for conservative legislation. The pundits called that sequence a double flip-flop.

But voters don't think like pundits—all they care about is that Jeb has a clear position. In particular, Hispanic voters care that the candidate advocates for a pathway to legalization, even with conditions, and even if full citizenship is disallowed—which is what Jeb has outlined. What the pundits call "flip-flopping," the voting public will likely view as "a full understanding of a complex issue."

To summarize what Jeb proposes in this book (which he does in chapter 1, entitled "A Proposal for Immigration Reform," and then details the policy and politics of that proposal for the rest of the book):

1. *Fundamental Reform*: Comprehensive interrelated approach because system as a whole is broken, and to achieve bipartisan consensus.

2. *A Demand-Driven Immigration System*: Replace overriding preference for family reunification with work-based immigration.

3. *An Increased Role for the States*: Share federal authority over immigration policy [such as] social services and providing benefits.

4. *Dealing With Current Illegal Immigrants*: We propose a path to permanent legal resident status for those who plead guilty to having entered our country illegally as adults and who have committed no additional crimes of significance.

5. *Border Security*: Broader immigration reform is an essential component of border security; we can't do one without the other.

6. *Toward a More Vibrant Future*: Getting immigration policy right will allow us to reclaim the prosperity that in recent years has eluded our grasp.

In summary, this book is an important early contribution to the 2016 race, and declares, loud and clear, that Jeb is preparing to run.

Book review written March 2013; full excerpts available online at: www.ontheissues.org/Immigration_Wars.htm

Book Review: The Obamians:
The Struggle Inside the White House to Redefine American Power by James Mann (June 14, 2012)

This book is a review of Obama's first term, published in June 2012 in time for the presidential election. The author, James Mann, previously published *Rise of the Vulcans*, the equivalent book at the equivalent time for President Bush's re-election. The problem with those types of books is their short shelf-life: What remains relevant after the election? We answer by focusing on Hillary Clinton and Joe Biden, two contenders for the 2016 presidential election who are featured here.

This book does provide some insight into major events of Obama's first term—and some insights into how Biden and Clinton participated in those major events too. But there's way too much focus on the 2008 election—it often feels like a rehash of the Democratic primary (which featured Obama, Biden, and Clinton). There were plenty of books about the 2008 Democratic primary—for example, *Game Change* and *The Battle for America 2008*—published well before 2012—why re-analyze several year old history just in time for the re-election campaign?

The key question for readers to ask of any retrospective political analysis is: "What is the author's bias?" Well, the *Rise of the Vulcans* book struck a reasonable political balance in analyzing the underpinnings of Bush's war policy. That implies that Mann is not too anti-Bush nor pro-Bush; and this book is not too anti-Obama nor pro-Obama. Like Mann's earlier book, this one focuses on war policy too. In that subject area, Mann's analysis is strong and unbiased. However, Mann hits some sour notes of bias in his political analysis, for example on p. 98, where Mann bashes McCain's choice of Sarah Palin as V.P:

> *McCain's decision to appoint Sarah Palin as his vice presidential nominee and her own utterances on foreign policy ("I can see Russia from my house") made it all but impossible to claim that he was the cautious, conservative candidate.*

That's the whole context—Mann seems to be quoting Palin verbatim, as an indicator of her inexpertise. But every journalist knows that Sarah Palin never actually said that phrase—it was uttered by the actress Tina Fey as a spoof of Sarah Palin on the TV show "Saturday Night Live." Here is what Palin actually said:

> *They're our next-door neighbors, and you can actually see Russia from land here in Alaska, from an island in Alaska.*

Palin was pointing out that Alaska borders Russia, and she was correct. It would be fair for Mann to mock Palin for ignorance of foreign policy based on misstatements she actually said—but it is unfair to use that phrase to mock Palin, since Palin never said it. And Mann knew that. And therefore Mann expresses anti-Republican bias. And that bias casts suspicion on his otherwise solid analysis.

Book review written Dec. 2012; full excerpts available online at:
www.ontheissues.org/The_Obamians.htm

Book Review: Jeb Bush:
Aggressive Conservatism in Florida
by Robert E. Crew, Jr. (Dec. 11, 2009)

This book is an academic analysis of Jeb Bush's political philosophy and policy actions during his two gubernatorial terms. The emphasis is on "academic": the author is a professor of political science at Florida State University. Hence this book does not read like a typical political book at all—it reads like a classroom study, with well-documented references and extensive footnotes.

Like any academic treatise, the professor injects lots of history and political theory:

- The history of Florida politics (converting from Democrat to Republican as part of the GOP "Southern Strategy" since the 1960s, pp. xiii-xvii);

- The history of the Florida legislature (8-year term limits passed in 1992, and hence took full effect in 2000, one year after during Jeb's first inauguration in 1999; that greatly empowered the Executive branch relative to the Legislative branch, pp. 64-65).

- A theory of privatization as a core principle of government (pp. 116-7 as a philosophy; p. 30 as a policy goal of reducing state worker headcounts).

- The theory of "aggressive conservatism," as indicated in the book's subtitle, permeates the book, even though Jeb himself never uttered the phrase (it presumably counters George W. Bush's phrase "compassionate conservatism"). An example of the heavily academic verbiage on this topic: "The theory of conservatism adopted by Jeb Bush was relentlessly consistent and carried with it an almost canonical list of specific agenda items to be checked off, many of which were viewed as moral absolutes rather than options open to debate and alteration." (p. 24)

The massive overuse of the passive voice, so common in academia, often leaves the reader struggling to figure out who exactly is doing what. That sentence from p. 24 could be translated as, "Bush did all the usual things that conservatives do, and did them because he thought they were the right thing to do, and wouldn't take 'no' for an answer." Massive parsing is required, when the passive voice is so massively overused. Here's the worst example (which we promise to parse and illustrate, so don't panic like we did):

> A variety of empirical measures permit an objective assessment of the political legacy left by a governor. These include the extent to which a political figure affects partisan attachments among citizens, and the degree to which he or she improves the electoral fortunes of his or her party.... An examination of these measures in Florida reinforces the view that Governor Bush left a modest political legacy in the state.

We *THINK* that means, "Political scientists measure governors by how well their party does, and by how well others of their party do, too; Bush didn't do so well by either measurement." In other words, fewer Floridians registered as Republicans after Jeb than did before Jeb, and the Republican Party of Florida's elective position got weaker as well. But the author substantiates that Jeb did accomplish his philosophical goals, using a massively academic chart:

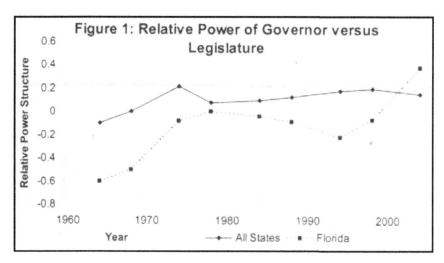

Figure 1: Relative Power of Governor versus Legislature

That chart (p. 68) indicates that when Jeb took office in 1999, the Florida governorship became a stronger office than the national average, whereas before Jeb the Florida legislature was the stronger branch. But if one reads the several paragraphs accompanying the chart, the author clarifies that the chart summarizes a multi-year survey of Florida executive branch officials. In other words, this chart indicates what state workers THINK about legislative power in Florida compared to other states—not anything that Jeb actually did, measured in some objective manner, or even anything that Jeb said. Reading the rest of the book, astute readers might note that the big swing in power came about because of the implementation of legislative term limits, which was passed in 1992 (the turning point of the chart) and threw out many long-time legislators in 2000 (pp. 64-65). The author doesn't make that connection—leaving it to the astuteness of the reader, or more likely leaving the reader to incorrectly assume that Jeb CAUSED the change.

I guess that's what "political science" means: making charts that readers must really study to understand. For most readers, that's way too academic—it'd be better to explain the political implications directly, rather than leaving so much to inference. We don't think the author is biased against Jeb—just too biased towards academia. But the author assuredly does not LIKE Jeb Bush: referring to Jeb's nickname as "King Jeb," the author cites a Republican legislator saying, "In his heart of hearts, the governor prefers dictatorship to Democracy" (p. 171). It's fine to have an anti-Jeb bias—we conclude that this book is a reasonably unbiased analysis of Jeb's governorship. But the reader should be prepared for an adventure in academia!

Book review written Dec. 2012; full excerpts available online at: www.ontheissues.org/Aggressive_Conservatism.htm

Book Review: God and Hillary Clinton:
A Spiritual Life
by Paul Kengor (Sept. 18, 2007)

OnTheIssues.org has reviewed several pro-Hillary books and several anti-Hillary books, but this book is in a category of its own. The author focuses exclusively on exploring Hillary's faith and how it affects her issue stances. One might not think that faith plays a large role—i.e., Hillary's detractors might want to reframe this book's theme as WHETHER faith affects her issue stances—but the author makes an honest appraisal and concludes that Hillary's faith is sincere, and sincerely affects many of her beliefs.

The author, Paul Kengor, has published two related books (among other publications): *God and Ronald Reagan*, and *God and George W. Bush*. There is no book entitled *God and Bill Clinton*, which leads us to believe that Mr. Kengor favors Republicans and is part of the religious right. While this book does not explicitly discuss the author's politics, there is little either to disavow that assumption. Despite the anti-Hillary stance inherent in that political philosophy, this book is balanced and thoroughly researched.

Important conclusions that Mr. Kengor draws include:

- Hillary is a devout Methodist who applies Methodist values to her daily life as well as to larger issues;

- Hillary is a member of the "religious left," which was a relevant force in the 1960s and may soon undergo a resurgence;

- Hillary sought pastoral guidance on several important issues, from capital punishment to dealing with Bill's infidelity, and would presumably do so as President.

Bill Clinton does make a substantial appearance in this book. While Mr. Kengor unambiguously concludes that Hillary is sincerely religious, Kengor is considerably more cynical about Bill's sincerity and beliefs. Kengor concludes, however, via the same methodology as with Hillary, that Bill applies the Biblical definition of social justice to his policy stances on poverty and welfare. We include several excerpts about Bill's stances, but the book focuses on Hillary.

We do omit several whole sections of the book from our excerpts. For example, Kengor explores in great detail Hillary's meetings with Mother Theresa and the Pope. Since no policy-based conclusions are drawn from these meetings, and no conclusions about Hillary's personal philosophy either, they are not relevant for our website. Those interested in a deeper religion-based analysis of Hillary's character should read the original book for further details. For all voters for whom religion is important or even moderately relevant, this book is a fascinating character study.

Book review written Oct. 2007; full excerpts available online at:
www.ontheissues.org/God_and_Hillary.htm

Book Review: Jeb: America's Next Bush:
His Florida Years and
What They Mean For the Nation,
by S.V. Dáte (February 15, 2007)

The author of "America's Next Bush," Shirish V. Dáte, is a Tallahassee journalist who covers Florida state government for the Associated Press and the Palm Beach Post. He does not like Jeb Bush, and he opens his preface with the warning, "Jeb Bush is going to hate this book." Hence this book is a critic's perspective on Bush's governorship, and of Bush's world view in general. Dáte does his share of bashing George W. Bush and George Bush Sr., too, (he claims the Bush family is "bent on global domination," p. xvi), in the context of analyzing why Jeb was "Born To Rule" as the "King Of Florida" (those are two chapter titles!).

However, Dáte is careful to balance his critiques with credit where credit is due. He praises Jeb (and points out the rest of Florida's praise) for Jeb's handling of disastrous hurricanes in 2005 (pp. 21-22 and again about Hurricane Katrina on pp. 168-169). He credits Jeb with registering 88,000 Hispanic voters in the 1980s, as part of his father's presidential campaign (Hispanics vote overwhelmingly Democratic, except in Florida, where Cubans overwhelmingly vote Republican). And he acknowledges that Jeb's use of $310 million in budget stimulus funds in 2003 were used well (for a biotech center) even though Dáte and others disagreed at the time. Dáte's balance, by praising some items and criticizing others, does make his criticisms seem more valid.

And Dáte's criticisms are very critical indeed. He feels that Jeb considers himself "Prince Jeb," (the title of Chapter 1) entitled to rule without dissent from the legislature or the judicial branch (and without much dissent possible from the public, since Jeb opposed the "Sunshine Laws," p. 41-42). Worse, Dáte accuses Jeb of receiving a large fortune from the 1980s Savings & Loan bailout (the same one which banned his brother Neil Bush from politics)—that Jeb benefited to the tune of $4 million from an S&L bailout, despite Jeb's protests of no wrongdoing. And Dáte gleefully details every time Jeb apologized over the years, such as when he overdid his criticism of his opponent for weakness on the death penalty in a TV ad (pp. 112-113).

The problem with Dáte's criticism is when he offers his own opinions, which is ok, but in criticizing those who oppose his own opinion, he isn't clear when the opponent is Jeb and when it is not. For example, Dáte describes his own stance against Jeb's proposed healthcare privatization (pp. 163-164) by defending whether Medicare and Medicaid are socialistic—but Jeb never described Medicare and Medicaid as "socialistic." Similarly, Dáte criticizes those who fly the Confederate flag, on grounds of "Southern heritage," as racist—for a page and a half (pp. 193-194)—before letting the reader know that Jeb *took down* the Confederate flag from the Florida Capitol (p. 195)—and did it quietly, to avoid a hullabaloo over "Southern heritage."

Overall, Dáte is reasonably journalistic in his criticism (usually), i.e. readers can read this book as valid criticism, not as simple Bush-bashing. But the reader needs to read carefully to avoid mixing up Dáte's opinions with those of Jeb or Jeb's opponents. Especially as one approaches the end of the book, where later chapters are less reporting and more speculation (about a possible presidential run). If Jeb runs for president in 2016, this will be an important book for his opponents to read, as background for how Jeb operated in Florida and as a prediction for how he will behave as a presidential candidate and as president. But before 2016, we hope there will be better books about Jeb that don't require the reader to be quite as cautious.

Book review written Dec. 2012; full excerpts available online at:
www.ontheissues.org/Next_Bush.htm

Book Review: For Love of Politics:

Bill and Hillary Clinton: The White House Years, by Sally Bedell (October 23, 2007)

Sally Bedell Smith's book, published in 2007, is a year-by-year account of how effectively Bill and Hillary work together to win elections, achieve political and policy goals, and contain scandal. In the author's own words, the book explores "how two intelligent, ambitious, and complex people confronted the challenges they faced in the White House, how they worked together and separately, and how the push and pull of their marriage affected the presidency."

The main point of the book is the idea of "two for one," almost a co-presidency, and less overtly, both Bill's and Hillary's use of the word "we" when describing policy positions and achievements. As illustration, the different styles, personalities, and approaches of Bill and Hillary are explored. Bill is depicted as a people-pleaser who avoided direct confrontation, and Hillary is more of a stern disciplinarian.

Bedell uses the "two for one" framework to describe election strategy, President Clinton's domestic and foreign policy agenda, Hillary's efforts to reform health care, and investigations ranging from Whitewater to Monica Lewinsky. In addition, Bill Clinton's relationships with other women and how they have impacted his career are discussed, including a long description of the Monica Lewinsky episode (including sexual details). Bedell also describes Hillary's successful campaign in New York to become a Senator, and the book ends with the idea that Hillary's run for the presidency is a continuation of the same mission—"high political office, a Democratic agenda, the accumulation of power, and the pursuit of the Clinton legacy"—even though Bill and Hillary had reversed roles.

Book review written by Dr. Naomi Lichtenberg Sept. 2007;
update below July 2014; full excerpts available online at:
www.ontheissues.org/Love_of_Politics.htm

Updated Book Review for 2016 race:

This book details, from the perspective of journalistic history, the events of Bill Clinton's presidential administration, in the context of Hillary Clinton's presidential run in 2008. It was published just prior to the 2008 presidential campaign, and the author notes in the introduction, "This is an opportune moment to try to unravel the mysteries of the Clintons' marriage and to assess the extent to which the country was governed by a co-presidency from 1993 to 2001." The book addresses the two issues in that introductory statement in great detail in its 608 pages:

- Yes, Bill and Hillary ran a co-presidency, much more than Al Gore got to participate in the co-presidency he dreamed of. All three of them could veto White House actions, according to the book, but Hillary was Bill's first adviser, with Gore a distant second.

- And yes, Bill and Hillary's marriage had some "mystery", if one questions why a wife would stay with a repeat philanderer. According to the book, it's because of Hillary's background (good Methodists don't divorce) and because she recognized that they could accomplish a lot together, including her future election, and would accomplish much less apart.

The author, Sally Bedell Smith, is a well-established political writer, and the book is relatively unbiased. Sometimes it feels anti-Hillary; sometimes it feels pro-Hillary; which means it's fair. It also sometimes feels anti-Bill and sometimes feels pro-Bill; which is also fair. But it's almost always anti-Al Gore; which feels a little unfair to the man who, towards the end of the book, won more votes for president than anyone prior in U.S. history.

The book reviews every fact and every rumor about every scandal of Bill's two terms. Given the 10- to 15-year lag time, fairness has finally become possible. Like any pundit over the age of 30, I remember the events presented, but have not discussed them myself for a decade; the book's summaries seem like accurate history and the few judgments made are always done by citing one of the players, rather than the author herself. But oh, there are *SO* many scandals, which is why the book stretches to *SO* many pages:

- Hillary's TravelGate scandal, tied to Vince Foster's suicide and the scandal surrounding his legal notes as her personal lawyer.

- Bill & Hillary's Whitewater scandal, in which they were accused of falsifying tax returns about profits and losses on a real estate development project on the White River in Arkansas. Vince Foster served as their lawyer for Whitewater also, tying Whitewater to the previous scandal.

- Bill's peccadilloes in Arkansas--he used his gubernatorial state troopers to transport women--became known as TrooperGate. This scandal led to all of the other sex scandals because Paula Jones based her lawsuit against Bill Clinton on TrooperGate.

- Paula Jones sued Bill for sexual harassment, and this was the only legal case ever involved with Bill Clinton's impeachment. Because of this civil lawsuit, Bill testified about Monica Lewinsky, with whom Bill claimed he never had sex.

- Ken Starr was appointed as Independent Counsel to investigate Whitewater and Vince Foster's death (not to investigate about Paula Jones nor Monica Lewinsky). According to the book, this investigation cost the taxpayers $65 million and occupied more than 3 years surrounding Bill's re-election -- but concluded that Bill had nothing to do with Vince Foster's death, and had no serious wrongdoing in Whitewater. The Independent Counsel law was not renewed in 1999, mostly as a result of this case.

- Nevertheless, Bill got impeached for lying about Monica Lewinsky in the Paula Jones case. His actual impeachment was for perjury and obstruction of justice -- neither of which he was ever charged with in court, but only in Congress. The House impeached him for those two charges (and not two others), and then the Senate denied convicting him of either one.

- The impeachment charges focused on Bill's misstatements in which he said there "is no sexual relationship" with Monica. The book excruciatingly explains Bill's Biblical definition of 'sex' (intercourse, not fellatio), as well as the "meaning of 'is'" (present tense, not past tense); hence Bill says his statement was legally true.

In summary, Bill was not impeached for any misconduct with Paula Jones, who presented the only actual lawsuit against him. And he was not impeached for any actions involving Whitewater or Vince Foster, which were the only original topics of Ken Starr's investigation. Monica Lewinsky never accused Bill of anything except breaking her heart, but Bill did get impeached for his statements about her. Reading this stuff retrospectively in a book was much less painful than I recall at the time of the events, when they went on interminably. At least here one could turn the page.

Overall, this book lays out everything a well-informed voter should know about Bill's presidency and Hillary's role in his administration and scandals. This book makes all other such books obsolete -- they are all biased or partisan in comparison. When Hillary runs in 2016, and these topics are reviewed again, no additional book should be necessary, because this book already exists. Alas, there are plenty of other books on all of the topics covered here, and probably more to follow before 2016 -- we review several of them below! -- the best advice to good citizens is to ignore all other scandal-ridden books and stick to this one!

That Bill and Hillary are aligned politically does not mean that they agree on the issues; looking at their agreements and disagreements....

Where Bill Clinton and Hillary Clinton agree on economic & foreign issues

- Both strongly pro-Green Energy
- Both strongly pro-progressive taxation
- Both strongly pro-cap-and-trade
- Both pro-comprehensive immigration reform
- Both pro-defense expenditures
- Both pro-minimum wage increase
- both pro-infrastructure investment

Where Bill Clinton and Hillary Clinton disagree on economic & foreign issues

	Bill Clinton	Hillary Clinton
Social Security:	Open to alternatives	No privatization
Free Trade:	Pro-NAFTA & GATT	Wary of NAFTA
Iraq War:	Opposed from beginning	Voted to authorize war
Corporatism:	Wary of corporate profit	Keep corporate tax low
Welfare reform:	Workfare-based reform	Faith-based welfare

Book Review: A Woman in Charge:
The Life of Hillary Rodham Clinton,
by Carl Bernstein (June 5, 2007)

"A Woman in Charge" is the definitive unauthorized biography of Hillary Clinton for the 2008 presidential season. It's written by Carl Bernstein, the reporter who (with Bob Woodward) broke the Watergate story in the Washington Post, earning a Pulitzer Prize, and thereby becoming the country's leading journalist.

Bernstein's method is simple. He goes through Hillary's autobiography, *Living History*, and investigates the veracity of each incident. Bernstein investigates incidents from several other sources as well, but *Living History* is his basic framework—hence Hillary has her version, and here Bernstein tries to present a fuller truth. Sometimes he confirms what Hillary wrote; sometimes he adds to it; sometimes he disconfirms it. Overall, Bernstein goes deeper than any other biographer into his background analysis, and maintains a journalistic neutrality along the way.

If you're only going to read one book about Hillary this campaign season, this is the one to read. (We would prefer if you read all of our excerpts, of course—a lot less reading for a lot more coverage!). It's actually better to read than "Living History," because Hillary's autobiography is obviously biased, especially towards what Hillary thinks she needs to present for her presidential run. If you'd like to check out all of our Hillary book excerpts, here they are, grouped by bias:

BIASED IN FAVOR OF HILLARY:

- *Living History*, by Hillary Rodham Clinton (2003)—her autobiography.

- *Talking It Over* (1998)—Hillary's columns while First Lady.

- *A Portrait in Her Own Words*, by Claire Osborne (1998)—a collection of speeches and fluff.

- *The Case For Hillary Clinton*, by Susan Estrich (2005)—a response to "The Case Against Hillary Clinton" by Peggy Noonan.

- *It Takes a Village*, 2006 edition, by Hillary Clinton (1996)—her political philosophy.
- *The Inside Story*, by Judith Warner (1993)—her biography as incoming First Lady.

NEUTRAL INVESTIGATION OF HILLARY:

- *Her Way*, by Jeff Gerth & Don Van Natta Jr. (2007)—from the New York Times.
- *God and Hillary Clinton*: A Spiritual Life, by Paul Kengor (2007)—a religious perspective.
- *For Love of Politics: The White House Years*, by Sally Bedell Smith (2007)—a joint biography.
- *Hillary's Choice*, by Gail Sheehy (2000)—an investigative biography.

BIASED AGAINST HILLARY:

- *The Extreme Makeover of Hillary (Rodham) Clinton*, by Bay Buchanan (2007)—a well-written attack book.
- *Condi vs. Hillary: The Next Great Presidential Race*, by Dick Morris (2005)—the predicted race didn't happen, but still a good analysis by Bill Clinton's former adviser.
- *Vast Right-Wing Conspiracy*, by Amanda Carpenter (2006)—every possible "Swift-boating" is here.
- *Partners in Power*, by Roger Morris (1999)—anti-Hillary, anti-Bill, and anti-Democrat.
- *Madame Hillary*, by R. Emmett Tyrell (2004)—anti-Hillary from a moderate perspective.
- *What Every American Should Know*, by the American Conservative Union (2000)—anti-Hillary during her Senate run.

Book review written August 2007; full excerpts available online at: www.ontheissues.org/Woman_in_Charge.htm

Book Review: It Takes A Village:
by Hillary Clinton
(Dec. 12, 2006, Tenth Anniversary Edition)

This book is Hillary's classic—not so much a political book as a definition of her view of the world. It was written in 1996, well before she was considering running for the presidency. Hence it does not have much in the way of policy prescriptions. However, Hillary added an introduction in December 2006, for the "10th Anniversary Edition," along with a new set of end-notes commenting on her updated thoughts on the original text. Those 2006 additions were written with her presidential run in mind, and constitute the bulk of our excerpts. (The 2006 additions are cited as roman-numeral pages for the introduction, and page numbers above 299 for the end-notes).

The theme of Hillary's book (and its title) is that children are raised not just by their parents, but also by all of the other people in the society around them. Therefore, according to Hillary, all the components of that society—the schools and the government, but the businesses too—have an obligation to consider their impact on children that they affect. Apparently Hillary's belief in this philosophy has been strengthened in the past 10 years, because her new commentary reinforces her original policy prescriptions with a decade of additional evidence.

On the left side of the political spectrum, one might view that philosophy as the underlying value of a compassionate society which is appropriately focused on child-rearing as its core focus. On the right side of the political spectrum, one might view that philosophy as a rationale for a government takeover of anything related to child-rearing, which can be expansively defined as anything at all. In either case, Hillary's philosophy is out in the open for public inspection—she has not hidden her beliefs since at least 1996.

Book review written November 2007
full excerpts available online at:
www.ontheissues.org/Takes_A_Village.htm

Book Review: My Father, My President:
A Personal Account
of the Life of George H. W. Bush
by Doro Bush Koch (Oct. 6, 2006)

Doro Bush Koch, the author of this memoir, is the younger sister of Governor Jeb Bush & President George W. Bush, and the daughter of President George H. W. Bush Sr. The book focuses on her father, but includes substantial personal insight into her two brothers as well. She has no political ambitions of her own, so this memoir represents the official Bush family line, without the bias inherent in autobiography. Therefore this book makes an interesting contrast to *All the Best*, President George H. W. Bush Sr.'s memoir, and *Decision Points*, President George W. Bush Jr.'s memoir.

Doro has her own unique insight into the three protagonists, and adds to her personal perspective that of numerous high-ranking aides, whom she cites extensively. Unlike with Kitty Kelley's joint biography of the same three protagonists, the high-ranking aides knew they could trust Doro to portray the Bushes in a sympathetic light (which Kitty Kelley often did not do), and hence were more forthcoming.

While there is some value to reading a presidential memoir by a "sympathetic insider," the book does have a larger purpose. Besides describing the official Bush family line on key historical events, this book also establishes the official Bush family legacy—i.e., how the Bushes want us to view Bush 41's and Bush 43's presidencies. And perhaps even more importantly, this book establishes the official Bush family dynasty—how the Bushes want us to perceive their future candidates (specifically, Jeb Bush for President, and George P. Bush for some other office later).

There is not a lot of material about Jeb, however—the book, as promised in its title and subtitle, focuses on Doro's father. For Jeb's future campaigns, this book sets more of a tone than a policy agenda. That tone could be summarized as the "Bush Political Doctrine:" maintain bipartisanship; exercise restrained prudence in important decisions;

remain resolute and loyal. All three of the protagonists want voters and historians to believe that they all followed all of those criteria whenever possible. Whether those are actually true of any of the three politicians in any given situation is up to the reader to decide—Doro makes the case here for just one side.

Book review written Jan. 2013; full excerpts available online at:
www.ontheissues.org/Father_President.htm

Book Review: Condi vs. Hillary:
The Next Great Presidential Race
by Dick Morris (Oct. 11, 2005)

Dick Morris is one of the foremost political analysts in America today. He was considered instrumental in Pres. Bill Clinton's winning strategy of "triangulation"—deciding how much was possible on his issues with the opposition party, then "triangulating" to that middle position and pushing it toward implementation. But Morris had a falling-out with the Clintons, and now he is one of Hillary's leading critics. This book reflects that.

Morris' idea that Condoleezza Rice would run for president was far-fetched when he proposed it, via this book, in 2005. Morris knew that—the purpose of the book was to lay out the case for drafting her, since she has not expressed a strong interest in running. The penultimate chapter is entitled "Drafting Condi," and lays out a plan for a grassroots Internet-based movement to build a volunteer organization. That organization would persuade Rice to run *AFTER* the primaries, like Dwight Eisenhower was persuaded, one month before the Republican convention in 1952.

Morris' "Draft Condi" idea was far-fetched but plausible in 2005. By 2007, the idea had become impossible. There will not be a draft movement now, because Condi does not have the popular support that she had in 2005. The Iraq War has gone substantially downhill since 2005, both militarily and in terms of popular support—so instead of Condi's big claim to fame, as Morris predicted, it became her primary reason *NOT* to run.

In any case, Morris' dream race was a wonderful dream. Morris assumes that Hillary will get the Democratic nomination—and analyzes several of her opponents' foibles accordingly (he did not predict that Barack Obama would enter the race). He makes the case that Hillary is unbeatable—except by Condi.

As with other books by Hillary's critics, this book acknowledges her strengths and points out her weaknesses—we detail some of them in our excerpts. And also like other critical books, many of the criticisms seem to actually be in Hillary's favor, when viewed from the perspective of Hillary's potential supporters. We detail some of those too. For example, in the chapter entitled "Hillary's Senate Record," Morris lists dozens of bills that Hillary supported—then says that even though they're each "good ideas," together they comprise a "wish list" spending spree. Then Morris criticizes Hillary for sponsoring only "symbolic" bills. Well, which is it? Either she's a big-spender for supporting too many bills, or a do-nothing senator for supporting only symbolic bills—but she can't be both!

Overall, this book is one of the better criticisms of Hillary in the 2008 race. Unfortunately for Dick Morris, the title makes it a low-seller. It *SHOULD* be as popular as some of the other well-thought-out and well-researched anti-Hillary books!

P.S. In the interest of full disclosure, OnTheIssues.org worked with Dick Morris' political website during the 2004 presidential race.

Book review written February 2007
full excerpts available online at:
www.ontheissues.org/Condi_vs_Hillary.htm

Book Review: The Family:
The Real Story of the Bush Dynasty
by Kitty Kelley (Sept. 14, 2004)

This is a joint biography of President George H. W. Bush Sr., and his son President George W. Bush Jr. It's also a briefer biography of Governor Jeb Bush (George W.'s brother) and Senator Prescott Bush (George H.'s father).

Of primary importance in understanding this biography is the author—Kitty Kelley, who was also the biographer for Jackie Onassis, Nancy Reagan, Frank Sinatra, and her other famous joint biography of the British royal family. In particular, Nancy Reagan told the Bush family to NOT participate with Kitty Kelley, because Kelley had some negative things to say about Nancy Reagan. Kelley has many, many negative things to say about the Bush family —perhaps more so because they listened to Nancy Reagan and forced Kelley to write an unauthorized biography.

Kelley digs up a lot of dirt about the senior President Bush in this book. (She digs up a lot of dirt about the junior President Bush too, but most of that dirt was already well-known.) For the senior President Bush, Kelley digs back to the 1960s, when Bush Sr. ran for Congress and the Senate in Texas.

At issue was that Bush was a "progressive Republican" in the mold of other Republican New Englanders like Sen. Olympia Snowe (R, ME) and Gov. Linc Chafee (R, RI). When Bush moved from New England to Texas, he had to change some of his stances in order to be eligible for high office—in particular on civil rights, contraception, and other social issues. Then when he ran as Reagan's Vice President in 1990, he had to change his stances again, to fit better with Reagan.

Kelley undertakes the clean method of digging up Bush's issue stances from old elections and comparing them to his current stances—that's real reporting, not gossip and not attacking. Readers might know Kitty Kelley from her past at *People* magazine and other gossip-focused reporting—and hence might (incorrectly) assume that this is a gossip-oriented biography. Kelley does summarize the gossip of the day—about Bush Senior's "girlfriend" while in office (never fully substantiated) and Bush Junior's well-known peccadilloes as well. But the real reporting vastly overwhelms the gossip—Kelley establishes herself as a serious biographer and a serious political reporter.

Book review written April 2012;
full excerpts available online at:
www.ontheissues.org/Kitty_Kelley.htm

Book Review:
The Faith of George W. Bush,
by Stephen Mansfield (April 30, 2004)

This book is about George W. Bush's faith as a candidate and president, but also about the faith of George H. W. Bush, the father. The two are intertwined, of course, since Bush Sr. chose Bush Jr.'s early church experiences. But the book outlines how their presidential politics continued that intertwining in adulthood.

The author claims (p. xiv) to have written this book because "the matter of his religious faith... is another likely pillar of George W. Bush's legacy." While that is not true for Bush Sr., the author does spend a lot of ink on the earlier president too. The author details (p. 19) how Bush Sr. considered his faith to be "personal", while Bush Jr., as indicated by the quote above, considered his faith to be a critical component of his policymaking.

This book is the first of a series by Stephen Mansfield on the faith of presidents and presidential candidates. Mansfield later authored The Faith of Barack Obama (2008) and The Faith and Values of Sarah Palin

(2010). Mansfield also writes faith-oriented biographies about non-politicians; but we hope he continues this insightful series on many more candidates.

Book review written Oct. 2011;
full excerpts available online at:
www.ontheissues.org/Hard_Choices.htm

Updated Book Review for 2016 race:

At issue in the upcoming 2016 election is what would be in a book entitled, *The Faith of Jeb Bush*. Assuming that issue arises — and it most certainly will, after the electorate spent so much of 2012 exploring the Mormonism of Mitt Romney and the habits of Barack Obama's pastor (Rev. Jeremiah Wright, remember?) — we expect the same in 2016. We outline below the policy differences between Jeb, his brother, and his father.

Jeb has one important distinction from the past two Presidents Bush: they were members of the Episcopalian Church, while Jeb is a Catholic. Jeb converted in 1995 to his wife Columba's religion. If elected, Jeb would be only the second Catholic President, after John F. Kennedy. Catholicism played an important role in Kennedy's 1960 election; but questions about Jeb's status as the would-be second Catholic president will likely take a back seat to issues about Hillary's status as the would-be first female president.

Where George W. Bush, Jeb Bush, & George Bush Sr. agree on Social issues

- All are hard-core pro-life
- All support faith-based social services
- All support character education
- All support abstinence education
- All support family values
- All support school vouchers

Where George W. Bush, Jeb Bush, & George Bush Sr. disagree on Social issues

	George W. Bush	Jeb Bush	George Bush Sr.
Stem Cells:	Compromised on stem cells	Hard core against stem cells	(No stance on stem cells)
Gay rights:	Hard-core for traditional marriage	Moderate for traditional marriage	Moderate for gay rights
Welfare:	Replace welfare with self-help	Replace welfare with work	Replace welfare with enterprise zones
Conservation:	Private land stewardship	State-run conservation	Personal conservation

Book Review: Living History:
by Hillary Rodham Clinton
(June 9, 2003)

This is Hillary's autobiography, published in 2003 in preparation for her presidential run. It is the book which is dissected and analyzed by all of her critics and supporters, in most detail in *A Woman in Charge* (by Carl Bernstein, who broke the Watergate story) and in *Her Way* (by the reporters who broke the Whitewater story). If you want to form your own opinions, rather than trust those of the pundits and/or Hillary's critics, this book is a must-read. Our excerpts, of course, will do.

This book traces Hillary's life from her girlhood in a Chicago suburb through her election to the Senate. She says in the introduction that it was originally intended to be only a portrait of her 8 years in the White House, but, she writes, "I quickly realized that I couldn't explain my life as First Lady without going back to the beginning." The book chronicles, in traditional chronological sequence, Hillary's years in college;

meeting Bill Clinton; as Arkansas' First Lady; the road to the White House; and finally her election in New York.

The book has chapters that will provide fodder for Hillary's supporters:

- "Class of '69," about her Wellesley graduation speech, her first claim to public fame;
- "East Wing, West Wing," about Hillary's expansion of the First Lady's role;
- "Women's Rights Are Human Rights," about Hillary's trip to China and her most famous speech there;
- "Conversations With Eleanor," about her identifying with Eleanor Roosevelt.

And the book has chapters that will provide fodder for Hillary's detractors:

- "Health Care," about her failed healthcare task force;
- "Independent Counsel," about the Whitewater investigation;
- "Soldiering On," the gently-named chapter about Monica Lewinsky;
- "Impeachment," about Bill's worst episode as President, and her reaction.

There's not much in the way of issues here—it's mostly personal history and personal impressions of historic events. But when you're running for President, those personal things are important too. So read on.

Book review written Dec. 2007
full excerpts available online at:
www.ontheissues.org/Living_History.htm

Book Review: Fortunate Son
George W. Bush and the Making of an American President, by J. H. Hatfield (Dec. 12, 2002)

This book is a negative biography of George W. Bush -- very negative. So negative that Bush attacked the author -- and hence the author became the controversy about this book, rather than the content of the book. At issue is the accusation that Bush was arrested for cocaine usage decades ago; Bush's allies responded by alleging that the author was arrested for even worse misdeeds. The counter-accusations against the author (and whether Bush was involved with them) deflected attention from the accusation against Bush -- which perhaps was the purpose of the counter-accusation, if one is a cynic.

Is attacking the author a good idea? Or more relevantly, is it good politics? This book was published just prior to the 2000 election; we have two examples for comparison, in the two subsequent elections. Bush suffered electorally because of the cocaine accusation -- but it never became enough of a full-fledged issue to lose him the election. In other words, the strategy of attacking the author worked.

In the 2004 election, John Kerry was similarly accused of horrendous behavior in what became known as the Swift Boat attack. Many Kerry allies attacked that book's author, Jerome Corsi, as unreliable, but Kerry himself did not respond. Kerry's lack of response is widely credited with contributing to his 2004 election loss. In other words, Kerry ignored Bush's lesson of responding by counter-attack, and paid the consequences.

After the 2008 election, Sarah Palin was the subject of an unfriendly biography called The Rogue, by Joe McGinnis. That author moved in next door to the Palins' home in Wasilla, Alaska. Palin made the author' the issue -- she attacked him for invasion of privacy, and by the time the book was published, the book's content had become irrelevant -- only the author's action in writing the book mattered. In other words, Palin took Bush's lesson and responded by counter-attack, and reaped the benefits.

So what about the content of this book? Why did Bush attack the author here, and not, say, the equally negative biographies *Shrub* or *Worse Than Watergate*? We think it's because this author went too far. Rather than restricting his attack to Bush's actions, the author questioned the entire Bush family. The Bushes feel entitled to high office, the author claims on pp. 2-5, because they feel like America's aristocracy.

The author goes on to attack George H. W. Bush too: questioning his actions in getting shot down over the Pacific in 1945. The author claims (pp. 306-17) that Bush Sr. ejected prematurely, and could have saved the other crew members from death. (The US Navy disagreed, and awarded Bush the Distinguished Flying Cross for that incident, as the author notes on p. 9). That sort of generic anti-Bush attack probably riled up the Bush family enough to go after the author -- and it certainly feels to the reader like the author overstepped the bounds of journalistic propriety.

We excerpt this book now, in preparation for the 2016 election, because the author would certainly include Jeb Bush as subject to the negative aspects of the Bush family legacy. We can anticipate a similar attack book, and a similar counter-attack, coming soon.

Book review written January 2013;
full excerpts available online at:
www.ontheissues.org/Fortunate_Son.htm

Updated Book Review for 2016 race:

At issue in the upcoming 2016 election is whether Jeb suffers from a similar sense of entitlement as George. In other words, is Jeb, too, a "Fortunate Son"? Presumably the author of *Fortunate Son* might include Jeb and any other members of the Bush family legacy: but let's look at some key facts about the two brothers' background of "entitlement":

- Jeb has no issues about his military service; he registered for the draft in 1971, but never got drafted because Vietnam was winding down. George Sr. served in WWII (with controversial medals, according to Hatfield) while George Jr. served stateside during Vietnam (by influence-peddling, according to Hatfield).

- Jeb was defeated for governor of Florida in 1994, then came back to win in 1998. Similarly, George Sr. was defeated in his first race for Congress in 1964, then came back to win in 1966. George Jr., on the other hand, won his first election for Governor in 1994, and never lost an election.

- Jeb graduated from the University of Texas at Austin; George Sr. graduated from Yale; and George Jr. graduated from Yale and Harvard.

Are those indicative that Jeb has less of a sense of entitlement than his father or brother? We'll let the reader decide, based on how those backgrounds translate into policy stances on entitlement-based economic and domestic issues:

Where George W. Bush, Jeb Bush, & George Bush Sr. agree on Economic / Domestic issues

- All agree on tax cuts
- All agree on federal spending cuts
- All agree on gun rights
- All agree on pursuing War on Drugs

Where George W. Bush, Jeb Bush, & George Bush Sr. disagree on Economic / Domestic issues

	George W. Bush	Jeb Bush	George Bush Sr.
Affirmative Action:	Affirmative access	Dismantle affirmative action	No quotas
Health Care:	Personal choice	Oppose ObamaCare	Optional Medicaid
Mandatory Sentencing:	Tough on crime	Alternatives to punishment	Limit appeals
Energy:	Drill offshore	Don't drill offshore	Pioneered drilling offshore

Book Review: Partners in Power:
The Clintons and Their America,
by Roger Morris (April 1, 1999)

This book is anti-Clinton. But more so, it's anti-Democrat. And even more so, it's anti-Republican, anti-Washington-DC, and anti-politician. In that context, I would not call this an anti-Hillary book, because that would mean the author, Roger Morris, believes Hillary would be a bad president, and we should vote for someone else. Morris believes, it seems, that the entire system is so corrupt that it's not possible to have a *GOOD* president, and therefore it hardly matters who we vote for. The book's theme can be summarized as, "All politicians are evil and therefore the Clintons are evil."

The book jacket describes Morris as working "in the finest tradition of investigative journalism," but I'd put that more accurately as working "in the worst tradition of cynical journalism." I can't find anything in this book that Morris believes in -- although I can find plenty of what he believes *AGAINST*. Morris seems to believe that *EVERYONE* is a bad president -- he bashes Bill Clinton and Ronald Reagan, and then bashes Hillary too. This book was written in 1996, and since it's about Bill and Hillary, they receive most of the bashing. But look, for example, at how Morris describes Washington DC: "Hard beneath Capitol Hill's oily deference and camaraderie was remorseless cannibalism."

The book calls itself "a dual biography" of Bill & Hillary Clinton, following their lives chronologically from their childhood homes in Hope AR and Park Ridge IL, to the White House. It's really more of a "triple biography," adding as the third character the American polity, from the Washington political establishment to the press to the Arkansas voters and then finally American society as a whole. The third subject of the biography is described as "a political system gone lethally wrong." Since me and you, dear reader, are members of that third subject, we are implicitly bashed also, which is perhaps why I feel this book is so negative.

The book isn't quite a biography (which would include positives as well as negatives), since it is strictly a negative examination, without ever acknowledging positive accomplishments. The book also deals heavily with Ronald Reagan, and a bit with George H. W. Bush Sr., who were presidents during Clinton's governorship. There's a whole chapter on the conspiracy theory of the Mena airport in Arkansas, where (Morris claims) the CIA ran cocaine to fund the Iran-Contra deal, under the explicit approval, of Reagan, Bush Sr., and Gov. Clinton. Everyone else the book touches on also gets bashed: from Roger Clinton (Bill's brother, whose drug habits are detailed) to Gerald Ford (who "laid the foundation for the bloated Pentagon budgets of the 1980s.") Even journalists get bashed: "American journalism managed little substantive understanding of or concern for governance and posed no genuine check to the real regime's billowing power," Morris describes the 1990s.

So who should read this book? Well, negativists, pessimists, and cynics will just eat this stuff up. Conspiracy theorists will just *LOVE* the Mena airport chapter. Anti-Hillary people should certainly add this to their repertoire, since Morris explicitly states, for example, that Hillary had an affair with Vince Foster (among numerous other scandals).

And who should avoid this book? Anyone who believes, still, that the press has a positive role; that government can change society for the better; or that people at their core are basically good.

I put myself firmly in this latter optimistic category, and I found this book to be needlessly pessimistic. In my work with OnTheIssues and elsewhere, I have dealt with hundreds of politicians, some of whom I've supported and many of whom I've opposed. But the one thing in common I've found, among all those politicians, even the ones I worked hard to defeat electorally, is that they all truly believe that they can change their part of the world for the better. I often disagree with *HOW* they want to change it, but I have never found any politician who's actually in it just for the money, or for the power, or for anything else. Politicians are in politics because they want to do some good. That's why they enter the arena, and put themselves on the line for criticisms like Morris'. And they all deserve a lot more respect than Morris gives them.

Book review written March 2008;
update below Feb. 2015; full excerpts available online at:
www.ontheissues.org/Partners_in_Power.htm

Updated Book Review for 2016 race:

Is Bill Clinton an asset for Hillary's 2016 campaign, or a liability? On the asset side, Bill Clinton is widely considered one of the best campaigners in the history of our country, and will certainly help Hillary raise money; get support from key people and organizations; and get voters to turn out to vote for her. On the liability side, Bill Clinton's presidency included (and some would say caused) the polarization of American politics: "before Bill Clinton" means "before Whitewater" but also "before Newt Gingrich and the Contract With America." The high level of political polarization began under Bill Clinton, and persists until today: and the current focus of much of that polarization is Hillary Clinton.

Al Gore chose to distance himself from Bill Clinton in 2000, both on moral issues and on policy issues. Hillary will not repeat that mistake. Bill and Hillary agree on some issues, and disagree on others; some examples follow (and see p. 235 for the economic and foreign issues):

Where Bill Clinton and Hillary Clinton agree on social & domestic issues

- Both pro-death penalty
- Both strongly pro-choice
- Both strongly pro-affirmative action
- Both strongly pro-ObamaCare
- Both strongly pro-environment
- Both strongly pro-gun control
- Both strongly pro-voting rights

Where Bill Clinton and Hillary Clinton disagree on social & domestic issues

	Bill Clinton	Hillary Clinton
Three Strikes:	Tough on crime	Limit mandatory sentencing
Gay marriage:	Supports some gay rights	Strongly supports gay marriage
School prayer:	No official school prayer	No religious instruction
School choice :	Supports charters for all	No private nor parochial choice
Legal marijuana:	Keep war on drugs	Open to legalization

Book Review: Profiles in Character:
by Jeb Bush & Brian Yablonski
(Jan. 1996)

This book was written in 1995, after Jeb Bush had narrowly lost the 1994 Florida gubernatorial election, and before he won the 1998 election. In other words, it outlines Jeb's policy stances with the focus on addressing issues he thought contributed to his 1994 loss and would contribute to his 1998 victory. The book is published by "The Foundation for Florida's Future," which is a think tank that Jeb founded after the 1994 loss. In other words, Jeb's Foundation was founded to publish this book, in conjunction with other projects focused on winning the next time around. Of course, those methods worked, and Jeb overwhelmingly won the 1998 election (and even more overwhelmingly won his 2002 re-election).

The title of this book is a take-off on John F. Kennedy's pre-presidential book, *Profiles in Courage*. Jeb's framing mechanism, focusing on "character" instead of "courage," implies that Jeb considers character the most important attribute of leadership, where JFK considered courage the most important attribute. JFK's concept of "Profiles" as an organizing theme continues its relevance, as illustrated by Caroline Kennedy's 2003 book *Profiles in Courage For Our Time*. All of these "Profile" books focus on individual inspirational stories.

We review this book in preparation for the 2016 presidential race. While the issue stances are from a different context (a gubernatorial run) and a different era (before Jeb's brother was elected President), they are relevant for 2016 because they show the longevity of Jeb's beliefs. In other words, voters can compare Jeb's issue stances from 1995 to those he holds closer to 2016. We summarize some of the similarities and differences:

- **Abortion:** In 1995, Jeb went on record calling abortion a moral issue. As governor, Jeb focused on more practical matters such as banning stem cell research.

- *Gay Rights:* In 1995, Jeb called the gay rights movement a "modern victim movement." As governor, Jeb did not push the issue (as he has not pushed other divisive social issues).

- *Corporations:* In 1995, Jeb used the term "corporate welfare," a term usually used by anti-corporate populists. As governor, Jeb pushed two major programs that could be considered corporate welfare: using state tax money for "Touchdown Jacksonville" (a Florida NFL team) and using federal stimulus money for the Scripps biotech center. Both of those projects were widely praised, but Jeb certainly did change his view on corporate welfare.

- *Crime:* In 1995, Jeb cited the "trivialization of crime"; as governor, he focused heavily on "tough-on-crime" enforcement.

- *Education:* In 1995, Jeb focused on "grade inflation"; but as governor, he focused on charter schools and education vouchers.

- *Welfare:* In 1995, Jeb proposed making welfare "shameful"; as governor, he pushed for faith-based organizations to provide welfare services.

Those differences are more about how the issues are framed: In 1995, Jeb used "character" as an organizing theme, and framed all of the issues as aspects of morals and values. As governor, Jeb had to actually govern, and hence had to translate those thematic issues into practical policy. This book demonstrates Jeb's consistency over the years, more than providing evidence of changing stances.

We presume Jeb will write another policy book in preparation for the 2016 presidential race (if Jeb authors a book in 2013 or 2014, that is strong evidence that he is planning to run). Until then, this book is all we can go by.

Book review written Dec. 2012;
full excerpts available online at:
www.ontheissues.org/Profiles_In_Character.htm

Hillary vs. Jeb on VoteMatch

Hillary Clinton and Jeb Bush disagree on many issues, but agree on some key stances as well: we discuss those summary agreements and disagreements in this final chapter.

Our "VoteMatch" quiz summarizes political views by analyzing responses to 20 questions below. Answers to the 20 questions are further summarized into a political philosophy, based on segregating the questions into a social axis and an economic axis (graphic on back cover; more detailed discussion below). That two-dimensional analysis concludes:

- *Hillary Clinton is a hard-core liberal* (not a progressive like Barack Obama and not a populist like Bill Clinton. We comment in other chapters that she is more centrist than Barack Obama, but that is because Obama campaigned as a progressive, although he governed as a centrist).

- *Jeb Bush is a populist-leaning conservative* (not a libertarian like Rand Paul, and not a hard-core conservative like George W. Bush, but also not a moderate conservative like their father).

Where do Hillary and Jeb disagree on the issues? They disagree on the core Democrat-versus-Republican list, including:

- *Abortion:* Hillary would promote reproductive rights and embryonic stem cell research; Jeb would not.
- *Gay Rights:* Hillary would promote same-sex marriage; Jeb would not.
- *ObamaCare:* Hillary would expand government-mandated healthcare coverage; Jeb would not.
- *Gun Rights:* Hillary would control guns; Jeb would not.
- *Union policy:* Hillary would push for unionization; Jeb would not.
- *Tax Reform:* Hillary would increase taxes on corporations and the wealthy; Jeb would not.
- *Technology:* Hillary would regulate the Internet; Jeb would not.

Where do Hillary and Jeb agree on the issues? They do agree on some, including:

- *Immigration:* both favor comprehensive reform.

- *Environment:* both support protecting environmental protection.

- *Common Core:* both support national education standards, despite their differences on local control.

- *Faith-based initiatives:* both support working with religious organizations for social services, despite their differences on the role of religion elsewhere in government.

- *Multilateralism:* both support an America engaged with allies around the world on both military issues and trade issues, with many differences on past wars and past trade agreements.

The bottom line: Hillary and Jeb are not diametrically opposed to each other on every issue. If you prefer a polar opposite to Hillary, Jeb should not be your chosen candidate. And if you prefer someone who will dismantle forever the Bush legacy, Hillary should not be your chosen candidate. Neither is the extremist their opponents make them out to be.

Hillary vs. Jeb on VoteMatch

VoteMatch is our 20-question quiz which summarizes the candidate's views on the controversial issues of the day. The 20 questions appear on the left, with our summary answers for Hillary and Jeb.

VoteMatch Social Issues

	Hillary Clinton	Jeb Bush
Abortion is a woman's unrestricted right	strongly favors	strongly opposes
Legally require hiring women & minorities	strongly favors	opposes
Comfortable with same-sex marriage	strongly favors	strongly opposes
Keep God in the public sphere	mixed opinion	strongly favors
Vouchers for school choice	strongly opposes	strongly favors

VoteMatch Domestic Issues

	Hillary Clinton	Jeb Bush
Expand ObamaCare	strongly favors	opposes
No 'rights' to clean air and water	strongly opposes	strongly opposes
Stricter punishment reduces crime	opposes	strongly favors
Absolute right to gun ownership	strongly opposes	favors
Never legalize marijuana	opposes	strongly favors

VoteMatch Economic Issues

	Hillary Clinton	Jeb Bush
Privatize Social Security	strongly opposes	mixed opinion
Higher taxes on the wealthy	strongly favors	strongly opposes
Stricter limits on political campaign funds	strongly favors	strongly opposes
Stimulus better than market-led recovery	strongly favors	opposes
Prioritize green energy	strongly favors	opposes

VoteMatch International Issues

	Hillary Clinton	Jeb Bush
Pathway to citizenship for illegal aliens	favors	favors
Support & expand free trade	opposes	favors
Maintain US sovereignty from UN	opposes	opposes
Expand the military	mixed opinion	favors
Stay out of Iran	favors	opposes

In our online quiz, you fill in your answers for these 20 questions, and we match you against all the candidates (including Jeb and Hillary and a dozen other contenders from both parties). Please see:

http://quiz.ontheissues.org/

Afterword

We hope that this book encourages you, as voters, to make your decisions based on the issues. We recognize the reality of American politics: voters make their decisions based primarily on whether they like the candidates. Accordingly, our goal is to get voters to compare their issue preferences in comparison to candidate issue stances when considering which candidates to like.

We intentionally omitted from this book any biographical background on Secretary Clinton and Governor Bush. Details of their birthplaces and religious affiliations — and minutiae of every other personal detail — are readily available in the mainstream media. Their issue stances are more challenging for voters to find.

Why does the mainstream media fail at this important function? Because they are "news" organizations which are poorly suited to covering political campaigns. "News" implies reporting on what is "new": Jeb's stance on criminal sentencing has not changed since 2009, and Hillary's stance on abortion not changed since 2008, so there's nothing in the news about those issues. But if you are impassioned about Three Strikes, or if you vote based on pro-life vs. pro-choice stances, then you cannot rely on the news media for those non-newsworthy issues. And that's where we come in.

This book represents an archive of where these two candidates stand on the key issues of our time. We don't consider whether candidates' issue stances are new — just what they say on each issue. That often requires a lot of digging on our part — we have a team of researchers to do that, but we invite you to volunteer any issue stances that we don't cover.

Our online website www.ontheissues.org covers many more issues than can fit in any book: many more stances from Jeb Bush and Hillary Clinton, as well as all of the other 2016 candidates, Governors, Senators, and House members. We score each candidate on a 20-question quiz called "VoteMatch." A representation of the VoteMatch quiz results for the presidential contenders appears on the back cover of this book. The mainstream media interpret candidates using a one-dimensional "right-left" analysis. That simplistic analysis comes to nonsensical conclusions like calling Hillary Clinton "extreme left-wing" even though she supported the Iraq War; supports free trade; and supports faith-based initiatives.

We find our two-dimensional analysis to be more accurate in differentiating candidates than that traditional one-dimensional analysis. We don't claim that our method is perfect — just superior to the simplistic mainstream media. VoteMatch uses a Social Issues dimension plus an Economic Issues dimension; we interpret candidates based on whether they believe in government involvement in either or both of those dimensions. Using the two-dimensional analysis differentiates five classes of political beliefs:

1. *Libertarian:*
    No government involvement in social issues
    No government involvement in economic issues
2. *Conservative:*
    Government involvement in social issues
    No government involvement in economic issues
3. *Liberal:*
    No government involvement in social issues
    Government involvement in economic issues
4. *Populist:*
    Government involvement in social issues
    Government involvement in economic issues
5. *Centrist:*
    Some government involvement in social issues
    Some government involvement in economic issues

Most importantly, you can answer the same 20 questions and see *your* political label and how the candidates match up with *you*. We invite you to try the VoteMatch quiz at:

http://quiz.ontheissues.org

Index

A

Abortion: 110,111,113
Abyssinians: 104
Accountability Review Boards: 144
Acquired Immune Deficiency Syndrome (AIDS): 117
ACT test: 95 *see also:* SAT
Adelson, Sheldon: 167
Adoption: 110-1,122 *see also:* Abortion
Adoption and Safe Families Act: 122
Affirmative action: 88,91
Afghanistan: 140,154-5
  War: 153-5,157,180
African Americans: 16,27,40,41,88,91,104,117
Aggressive Conservatism in Florida, by Robert Crew (2009): 13,17,29,39,
  63,67,79,81,87,91,101,105,113,115
  Book review: 209
Ahmadinejad, Mahmoud: 148
Alaska: 174
Alliances: 180
Al-Qaeda: 141,143
Alternative energy: 58,60-1
America's Next Bush, by S.V. Dáte (2007): 19,25,27,39,41,59,67,69,
  83,87,89,127,129,131,133,163,177,191
  Book review: 213
American Exceptionalism: 179
American Federation of State, County and Municipal Employees
(AFSCME): 62
American Institute in Taiwan: 187
American Israel Public Affairs Committee (AIPAC): 153
Anthrax: 185
Anti-discrimination laws: 119
Arab League: 180
Arctic National Wildlife Refuge (ANWR): 58,172
Aristotle: 103
Arizona Supreme Court: 99
Arkansas: 94
Armed Services Committee: 156
Army Reserve: 156
Assad, Bashar: 142
Assange, Julian: 37
Assisted suicide: *see:* Death With Dignity
Association of Southeast Asian Nations *(ASEAN): 164*
Atlanta: 189

Atomic power *see:* Nuclear power
Automakers: 47,61 *see also:* Chrysler, Ford, General Motors

B

Bailouts
   Banks: 51,53
   Automotive: 51
Bankruptcy: 46
Banks: 50-1
BASE REALIGNMENT AND CLOSURE (BRAC): 157-9
   see also: Military Bases
Benghazi: 144-5
Bennett, William: 111
Bible: 124
Biden, Joseph: 154
Billionaires: 90
Birth control: 110,112,113 *see also:* Abortion
Blacks: *see:* African Americans
Blaine Amendment: 99
Bosch, Orlando: 161
BRICs (Brazil, Russia, India, China, South Africa): 186
Brady Campaign: 13
Brazil: 186,189,190
Brown, Gordon: 172
Budget deficit: 54-5
Budget, Federal: 54
Burnham Institute: 115
Bush, Barbara: 193
Bush, George Herbert Walker: 71,161,163, 227, 232
Bush, George W.: 53,68,115,134,140,146,148,155,167,198, 227, 232

C

Cain, Herman: 136
California: 115,194
Campaign
   Donations: 65
   Finance: 39,64,65
Canada: 192
Cap and Trade: 174
Capital gains: 66,67
Capital punishment *see:* Death penalty
Carbon emissions: 172,174
Casinos: 132,133
   Regulation: 132
Castro, Fidel: 160,161
Castro, Raul: 160

D

Death penalty: 18-9
Death tax: *see:* Taxes
Death With Dignity: 111
Debt ceiling: 55
Defense: 135 *see also:* US Department of Defense
    Spending: 156-7
Defense of Marriage Act (DOMA): 116,118 *see also:* Gay Rights
Democratic party: 3,8-9,36-7,41-2,47,51,53,62,7-8,102,120-
1,125,133,150-1, 162,178,183,209
Department of Children and Families: 123
Department of Energy (DOE): 31
Disabilities: 123
Discrimination: 40
Dixon, Ymelda: 193
DNA (deoxyribonucleic acid) testing: 18
Dodd, Chris: 198
Dole, Bob, 120
Domestic issues: 8
Domestic violence: 13
Don't Ask, Don't Tell (DADT): 116 *see:* Gay Rights
Drug cartels: 21
Drug treatment: 20-1
Drugs, illegal: 20-1

E

Ebola: 184-5
Economic inequality: 48
Economy: 54
Educate America Act: 92
Education: 90-5,166
    see also: Common Core, No Child Left Behind, University
Education savings accounts: 99
Edwards, John: 56
Egypt: 153
Elementary and Secondary Education Act: 92
El Salvador: 187
Eminent domain: 57
Employ American Workers Act: 85
Employment *see:* Jobs
Energy conservation: 61
Energy policy: 30,58
English language: 103,194
Environment: 28-9
Environmental Protection Agency (EPA): 28,62
Equal pay: 88

Free Trade: 188-9
Free Trade Area of the Americas: 189

G

Gangs. 111
Garnica, Columba: 194
Gates, Robert: 154
Gay marriage: 118 *see also:* Gay rights
Gay rights: 111,116-8
Gaza: 153
General Motors: 47,61
Gerald B. H. Solomon Freedom Consolidation Act of 2001 *see:* HR 3167
Gingrich, Newt: 122
Giuliani, Rudolph: 146
GLBT *see:* Gay Rights
God: 128,179
God and Hillary Clinton, by Paul Kengor (2007): 118,128,152,220
   Book review: 211
Goldman-Sachs: 186
Goldwater Institute: 99
GOP *see:* Republican Party
Government downsizing: 28,63
Great Britain: 146,174
Great recession *see:* Recession, great
Gulf of Mexico: 177
Gun control: 12,13 *see also:* gun crimes, 2nd Amendment
Gun crimes: 12,14-5
Gun rights *see:* 2nd Amendment

H

Hamas: 153
Hard Choices, by Hillary Clinton (2014):
36,142,148,150,152,154,164,166,172,180,182,190
   Book review: 202
Hate crimes: 119
Healthcare *see:* Medicaid/ Medicare, Mental health care, ObamaCare
Heller decision: 12
Hendrix College: 130
Hezbollah: 143
High School Diploma: 92
HILL-PAC: 64
Hispanic: 41,47,88,89, 104,121,204-6,213
Home Instruction for Parents and Preschool Youngsters: (HIPPY) 94
Homosexuality: *see:* Gay Rights
Hourly wage: 87

Japan: 151,164
Jews: 152
Jinping, Xi: 187
Jobs: 24,86-7
 Creation: 132
 Green jobs: 56
 Growth: 87
Johnson, Lyndon B.: 163

K

King, Martin Luther: 117
Korea: 151,164
 Korea, North: 164
 Korea, South: 164-5
Kosovo: 180
Kurds: 158
Kuwait: 151
Kyl-Lieberman Amendment: 148
Kyoto Treaty: 173-5

L

Labor shortage: 194
Latin America: 160,190-1,194
Latino *see:* Hispanic
Lazio, Rick: 132
Levant: 141
Lewis, Ann: 130
Libertarian party: 8
Libya: 144,180
Living History, by Hillary Rodham Clinton (2003): 78,102,112, 120,122,134,203,219
 Book review: 228
Lu, Annette: 187

M

Management Privatization Act: 63
Mandatory prison sentences *see:* Prison incarceration
Marijuana, legalization: 22-3
Marriage: 119 *see also:* Gay marriage
Martin, Trayvon: 13
Mass spectrometer: 123
Mass transit: 25,174 *see also:* Transportation infrastructure
McCain, John: 51,65,150,155-6,174
McChrystal, Stanley: 154

Medical doctor: *see:* Physicians
Medical malpractice: 82-3
Medical marijuana *see:* Marijuana, legalization
Medicaid: 78-9, 101
Medicare: 78-9
Mental health care: 80-1
Mercenaries: 151
Mexico: 136,190,192,194
Mexico border: 192-3,199
Miami: 161,189
Middle East: 37,143
Military: *see:* US Department of Defense
Military Bases: 158-9 *see also: Base Realignment and Closure (BRAC)*
Minnesota: 97
Morality: 111,121
Morris, Dick: 134
Mortgage Bankers Association: 53
Mortgages: 52,53
Mother Theresa: 112
Muslim: *see:* Islam
My Father, My President, by Doro Bush Koch (2006):
  Book review: 222

N

National Center for Education and the Economy (NCEE): 92
National Governors Association (NGA): 33, 175
National Guard: 136,156,179
National gun registry: 14
National Rifle Association (NRA): 13
National security: 37
NATO: 144,180-1
Nazis: 111
Netanyahu, Benjamin: 152
New American Moment: 178
New Jobs for New York: 86
New Hampshire: 130
New York (NY): 86,104,132,140,174
New York City (NYC): 94,104,115,146
Newborn: 123
Newtown, Connecticut shootings: 14
Niagara Falls, Canada: 132
Nixon, Richard M.: 163
No Child Left Behind: 94-6
No Place Like Home: 123
Non-violent criminal offenders: 20
Norquist, Grover: 71
North America Free-Trade Agreement (NAFTA): 169,188-9

Norway: 174
Nuclear Non-Proliferation Treaty: 149
Nuclear power: 30 see also: Energy policy
Nuclear waste: 30-1 see also: Yucca Mountain
Nuclear weapons: 148-9

O

Obama, Barack: 69.92,143,148-9,154,157,164,167,181,185-6
ObamaCare: 49,76-7,81
   Ten Essential Health Benefits: 81
The Obamians, by James Mann (2012): 154,162,178,186
   Book review: 207
Office of the Governor: 105
Oil companies: 90,172
Oil drilling: 58,59,60,172
Oman: 188
Open government: 38
Organized labor *see:* Unions
Organization of Petroleum Exporting Countries (OPEC): 58

P

Palin, Sarah: 136
Palestine: 153
Palestinian Liberation Organization (PLO): 153
Parental notification *see:* Abortion
Partisanship: 134-5
Partners in Power, by Roger Morris (1999): 220
   Book review: 233
Patriot Act: 140
Paul, Rand: 8,183
Pentagon: 146
Pharmaceutical companies: 90
Philosophy: 131
   Political: 130
Physicians: 112
Planned Parenthood: 112
Police: 13
Political Action Committees (PAC): 64
Poor: 103
Positive Aging Act: 80
Powell, Colin: 154
Pregnancy: 113
   Teenage: 110
Prevention First Act: 112
Principles: 130
Prison incarceration: 17,23

Virtues: 111,121,129
Visas: 85
Voter identification: 40 *see also:* Voter registration
Voter registration: 38,40,41
Voting Rights Act: 40 *see also:* Voter registration

W

Walker, Scott: 85,135
Wall Street: 186
War on drugs *see:* Drugs, illegal
War on Terrorism: see: Terrorism
Welfare: 122
  Reform: 102-3
  Work requirement: 102
Wesley, John: 130
Wesleyan Credo: 130
West Bank: 153
WikiLeaks: 36-7
Wisconsin: 85
Wisconsin Supreme Court: 85
A Woman in Charge, by Carl Bernstein (2007): 48,228
  Book review: 219
World Trade Center: 146
World Trade Organization (WTO): 58,162
World War II: 151

Y

Yucca Mountain: 30

Z

Zero-sum game: 166
Zimmerman, George: 13

1 to 9

911 (September 11, 2001): 129,140-1,146-7,153,174,192

Other Books in This Series

Acknowledgments

This book would not have been possible without the tireless efforts of the entire OnTheIssues team: Nicholai Alexandrovich (our indexer), Jay Camara, Derek Camara (our cover artist), Janice Gordon, Michele Gordon, Joshua Hoerr (our App designer), Marissa Hoerr (our Facebook consultant), Peter Hoerr, Ram Lau, Rachael Lawrence, Jamie Leighton, Naomi Lichtenberg, Ogden Porter, Will Rico, Dan Teittinen, Irma Teittinen, and especially Kathleen Camara.

About the Editor

Jesse Gordon has been the editor-in-chief of OnTheIssues.org since its formation in 1999. His passion revolves around providing issue-based coverage on political races, to combat the mainstream media's growing lack of such coverage.

Mr. Gordon holds a Master's degree in Public Policy from Harvard University's Kennedy School of Government. He and the website OnTheIssues.org are based in Cambridge, Massachusetts. He resides with his fiancée, Kathleen; his son Julien; Kathleen's son Derek; their cat Chanel; and four fish with whom Chanel is obsessed.

Mr. Gordon's politics are, on the VoteMatch chart, a libertarian-leaning progressive (upper left quadrant). He is a registered Independent, but has voted for Democrats, Republicans, Greens, and Libertarians. He was the founder of both the Progressive Democrats of Cambridge, and the Harvard University Libertarian Caucus. His most important political values are open government, as reflected in the open issues concept underlying the OnTheIssues website.

Mr. Gordon replies to email personally, at jesse@ontheissues.org — whether to suggest improvements to the website or to order one of the other books above.

Made in the USA
Coppell, TX
15 July 2023

19223845R00152